THE CAJUN GOURMET
AFLOAT AND O

TREASURED MASTERPIECE
FOR A SOCIETY ON THE MOVE!

author / illustrator
Carlo DiNapoli

edited by
R. Constantine

Hawk Publishing & Distributing
Longboat Key, FL
Birmingham, AL

Other works by Carlo DiNapoli:

Cooking Country With Shotgun Red, 2nd printing
All I Ever Wanted To Know About Cooking I Learned From Momma, 4th printing
The Upper Crud Cookbook, 4th printing
Is This Country Cooking? This Is Country Cooking!, 2nd printing
How They Owned A Boat And Didn't Spend Any Money, 2nd printing

Coming Soon:

The Damned Well Do's And Don'ts For a Perfect Lifestyle

Yankee Cooking Conch And All Dem Other Critters

Other works by pen name, Jonathan Woe—Children's Books:

The Wing'ed Whale From Woefully
The Longneck Bird Of Longboat Key, One Of The Privileged Class

COPYRIGHT 1991

Published by

HAWK PUBLISHING INC.
P.O. BOX 8422
LONGBOAT KEY, FL 34228

First printing	May 1991
Second printing	July 1991
Third printing	August 1991
Fourth printing	October 1991
Fifth printing	March 1992
Sixth printing	October 1992
Seventh printing	June 1993
Eighth printing	May 1994

Dedication

To my darling wife.
At times it is impossible to write with her.
But, I have found it is always impossible to write without her.

And,
To those wonderful Cajuns who contributed their recipes so generously to this book.

ABOUT THE AUTHOR/ILLUSTRATOR

Carlo DiNapoli grew up in the French Market in the days of the vegetable pushcarts and worked in various restaurants in the Vieux Carre. After school assisting the various skilled chefs in the arts of Cajun Creole cooking, Carlo received his deep embedded roots in this culinary mastery of Cajun Creole cooking. He later advanced to a caucier for these great masters.

He entered the Navy at the end of World War Two, and though he was not a cook in the service, his artistic abilities with food were soon recognized. He handled the Cajun delights at many elaborate parties.

When the Korean War broke out, he joined the Marine Corps as a cook, graduating from Cook's and Baker's School. He was placed in charge of the mess hall and became in great demand for his Cajun cooking.

Returning to New Orleans his mother owned the famous Momma D's restaurant during the 50s and 60s. It was here that he expanded his abilities under the creative genius of his mother's cooking and other great chefs.

From that point, his investments in industry brought him to the ownership and president of an industrial complex. His table was always "the place" to eat. His adventures as a sportsman allowed him to pursue his never ending love for the art of cooking. His success in industry then in ghostwriting, allowed him to retire with his wife to write and pursue his four great loves: writing, cooking, hunting, and fishing.

FOREWORD

Cajun Creole cooking is the anticipation of the next delicious bite. It is a melody of aromas and the song of contented dining.

The background of Cajun and Creole cooking is like a Cajun song full of wild melodies of taste and exciting aromas. When the Cajuns arrived from Canada in the 1700s they brought their French ingredients. They were added to the French cooking already in place in Louisiana. To this was added a sprinkling of seasonings from the Spanish influence, one of the seven flags that flew over Louisiana. Stirred into this mixture was the marvelous black influence from the slave cooks. One of their ancestors was instrumental in teaching my mother and I that gauntlet of tastes, Creole cooking. Then, added to this grand melting pot was the Irish melodies of taste from the Irish Channel of New Orleans.

Among these notes, you must add the influence of Sicilian cooking carried with my ancestors from those shores of New Orleans. Never for a moment forget the generosity of the Jewish influence on Louisiana cooking.

In the kitchens of Louisiana and the dishes created there, though the melodies and aromas are French, many of the notes to this beautiful song called Cajun Creole cooking contain the ethnic background of other tunes.

I researched diligently to perfect these recipes and bring to light the true taste of Cajun Creole cooking and modernize the techniques of its preparation. I questioned a wide spectrum of personalities and backgrounds throughout Louisiana and sought comments on the authenticity of the recipes from the Creole and Cajun world. Their colorful comments created a character. Their stories will be told by that character whom I call Clovice. He is a combination of the Delacroix Island Spanish Creoles, the New Orleans Ninth Ward black Creoles, and the Cajuns of the Thibodeaux, Houma and Grand Couilleau area of Louisiana.

Clovice, in the beautiful language of Creole, will add a wonderful taste of color, humor, and reality to each chapter. His satire contains many of the deep seated beliefs of these wonderful people. I hope you will enjoy his explanations and benefit from his remarks as much as I have.

NOW DAT YOU DONE SEEN MY FACE ON DE COVER AND KNOW HOW BEAUTIFUL I IS AND DEY DONE TOLD YOU WHO I IS, YOU MUST REALIZE THAT I IS DE STAR OF DIS BOOK. I WILL DO MY BEST TO ES'PLAIN DE MOST IMPORTANT PARTS OF DE RECIPES.

SECRET CAJUN AND CREOLE PHILOSOPHIES
BY ME, CLOVICE

All difficult questions oughta be answered . . . wit absolutely maybe's.

De proper way to answer an in-law . . . wit a definite maybe's.

De safe way to answer your mudder-in-law . . . with a non-committal grunt.

De way out of a difficult situation . . . 'member, nobody's been wrong since dey invented excuses . . . so . . . be inventive.

De safe way to answer your wife when she catches you doin' sometin' wrong . . . be . . . real inventive.

De Creole way of answerin' a politician . . . be as sincere as he is an he'll never asks you fuh anytin' again.

A Creole's answer to how many times you should lie to your girlfriend . . . I ain't reached dat number yet.

INTRODUCTION TO GOOD EATING HABITS
BY ME, CLOVICE

A man must limit hisself in his eating habits if'n he wants to stay healthy. So' if you follow de precise eating habits of a Creole Cajun dis limits you to eatin' everytin' on four legs but de kitchen table and anytin' on two legs dat has feathers and anytin' dat wears skins, dat creeps, crawls, slithers and slides. And if'n it's in a shell you are strictly limited to removin' same before eating. Case in ex'ception: if at present time de shell is soft.

So, fuh good eatin' habits follow de strict rules of a Creole Cajun country boy.

P.S. If'n it comes out of de water and it's not a tree stump or a rock, den it's edible.

CHAPTER ONE
CARLO IS GOIN' TO
EXPOUND ON DE MYSTERY OF ROUX

Roux is not a mystery; it is simple and has an unlimited variety of uses. In this chapter I will give you the basic recipe for roux, along with variations and techniques for changing its taste.

First, one must understand that roux has a life of its own in Creole Cajun cooking. Its principal use is to convey texture, taste, and color. The basic colors of roux are white, cream, light brown, dark brown, and rich dark red brown. Each has its own taste and is controlled by the time and temperature of cooking.

The basic form of roux consists of one-half plain flour and one-half oil. In the old days only animal fats served this purpose. For diet purposes, I use a good margarine or a polyunsaturated oil.

Here are some suggestions for its use. White roux is a conveyor of light taste and can be blended with light white wines, mushroom soups, chicken soups, and a cream of just-about-anything. I use this extensively as a basis for fish, wine sauce, and creamy vegetables. I vary my texture of white roux with sour cream and skimmed milk.

Cream colored roux along with light brown roux is my grand textured base which can be used in an endless variety of sauces and gravies. I consider it outstanding for ground meat sauces, liver, and veal. Light brown roux is the float for my casseroles. To increase the color, I merely allow the light cream roux to remain over the heat a little longer. When it becomes nutty brown, I remove it from the heat and add hot water, blending briskly.

We now enter the nutty flavors of dark roux: rich brown, dark brown, and dark red brown. They create a base for my light colored meats: veal, pork, rabbit, quail, and fish. Gumbo should never be without it.

These are suggestions, not hard and fast rules. Vary your approach to each dish and with your imagination seek the color, texture, and taste of your choice. Please forget the old adage; dark meat—dark roux, white meat—white roux. Experiment like a child in a room full of toys.

There is a plague phrase which I avoid called "proper thickness." In my research, no two people see thickness with equal density. I hope I'm not oversimplifying—choose your own thickness, friends.

Now, the weapons for attacking roux. I will declare here and now, it is the amount of heat transferred to the ingredients that form the color and taste, NOT THE TYPE OF PAN. I have a favorite weapon—it is the hot bottom of my electric wok which has a thick metal base.

I will mention a misconception—special equipment is not necessary to prepare roux. Many famous cooks feel that preparing a meal requires creative chemistry in special containers and not a delightful adventure. I use non-stick surfaces and wooden spatulas. I blend liquids with any type of good whisk.

Let's start with white roux which consists of equal amounts of the oil of your choice and plain flour. If you intend to use margarine, make sure it's heated until the moisture is removed. Next, reduce the heat and add flour. Remember, roux is an on-the-move mixture. In other words, never stop stirring, blend it thoroughly. A white roux is created with the least amount of heat, about 350 degrees for two minutes. When the flour gels with the oil and reaches the desired color, slowly blend in extremely hot liquid—never use cold liquid. Whatever type saucepan you use, make sure it has high sides. This is the point where variances in color can take place.

For chicken, I like to add a teaspoon of powdered chicken bouillon. For white wine sauces, I add a cup of white wine, the juice of one lemon, and a variety of seasonings.

Like all roux, once the liquid is added you can establish the density by additional cooking time to remove moisture. I run the gauntlet from a sticky heavy paste in some dishes to a thin creamy texture for oyster soup.

From this point on, the mystery of roux is controlled by temperature and the time of cooking. I work at 450 degrees on the darker roux. Again, I deviate from other cooks. I never let the oil burn or smoke. It is the TOASTING OF THE FLOUR, NOT THE BURNING OF THE OILS that creates the rich nutty flavors of dark roux.

Roux may be prepared ahead of time. It is easily stored and keeps well in airtight containers. I always preheat roux before adding it to any dish. I keep roux in its thickest form. Moisture and a whisk will create the thickness you desire.

Roux and sauces are the stage upon which Cajun and Creole cooking rush to perform. It is here that they display their talents in taste. And so, my friends, enter upon this stage with this diversified actor called roux and create a performance of delightful tastes.

TABLE OF CONTENTS

FAVORITE RECIPES
FROM MY COOKBOOK

Recipe Name	Page Number

"So that's how you make roux!"

Sauces, the Kissing Cousin of Roux

CLOVICE'S HIDING SAUCE

A Good Hiding Sauce For Bad-Tasting Food

Calorie count—who cares?

De definition of dis sauce is de Creole method of hidin' bad-tastin' food.

Ingredients:

2 c. white roux

2 c. white wine (for me)

1 c. tabasco sauce

1 bunch of half-bombed guests

1 bunch of appetizers

1 bunch you owe money to

Combine ingredients. Bring to a boil. Serve guests as many appetizers and drinks as possible. Fill them up wit liverwurst, ham and all 'kinda of stuff. Lead them to de table. Place large portions of bad tasting food on their plate. You don't want any leftovers anyway. Cover generously wit de a'bove sauce and watch dem fools say de meal was good.

INTERESTING HINTS FOR FOOD PREPARATION

1/2 pound of fresh mushrooms will yield 2 1/2 cups, sliced and 2 cups, finely chopped. When rinsing mushrooms, quickly dry them or they will turn brown and wilt.

One of the best ways to cook bacon is to start in a cold skillet, heated with a low flame. This will pull out more fat. Six ounces of bacon will yield 1 cup, diced. Bacon will lie flat if you prick it with a fork before frying. It drains well on several layers of newspaper placed under a sheet of paper towels.

Cheese that you intend to serve should be at room temperature. Remove it from the refrigerator 1 hour or more ahead of time. There are 4 ounces of cream cheese in 1/2 cup. If you serve cream cheese as a spread, mix with milk, buttermilk, sour cream or yogurt.

For a better flavor to fresh beets, try baking them like a potato.

You can cook beets with their skins and greens on, then plunge them in cold water; the skins will come off easy. Retain the greens for a delicious extra dish. Add a little cream of tartar or vinegar to the cooking water it will keep the beets from fading. To keep the color of other ingredients in a mixed dish, add the beets last. They stain everything including your wooden cutting board.

* *

SAUCES, THE KISSING COUSIN OF ROUX

CREOLE REMOULADE SAUCE

4 Tbsp. lemon juice
4 Tbsp. Creole mustard
4 Tbsp. fresh horseradish
½ c. green onions, minced
½ c. celery, chopped fine
¼ tsp. garlic powder
¼ tsp. Tabasco sauce

¼ tsp. Louisiana hot sauce
¼ tsp. oregano
¼ tsp. basil
4 Tbsp. tarragon vinegar
2 Tbsp. paprika
6 oz. thick tomato ketchup
10 oz. mayonnaise or olive oil

In a blender, combine all liquid ingredients thoroughly. Add mustard and horseradish. Slow blender down and add remaining ingredients. Chill before serving.

There is nothing I like better than dipping boiled shrimp or fish sticks into this sauce.

BUTTER PECAN SAUCE

1 c. dry roasted pecans,
   chopped fine
¼ stick margarine
Juice of 1 lemon
⅛ tsp. red pepper

⅛ tsp. white pepper
¼ tsp. garlic powder
½ tsp. onion powder
¼ c. sour cream

Melt margarine at room temperature. Place entire ingredients in a blender. Blend until creamy and smooth.

CREAM OF WHITE WINE SAUCE

½ stick margarine
1 pt. sour cream
4 Tbsp. flour

8 oz. dry wine
½ c. milk

In a saucepan, melt margarine at 350° until moisture is removed. Reduce the heat and add flour, slowly blending continuously until it gels. Add milk, but do not boil. This will spoil the sauce. Add sour cream and bring to simmer. Remove from heat and add wine. Return to the heat at 175° and simmer to desired thickness.

CAJUN HOLLANDAISE SAUCE THAT NEVER FAILS

4 egg yolks, beaten
2 sticks margarine, cut into
   small pieces
¼ tsp. Tabasco sauce

1 Tbsp. cornstarch
¼ tsp. white pepper
¼ tsp. basil
Juice of 1 lemon

Heat water in the top of a double boiler. Add seasonings, lemon juice and Tabasco. Dissolve cornstarch in a small amount of cold water. Add to the above mixture, stirring constantly. When mixture is thickened, remove from hot water. Add the beaten egg yolks and 1 tablespoon margarine. Stir in thoroughly; place over hot water again until thickened. Blend in another tablespoon of margarine before serving.

Too high a temperature, cooking too long or remaining over the heat may cause the sauce to curdle. If this happens, add 1 teaspoon of boiling water and beat thoroughly.

CREOLE BROWN CONSOMME

1 c. brown roux
2 cans beef consomme
¼ c. green onions, finely
   chopped

3 Tbsp. parsley, chopped
¼ tsp. salt
¼ tsp. black pepper

Bring beef consomme to simmer in a shallow saucepan; blend in roux with a whisk. In a separate pan, saute parsley and green onions until soft, not brown. Blend all ingredients together. Bring to a rapid boil for 5 minutes. Control the thickness of your choice by adding hot water.

BEARNAISE SAUCE ST. CHARLES

4 egg yolks, beaten
Juice of 1 lemon
1 Tbsp. tarragon or wine vinegar
1 c. margarine
1 tsp. parsley, finely chopped

¼ tsp. Tabasco sauce
1 tsp. onion juice
¼ tsp. salt
⅛ tsp. white pepper
⅛ tsp. red pepper
⅛ tsp. dry mustard

Melt margarine, using a double boiler. Slowly blend in egg yolks, constantly stirring. Keep the water hot at the bottom of the double boiler; do not boil. Add remaining ingredients, continuing to stir until sauce thickens. Serve over fish.

CREAMY BAYOU VEGETABLE SAUCE

1 c. small shrimp, peeled and deveined
1 c. asparagus or cucumber or spinach, finely chopped
¼ stick margarine
2 Tbsp. flour
Juice of 1 lemon

Grated rind of ½ lemon
¼ tsp. onion powder
¼ tsp. garlic powder
¼ tsp. white pepper
⅛ tsp. red pepper
¼ tsp. oregano
⅛ tsp. thyme
1 c. hot water

In a saucepan, melt ⅛ stick margarine at 400°. Add shrimp and saute for 1 minute. Reduce heat to 250°. Add 1 cup hot water; saute for 4 minutes to create a stock. Set aside. In a medium size saucepan, cook the vegetables until tender, but not soggy. Drain all excess moisture; do not allow to dry. Melt remaining margarine in a separate pan. Add vegetables and remaining ingredients including shrimp stock. Blend well. Bring to a simmer for 3 minutes. Serves 6.

Serve as a bed or over seafood. I often tempt this dish by adding a little white wine.

CAJUN COUNTRY MUSHROOM SAUCE

1 c. light brown roux
2 egg yolks, beaten
1 can mushrooms
1 can cream of mushroom soup
Juice of 1 lemon
2 Tbsp. parsley leaves, chopped

Water or milk to control thickness
¼ tsp. white pepper
⅛ tsp. black pepper
⅛ tsp. oregano
⅛ tsp. thyme

Heat ½ cup water in a saucepan; bring to a simmer. Blend in roux at 200°. Add all ingredients except egg. Blend this, using a whisk, and simmer for 15 minutes at 250°. Remove from heat and allow the temperature to drop a few degrees. This will avoid the curdling of the egg when it is added. Blend in egg and tempt with brandy.

CREAM OF WINE SAUCE FOR CASSEROLE DISHES

1/2 stick margarine
2 Tbsp. flour
1 pt. sour cream
6 oz. white wine
1 can cream of mushroom soup
1/4 tsp. white pepper

1/8 tsp. red pepper
1/8 tsp. oregano
1/8 tsp. thyme
2 heaping tsp. grated cheese
   (your choice)
1/2 c. hot milk
1/2 c. hot water

At 400°, melt margarine in a deep saucepan. Allow the moisture to evaporate. Blend in flour until it gels. Reduce heat to 200°. Add milk and blend in sour cream. Bring to a simmer. Add soup and 1/2 cup hot water; whisk thoroughly. Add additional hot milk if needed to control thickness. Blend in cheese; make sure cheese is thoroughly melted. Bring to simmer; add wine. Blend well and add seasonings. Simmer to desired thickness. Serves 8. *Outstanding with shrimp and crabs!*

RICH CAJUN BUTTER SAUCE

1/2 stick margarine
Juice of 1 lemon
3 Tbsp. flour
1/8 tsp. red pepper

1/2 tsp. white pepper
1/8 tsp. oregano
1/8 tsp. sweet basil

In a shallow saucepan, melt 1/4 stick margarine at 400°. Blend in flour until it gels. Toast the flour to a light brown, whisking thoroughly. Add lemon juice and seasonings. Add 1 cup boiling water; whisk in continuously. Reduce the heat to 200° and simmer for 5 minutes. Add remaining margarine; blend until melted. Serve. Serves 6.

TART GRAND COUILLEAU WINE SAUCE

1/3 c. good sherry wine
1/4 c. sweet pickles, drained (or relish)
3 Tbsp. pimento olives, finely chopped
2 Tbsp. minced onion

1/2 tsp. Tabasco sauce
3 Tbsp. parsley, finely chopped
1 c. mayonnaise
1/4 c. sour cream

Blend the whole darn thing together real good.

I like sour pickle relish; my wife likes sweet pickle relish. So whoever prepares this dish gets to choose what type of relish goes in!

MORGAN CITY CREAMY HORSERADISH SAUCE

4 Tbsp. horseradish
1 c. sour cream or heavy cream
1½ tsp. dry mustard

1 Tbsp. vinegar
1 heaping tsp. sugar
¼ tsp. white pepper

Heat entire ingredients in a saucepan. Blend well, using a whisk. Immediately upon simmer, remove from heat.

BAYOU BLUE SEAFOOD SAUCE DELIGHT

2 c. cream roux
½ c. dry white wine
⅛ tsp. red pepper
⅛ tsp. white pepper

1½ c. shrimp or crawfish or other solid shellfish, finely chopped

Bring roux to simmer and remove from heat. In a separate saucepan, saute seafood until pink. Add wine and seasonings; blend well. Add roux slowly, blending well. Control thickness with hot water. Simmer, do not boil, for 5 minutes. Pour over any kind of seafood.

JEANERETTE PEPPERY CRAB CASSEROLE SAUCE

1 c. light brown roux
2 eggs, well beaten
1 c. sour cream

¼ tsp. white pepper
½ tsp. Tabasco sauce
¼ tsp. thyme

In a deep saucepan, bring roux to simmer. Add sour cream, whisking all the time. At this point, be careful the sour cream does not curdle from excess heat. Remove from heat. Blend in beaten eggs and seasonings.

I like to pour a layer of this as a bed for crabmeat. In a casserole dish, add a succession of layers consisting of cream sauce, oysters or crabmeat and a layer of bread crumbs. Repeat same process. Bake slowly at 300° for 20 minutes.

SPICY ST. CHARLES TARTAR SAUCE

1 Tbsp. onion, finely chopped
⅛ tsp. red pepper
⅛ tsp. white pepper
3 Tbsp. sour pickles, chopped
2 Tbsp. minced green onion

1 clove garlic, chopped
2 Tbsp. parsley, finely chopped
1 tsp. dry mustard
8 oz. mayonnaise
2 tsp. capers, chopped

Combine all ingredients; mix extremely well. Chill before serving.

Wonderful with any kind of seafood.

VEGETABLE SAUCE MANDEVILLE

½ stick margarine
½ c. onions, chopped
½ c. celery, chopped
3 Tbsp. green pepper, chopped
⅛ c. green onion leaves, chopped
3 Tbsp. parsley leaves, chopped

1 c. dry white wine
⅛ tsp. white pepper
⅛ tsp. red pepper
¼ tsp. basil
¼ tsp. oregano
¼ tsp. thyme
2 Tbsp. Worcestershire sauce
1 c. sour cream

In a shallow saucepan, melt margarine. Saute vegetables until soft. Do not brown or it will spoil the taste. Reduce heat to 200°. Add sour cream, blending well. Keep stirring and add wine slowly. Add remaining ingredients, one at a time. Keep at simmer for 5 minutes. Control thickness with additional wine or sour cream if you wish a heavy base.

SEAFOOD SAUCE PIQUANT JENNINGS

2 lb. peeled shrimp or other solid shellfish (scallops or crabs)
2 cans creamy seafood soup
¼ stick margarine
1 c. green peppers, chopped
2 c. onions, chopped
1 c. celery, chopped
1 large can tomatoes
1 c. tomato sauce
4 jalapeno peppers, chopped

½ tsp. ground bay leaf
¼ tsp. sweet basil
¼ tsp. oregano
¼ tsp. thyme
1 tsp. minced garlic
2 tsp. dark brown sugar
1 tsp. black pepper
1 tsp. white pepper
1 tsp. Tabasco sauce
4 c. cooked rice

In a large saucepan, melt margarine at 350°. Saute seafood for 3 minutes. Remove from pan; set aside. Saute all vegetables until soft with light brown edges. Add tomatoes, tomato sauce, seafood, and remaining ingredients except rice. Control thickness with hot water and bring to a boil. Reduce to simmer immediately. Add 4 cups hot cooked rice; blend well. This will stick quickly if moisture is not controlled or heat is in excess. Cook for 20 minutes at 200°; remove from heat. Cover, allow to thicken and serve. Serves 8.

BAYOU CATHERINE GROUND MEAT SAUCE

1 lb. ground meat
¼ stick margarine
1 c. brown roux
½ c. celery, chopped
½ c. onions, chopped

2 cloves garlic, chopped
1 Tbsp. Tabasco sauce
½ tsp. black pepper
1 can cream of mushroom soup

In a large frying pan at 400°, saute ground meat until brown. Remove from pan; set aside. Leave drippings in pan. Add margarine and melt on low heat. Add vegetables; saute until lightly browned. Add soup; blend well. Add hot water to control thickness. Add roux slowly, a tablespoon at a time. Bring to simmer. Add seasonings and blend well. Add ground meat and bring to simmer for 5 minutes.

Note: You may vary the meat with ground turkey or chicken; if so, brown until crisp.

RAISIN SAUCE METAIRIE

¾ c. raisins
½ c. red wine
2 c. water
½ c. dark brown sugar
1 Tbsp. flour

½ tsp. salt
¼ tsp. black pepper
½ tsp. dry mustard
¼ tsp. nutmeg
⅓ tsp. cinnamon

Combine all seasonings in a measuring cup. Bring water to a simmer in a shallow saucepan. Add raisins and sugar; bring to simmer. Add seasonings and remaining ingredients. Cook until thickened at 250° or until raisins swell.

Delicious served with roast. I tempt this dish with apricot brandy.

NAPOLEANVILLE BECHAMEL SAUCE

2 Tbsp. margarine
2 Tbsp. flour
1 c. chicken broth
1 c. heavy cream
1 c. chicken broth
1 small onion, sliced

1 small carrot, sliced
½ bay leaf
1 sprig parsley
1 tsp. salt
½ tsp. white pepper
¼ tsp. red pepper

Melt margarine in saucepan at 400°; whisk until frothy. Reduce heat to 200° and add flour, stirring constantly for 3 minutes. In a separate pan, add chicken broth and simmer with onion, carrot, bay leaf, and parsley. Remove from the heat and strain. Return to the heat and add to margarine and flour mixture, stirring constantly. Blend in seasonings. Cook slowly until thickened. Stir in cream and cook for 4 minutes.

BAYOU LOUIE LEMON BUTTER SAUCE

1 lemon, peeled, seeded and
    thin sliced
⅛ tsp. salt
2 sticks margarine
1 chicken bouillon cube

1 egg yolk
2 Tbsp. flour
Juice of ½ lemon
1 c. hot water

    Melt bouillon in 1 cup hot water; set aside. In a shallow saucepan, melt 1 stick margarine at 350°. Add lemon slices and lemon juice. While whisking consistently, add flour until it gels. Remove from the heat; blend in egg. Blend in bouillon liquid. Return to the heat at 250°. Add remaining margarine and salt. Stir well and do not allow to boil. Simmer to desired thickness.

CREOLE ONION SAUCE

1 c. roux
3 medium size sweet onions,
    peeled and chopped
3 Tbsp. margarine
1 tsp. brown sugar
½ tsp. dry mustard
2 beef bouillon cubes

1 qt. hot water
¾ c. white wine
Salt and pepper to taste
French bread, sliced
Parmesan and Swiss cheese
    (optional)

    Dissolve bouillon in 1 quart hot water; set aside. Slice 1 onion into 4¼ inch rings from the center; chop remaining onions. In a large saucepan, melt margarine at 400° until moisture is removed. Carefully add onion rings; saute on one side for 1 minute. Remove from the pan and set aside. Add remaining onions and saute for 2 minutes or until light brown. Reduce heat to 200°. Add sugar and mustard; simmer for an additional 15 minutes. Slowly blend in roux. Add beef broth and wine, blending slowly. Bring to simmer for 20 minutes until sauce thickens to a heavy syrup. Place buttered French bread under broiler until golden brown (garlic bread if you choose). Ladle sauce into cups and top with French bread. Add onion rings, then top with Swiss or Parmesan cheese.

    You can vary this as a soup by adding additional hot water.

CREOLE OYSTER SAUCE

2 doz. oysters
1 tsp. white pepper
1 tsp. Worcestershire
¼ tsp. red pepper
1 tsp. salt
6 cloves

¼ c. celery, chopped fine
1 qt. hot milk
½ c. green onions, chopped fine
3 Tbsp. flour
½ stick margarine

In a saucepan, melt ¼ stick margarine at 350°. Add flour and stir until it gels. Add hot milk slowly, blending with a whisk. Add chopped celery, cloves and seasoning. Cook slowly until it thickens. In a separate saucepan, melt ¼ stick margarine at 400°. Add oysters and saute for 1 minute. Add oyster water and simmer for 2 minutes. Remove from the heat and dice. Combine all ingredients and simmer until sauce reaches your desired thickness.

SAUCE BAYOU TECHE

2 Tbsp. margarine
3 Tbsp. plain flour
2 c. hot milk
4 Tbsp. tomato paste
2 Tbsp. softened margarine

¼ tsp. salt
¼ tsp. black pepper
2 tsp. minced parsley
1 tsp. tarragon

In a saucepan, melt margarine at 250°. Blend in flour, stirring slowly until it gels for 2 minutes. Avoid browning. Remove sauce from heat. When no longer simmering, add hot milk immediately. Beat vigorously with a whisk, blending in thoroughly. Do not allow residue to form on edge of pan. Return saucepan to moderate heat, approximately 200°, and whisk slowly until sauce begins to simmer for 1 minute. Reduce heat and stir in tomato paste slowly until you have the color and flavor you wish. Remove from heat and stir in remaining ingredients.

DELCAMBRE PREMIER HOLLANDAISE SAUCE

2 sticks margarine
¼ tsp. salt
⅛ tsp. red pepper

5 egg yolks
2 Tbsp. lemon juice
⅛ tsp. white pepper

Slice margarine into 8 separate pieces. In the top of a double boiler, beat egg yolks until smooth. Blend in lemon juice and allow to reach a low simmer. Add margarine, one piece at a time. Stir constantly until all margarine has been added and sauce thickens. Add seasoning; remove from heat.

FRENCH ONION SAUCE PIERRE

¼ lb. ground meat, ground fine
6 medium onions, peeled and
   sliced
⅛ tsp. white pepper
⅛ tsp. black pepper
1 bay leaf
¼ tsp. thyme

3 Tbsp. margarine
2 beef bouillon cubes
2 c. hot water
¼ c. roux
¼ tsp. salt
4 slices French bread, cut 1 inch
   thick
1½ c. Monterey Jack, grated

Dissolve bouillon in 2 cups hot water; set aside. In a saucepan, melt 1 tablespoon margarine at 400°. Add ground meat and saute until brown. Reduce heat to 200° and add bouillon liquid; set aside. In a large saucepan, melt 2 tablespoons margarine at 250°. Add onions and saute until tender, stirring constantly. Add beef broth, water, salt, pepper, bay leaf, and thyme. Add roux slowly, blending well. Bring mixture to a simmer for 20 minutes. Butter bread and brown until golden on both sides under a broiler. Place bread in 4 deep ovenproof sauce bowls. Cover with sauce, top with Monterey Jack and place in oven until cheese melts.

Note: Cauliflower and other vegetables may be added to replace bread. Makes a wonderful vegetable dish or an excellent sauce to top with meatloaf.

CREAMY MUSTARD SAUCE CARONDELET

2 Tbsp. margarine
2 Tbsp. flour
½ tsp. white pepper

½ c. stone ground mustard
1 c. sour cream
¼ c. dry white wine

In a saucepan, melt margarine at 200°. Add flour slowly, blending well. Do not allow to brown. Add sour cream; bring to a slow simmer. Add white pepper; continue to simmer. Add mustard; simmer until sauce has a heavy density, about 5 minutes. Slowly blend in wine. When sauce returns to simmer, remove after 1 minute. Serve. *Delicious over seafood.*

MUSTARD PARMESAN SAUCE THIBODEAUX

1 bottle Creole mustard
1 c. sour cream
½ c. Parmesan cheese

¼ stick margarine
½ c. hot milk
1 Tbsp. flour

In a saucepan, melt margarine at 200°. Blend flour in until it gels. Add hot milk. Add mustard and bring to a low simmer for 2 minutes. Blend in sour cream; simmer for an additional 3 minutes. Add Parmesan cheese slowly. Blend thoroughly. If sauce appears too thick, add warm milk. Do not boil. *Delicious over chicken.*

CREAMY PEANUT SAUCE

¼ c. peanut butter
1 tsp. minced onions
2 Tbsp. flour
2 Tbsp. margarine

2 c. scalded milk
1 chicken bouillon cube
1 c. hot water
½ tsp. white pepper

Dissolve bouillon in 1 cup hot water. In a saucepan, melt margarine at 200°. Add peanut butter and onions; stir briskly for 5 minutes. Add flour; blend until smooth. Add bouillon liquid; stir well. Add milk and seasoning. Remove from heat. Place in a double boiler and simmer until sauce thickens. Special attention should be paid to the stirring. Serve.

MONROE SWEET ONION AND CELERY SAUCE

2 c. light brown roux
2 c. sweet onions, minced
¾ c. celery, minced
¼ c. hot chicken bouillon
1 tsp. salt
2 c. hot milk or warm sour
     cream

⅛ tsp. white pepper
⅛ tsp. red pepper
¼ tsp. nutmeg
¼ c. heavy cream, warmed
2 Tbsp. pistachio nuts

In a large saucepan, add onions, celery, ½ teaspoon salt, and hot bouillon. Bring to a simmer at 250°. Reduce heat to 200°. Cover until onions and celery become soft. Place in a blender and puree. Place roux in a saucepan and bring to a light simmer. Blend in milk. Add remaining salt and add pureed vegetables. Bring to a simmer. Stir in warm cream. Sprinkle with pepper and nuts. *Fabulous served over steak.*

ASCENSION PARISH CRAB SAUCE WITH SWEET ONION

This is a masterpiece over baked grouper or redfish!

½ c. white roux
¼ lb. bacon
3 medium sweet onions, finely
     chopped
2 bell peppers, finely chopped

1 lb. chunky crabmeat
2 qt. milk
1 can cream of celery soup
½ tsp. salt
½ tsp. white pepper

Fry bacon until crisp. Add onions and bell peppers; saute until soft and brown. Reduce heat to 200°. Add crabmeat, milk and cream of celery soup. Add roux and seasonings. Allow to simmer; do not boil. The amount of milk will determine whether this dish should be used as a sauce or soup.

Note: Thin sliced canned potatoes added to this sauce makes it outstanding.

CRAWFISH SAUCE BURGUNDY

2 c. cooked crawfish, quartered
½ c. dry white wine
½ stick margarine
4 Tbsp. flour

2 c. milk
1 tsp. salt
¼ tsp. white pepper
¼ tsp. red pepper

In a large saucepan, melt margarine until moisture is removed at 300°. Add flour; blend well until it gels. Add milk slowly and bring to a simmer for 5 minutes or until sauce thickens. This dish requires constant stirring. Add crawfish; stir in for 2 minutes. Blend in wine. Add salt and pepper; simmer slowly for 5 minutes. Pour over crawfish. Croutons or cheese may be sprinkled on top.

CAJUN TOMATO SAUCE DUPONT

1 can tomato sauce
1 small pkg. frozen vegetables,
    finely chopped
⅛ tsp. white pepper
⅛ tsp. red pepper
⅛ tsp. thyme

⅛ tsp. basil
⅛ tsp. black pepper
1 Tbsp. Worcestershire sauce
1 tsp. brown sugar
1 Tbsp. lemon juice
½ stick margarine

In a saucepan, melt margarine at 250°. Add tomato sauce, bringing to a simmer. Add sugar; blend well. Bring to a simmer for 7 minutes. Add remaining ingredients, mixing well. Bring to a brisk simmer for 45 minutes.

Watch the thickness of this sauce. If necessary, add hot water. Serve over ground meat.

SHRIMP SAUCE LE POUPON

1 lb. shrimp, peeled and
    quartered
1 can sliced mushrooms
¼ c. green pepper, chopped fine
2 c. light brown roux

½ tsp. salt
¼ tsp. cayenne
2 c. milk
2 Tbsp. pimento
3 Tbsp. margarine
1 Tbsp. parsley, chopped fine

In a saucepan, melt margarine at 300°. Saute mushrooms and green pepper until tender. Add shrimp and continue to saute until pink. Reduce heat and add roux slowly. Add milk gradually and cook until sauce thickens. Stir constantly; this dish needs your attention. Add pimento and remaining ingredients. Allow to simmer. Remove from heat, blend in croutons and serve.

SHRIMP BAYOU LABELLE SAUCE

1½ lb. shrimp, peeled, deveined
    and quartered
1 bell pepper, chopped
2 medium onions, chopped
2 sticks celery, chopped
2 medium potatoes, diced
¼ tsp. powdered bay leaf
½ lb. bacon, diced

2½ c. hot milk
2 c. brown roux
½ tsp. white pepper
½ tsp. red pepper
⅛ tsp. thyme
⅛ tsp. basil
⅛ tsp. oregano
Parsley for garnish

Place green pepper in a saucepan with ½ inch water; bring to a simmer for 1 minute. Rinse with cold water and allow to drain. In a large saucepan, fry bacon at 450° until brown. Add onions and celery; saute until golden brown. Add green pepper, potatoes, bay leaf, and 2 cups hot water. Bring to a boil. Slowly blend in roux. Add seasonings, mixing well. Reduce heat to 200°. Add milk. Simmer until potatoes are tender. Remove from heat. Add shrimp and simmer 10 minutes or until sauce thickens before serving. Sprinkle with parsley. Serve over rice.

CHERRY SAUCE CHENEYVILLE

1 can black cherries
1 c. sour cream

¼ c. dry red wine

Mix thoroughly in a blender.

Use as a cold dip with leftover cold meat.

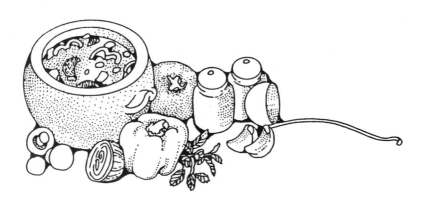

Notes

"What's your problem . . .
we're just as pretty as a shrimp!"

Appetizers

ADVICE FROM CLOVICE:

The definition of appetizers are sometin' dat is served at a party about de time when you're so hungry your belly thinks your throat is cut. If it's your party and you prepared exceptionally good appetizers like I'm going to suggest, wait till your company is finished eatin' dinner wit their bellies full. Den serve de appetizers, they definitely won't eat many and you can keep dem for yourself.

Another time to serve appetizers so dat everybody will think you are a good cook is wait till dey had plenty to drink and are starving to death. Dey will eat everythin' and say dis is good.

Dis is the simplest way to make dem Greek, Italian, Cajun Creole collection of delicious appetizers. Dat mean or' durbies.

KITCHEN WISDOM

To keep celery crisp and white for serving, place it upright in a pitcher of water with a little lemon juice in the refrigerator. Remember, boiling celery fast makes it tough. To rid celery of strings, scrape the outside ridges with a knife.

Crabmeat like all seafood should never be overcooked. When preparing a marinade, always make enough to completely cover the food. If the food is light and floats, weigh it down with a flat dish.

The meat of a blue crab is generally sold in fish markets, cooked and packed in cans. Alaskan king crab is more like lobster in taste and texture and not as sweet and tender as blue crab.

Small shrimp have the better flavor and are preferred for dip. When buying fresh shrimp look for those with a grayish green color and shells that fit tight.

Watch the temperature of oil when frying croquettes. Overcooking will make them hard. Undercooking will leave them mushy in the center.

Fresh bread crumbs are a must. One slice of toast will yield 1/3 cup of fine crumbs.
If your recipe calls only for mushroom caps, save the stems by freezing.

APPETIZERS

MUSTARD SHRIMP

2 lb. shrimp, peeled and
   deveined
1/2 c. dry red wine
1 Tbsp. ketchup
1/2 tsp. garlic powder
1/4 tsp. black pepper
1/4 c. salad oil

1 tsp. chives, chopped fine
1/2 tsp. horseradish
2 Tbsp. hot Creole mustard
1 tsp. salt
1/2 tsp. ground red pepper
1/4 stick margarine

In a saucepan, melt margarine at 400°. Add shrimp and saute until pink. Remove from pan, allow to cool and chop. In a bowl, combine all ingredients; mix well. Chill for 45 minutes. Line salad bowls with lettuce leaves. Serve. Serves 12.

A variation of this theme: Slice in half 1 loaf of French bread. Cover with Mustard Shrimp. Place in a hot oven for 10 minutes.

MUSHROOM STUFFED SHRIMP

2 lb. shrimp, peeled and
   deveined
2 pkg. large fresh mushroom
   caps
2 eggs, beaten
1/4 c. milk
2 Tbsp. onion, grated

1/2 stick margarine
1/4 tsp. white pepper
1/4 tsp. red pepper
1/4 tsp. Louisiana hot sauce
Juice of 1 lemon
1/2 c. bread crumbs

Wash mushrooms thoroughly. Remove stems and chop fine. Place mushroom caps in a lightly oiled casserole dish. In a saucepan, melt margarine at 450°. Add shrimp; saute until pink. Remove from heat and chop; return to pan. Add remaining ingredients except bread crumbs; mix well. Remove from heat. Blend in bread crumbs. Stuff mushroom caps. Bake for 20 minutes at 350°. Serves 12.

FRIED CRAB CLAWS ANOTHER WAY

2 doz. peeled crab claws
1 egg, beaten
1/2 tsp. white pepper
1/2 tsp. red pepper

1/8 tsp. oregano
1/8 tsp. sweet basil
3/4 c. bread crumbs

In a bowl, combine seasonings. In a separate bowl, combine 1/2 seasonings with egg. Dip crab claws in egg mixture. Roll into bread crumbs, mixed with 1/2 seasoning mix. Fry until golden brown. Serve with tartar sauce. Serves 6.

MARINATED CRAB CLAWS

2 doz. peeled crab claws,
  cooked
1 c. onions, finely chopped
1 c. parsley, finely chopped
¼ c. celery, finely chopped
2 Tbsp. tarragon vinegar
½ c. white wine

Juice of 1 lemon
⅛ tsp. oregano
1 Tbsp. steak sauce
1 Tbsp. Worcestershire sauce
¼ c. salad dressing (your
  choice)

Blend ingredients thoroughly. Marinate for 4 hours. Serve. Serves 6.

CRAB DIP

3 cans king or blue crabmeat
8 oz. cream cheese
½ tsp. garlic salt
½ c. mayonnaise
½ c. dry white wine

2 Tbsp. Creole mustard
2 Tbsp. brown sugar
Juice of ½ lemon
¼ stick margarine

In a saucepan, melt margarine at 350°. Add crab and saute for 3 minutes. Remove from heat and allow to cool. Return to heat at 150°. Add cream cheese. Blend in wine. Add sugar, whisking in well. Add remaining ingredients, blending thoroughly. Chill. Serve over crackers. Serves 24.

CAJUN SHRIMP BALLS

1½ lb. shrimp, finely chopped
2 eggs, beaten
½ c. onions, chopped
4 cloves garlic, finely chopped
2 Tbsp. parsley, chopped
1 Tbsp. green onions, chopped

1½ Tbsp. Worcestershire sauce
¼ tsp. white pepper
¼ tsp. black pepper
½ tsp. red pepper
1 c. flour

In a bowl, combine seasonings; set aside. In a separate bowl, combine all ingredients except flour and ½ seasoning mix. Mix well and roll into balls. In a separate bowl, combine flour and remaining seasoning mix. Roll into flour. Fry until golden brown. Serve with cream of wine sauce. Serves 12.

CREOLE SHRIMP DIP

1 c. shrimp, peeled and
    deveined
10 oz. sour cream
1/2 c. bourbon
1/2 tsp. paprika
1 Tbsp. dill pickle, chopped
1 tsp. salt

1/8 tsp. oregano
1/4 tsp. white pepper
1/4 tsp. red pepper
1 Tbsp. chives, chopped
2 Tbsp. parsley, finely chopped
1/4 stick margarine

In a saucepan, melt margarine at 400°. Chop shrimp and saute until deep pink. Remove from heat and allow to cool. Place ingredients, except chives, in a blender. Whip until smooth. Chill. Stir in chives. Serve. Serves 24.

SEAFOOD CREPES

12 crepes
1/2 lb. crabmeat
1 lb. peeled crawfish
3/4 lb. shrimp, peeled and
    deveined
1 1/4 c. heavy cream
1/4 stick margarine
1/4 c. onions, chopped fine

1/2 c. green pepper, chopped fine
1 Tbsp. all-purpose flour
1 tsp. salt
1/2 tsp. red pepper
1/2 tsp. white pepper
1/8 tsp. oregano
1/8 tsp. thyme
1/4 tsp. sweet basil

In a bowl, combine seasonings and set aside. In a saucepan, melt margarine at 450°. Add onions; saute until tender. Add seasoning mix; blend in for 2 minutes. Add green pepper and flour, blending well. Stir in cream; bring to a brisk simmer. Add crabmeat; stir, but do not break up lumps. Reduce heat to 350°. Add crawfish and shrimp; saute until pink, about 5 minutes. Remove from heat. Serve over crepes. Makes 12 crepes.

BREADED SHRIMP

2 doz. jumbo shrimp, peeled and
    deveined
2 eggs, beaten
1/2 c. milk
Juice of 1/2 lemon
1/2 c. flour
1 tsp. salt
1/2 tsp. red pepper

1/4 tsp. sweet paprika
1/4 tsp. garlic powder
1/2 tsp. black pepper
1/4 tsp. oregano
1/4 tsp. thyme
1 tsp. baking powder
1/2 c. seasoned bread crumbs

In small bowl, combine seasonings; set aside. In a separate bowl, combine 1/2 seasoning mix, baking powder and eggs. Form a thick batter. Combine remaining seasoning mix with bread crumbs. Dip shrimp into batter, then pat into bread crumbs. Shake off excess. Fry until golden brown. Serves 12.

GUACAMOLE AND SHRIMP DIP

1 lb. shrimp, peeled and
  deveined
2 avocados, diced
¼ tsp. chili powder
½ tsp. red pepper
¼ tsp. black pepper

¼ tsp. white pepper
½ tsp. garlic powder
1 tomato, chopped
Juice of ½ lemon
¼ stick margarine
4 Tbsp. onions, chopped

In a bowl, combine seasonings; set aside. In a saucepan, melt margarine at 450° until a light smoke appears. Add seasonings; blend in well. Add shrimp and saute until deep pink. Remove from heat and allow to cool. Combine all ingredients in a blender. Whip until smooth. Serve with crackers. Serves 24.

CRAB CROQUETTES

1 lb. crabmeat
2 hard-boiled eggs, finely
  chopped
¼ tsp. white pepper
¼ tsp. red pepper
¼ tsp. black pepper
⅛ tsp. garlic powder

⅛ tsp. onion powder
1 c. cream of wine sauce
¾ c. bread crumbs
2 eggs, beaten
2 Tbsp. flour
¼ c. hot milk
¼ stick margarine

In a bowl, combine seasonings; set aside. In a saucepan, melt margarine at 200°. Add flour until it gels. Add milk slowly to form a cream. Add ½ seasoning mix, hard-boiled eggs and crabmeat; blend together well. Allow to cool. Form into croquettes. In a separate bowl, add ½ seasoning mix and eggs; blend well. Combine remaining seasoning mix with bread crumbs. Dip croquettes into beaten eggs, then into bread crumbs. Fry until golden brown. Pour over with cream of wine sauce. Serves 24.

CRABMEAT MUSHROOMS

1 lb. crabmeat
¼ c. seasoned bread crumbs
2 Tbsp. parsley, finely chopped
1 Tbsp. onion, finely chopped
2 eggs, beaten

2 packs fresh mushrooms
¼ c. Parmesan cheese
¼ tsp. red pepper
¼ tsp. white pepper
¼ tsp. tarragon

Combine crabmeat, bread crumbs, onion, parsley, and seasonings. Blend well. Add eggs; mix well. Fill mushrooms. Arrange in a lightly oiled casserole dish. Cover with Parmesan cheese. Bake at 350° until brown. Serves 12.

MINIATURE SOFT CRABS

18 small crabs (1½ inches in
    size)
2 eggs, beaten
1 c. milk
1 c. flour
½ tsp. red pepper

½ tsp. salt
¼ tsp. black pepper
¼ tsp. white pepper
¼ tsp. thyme
⅛ tsp. oregano
Juice of 1 lemon

In a bowl, combine seasonings. In a bowl, add ½ seasoning mix, milk and eggs; blend together well. Marinate crabs in mixture for ½ hour. Make sure crabs are covered thoroughly with marinade. Combine flour and ½ seasoning mix. Pat crabs thoroughly in flour. Fry until golden brown. Squeeze with lemon juice. Serve. Serves 18.

AVOCADO WITH CRABMEAT CANAPES

1 lb. crabmeat
½ c. mayonnaise
4 large avocados
1 Tbsp. parsley, chopped

½ c. celery, finely chopped
¼ tsp. white pepper
⅛ tsp. red pepper

Chop avocado fine and combine with crabmeat. Add remaining ingredients except parsley. Mix well. Stuff mixture into canapes. Garnish with parsley. Serve chilled. Serves 24.

CATFISH FINGERS

3 catfish fillets, cut into 1 inch
    fingers
2 eggs, beaten
½ tsp. red pepper
1 tsp. salt
½ tsp. black pepper

¼ tsp. thyme
½ tsp. oregano
½ tsp. baking powder
½ c. corn meal
½ c. flour

In a bowl, combine seasonings. In a separate bowl, combine ¾ seasoning mix with eggs. In another bowl, combine remaining seasoning, baking powder, flour, and corn meal. Dip fingers into egg mixture. Dredge in corn meal. If a heavier crust is required, repeat dipping process. Fry until golden brown. Serves 24.

OYSTER HONEY BROCHETTES

2 doz. oysters
½ c. honey
½ tsp. red pepper
½ tsp. black pepper
¼ tsp. thyme

½ tsp. white pepper
⅛ tsp. oregano
6 slices bacon, cut in halves
1 c. bread crumbs

In a bowl, combine seasonings; set aside. Sprinkle oysters generously with ¾ seasoning mix. Dip in honey. Combine remaining seasoning with bread crumbs. Dredge oysters in flour; shake off excess. Wrap with bacon pieces. Skewer with toothpick. Broil until golden brown. Serves 12.

SPICY CREOLE OYSTERS

2 doz. oysters
2 eggs, beaten
½ tsp. black pepper
¼ tsp. oregano
⅛ tsp. sweet basil

¾ c. flour
¾ c. seasoned corn meal
½ c. milk
½ tsp. white pepper
½ tsp. red pepper

In a bowl, combine seasonings. In a separate bowl, combine ¾ seasoning mix, milk and eggs. In a separate bowl, combine flour, corn meal and remaining seasoning. Dip oysters in egg mixture, then dredge in flour mixture. Repeat process until fully coated. Fry until golden brown and crispy. Serves 12.

CREOLE GIBLETS

1 lb. giblets
¼ c. margarine
2 tsp. Worcestershire sauce
½ tsp. black pepper
½ tsp. white pepper

1 tsp. onion flakes
¼ tsp. garlic flakes
¾ c. red wine
1 tsp. salt
½ c. sour cream

In a bowl, combine seasonings; set aside. In a saucepan, melt margarine at 400°. Stir in ½ seasoning mix. Add giblets and saute until light brown. Add Worcestershire sauce; stir for 1 minute. Reduce the heat to 225°. Add wine and remaining seasoning; saute until giblets are tender. Reduce the heat to 150°. Blend in sour cream until giblets are well coated. Pour into a flat serving dish. Serve with toothpicks. Serves 12.

CAJUN CHICKEN WINGS

3 lb. chicken wings
1 c. flour
3 eggs
½ tsp. red pepper
1 tsp. white pepper
½ c. gin

½ tsp. lemon juice
½ tsp. soy sauce
1 tsp. garlic powder
½ tsp. onion powder
2 c. corn oil

Cut chicken wings at the joint and separate. Combine all ingredients except for flour and eggs. Marinate chicken wings for 4 hours. Remove chicken from marinade; drain and retain marinade. In a bowl, beat eggs. In another bowl, add flour. Dip chicken in marinade, then in flour, in eggs and then again in flour. Fry until golden brown. Serves 12.

CREOLE SESAME CHEESE ROLLS

½ lb. cream cheese
½ lb. Blue cheese
½ lb. butter
¾ c. salad olives, chopped
½ tsp. garlic powder
1 Tbsp. chives, chopped fine

1 Tbsp. parsley
2 Tbsp. cognac
½ c. sesame seeds
½ tsp. white pepper
½ tsp. red pepper

In a bowl, combine cream cheese and butter; blend together with a hand mixer. Blend in remaining ingredients, except sesame seeds, one at a time, blending well. Place in refrigerator and allow mixture to chill until it stiffens. Remove and roll into dollar- size rolls.

To toast sesame seeds, pour into a shallow baking pan and toast at 350° until golden brown. Roll cheese rolls into sesame seeds and serve. Serves 24.

SPICY CHEESE FONDUE

1½ lb. cheese (your choice)
2 c. dry white wine
3 Tbsp. cornstarch
½ tsp. garlic powder
2 oz. Swiss brandy
⅛ tsp. nutmeg

1 tsp. red pepper
½ tsp. white pepper
1 Tbsp. butter
1 loaf French or Italian bread,
    cut into 1 inch cubes

Mix garlic powder with 1 tablespoon butter and thoroughly coat inside of fondue dish. Pour in wine and heat until it simmers. Add cheese, small amounts at a time, until cheese is melted, avoiding boiling cheese. In a separate bowl, dissolve cornstarch into brandy. Add to cheese mixture and blend well for 3 minutes. Add seasonings.

It's important to make sure seasonings are completely blended. Toast bread cubes, place on a long fondue toothpick and serve. Serves 12.

OYSTER CUPS

2 doz. oysters
2 doz. aluminum muffin cups
1 c. seasoned bread crumbs
½ c. Italian cheese, grated

½ c. sour cream
1 tsp. white pepper
¼ stick margarine
Tabasco sauce

Melt margarine in a wide pan. Saute oysters on one side for 2 minutes and other side for 1 minute. Remove from pan. Combine remaining ingredients in the pan. It may be necessary to add more moisture; if so, add warm milk. Blend well. Remove from heat. Fill muffin cups ¼ full. Lay oysters on top. Sprinkle with a dash of white pepper. Fill with additional mixture. Top with a dash of Tabasco sauce. Bake for 10 minutes at 350°. Serve. Serves 12.

GREEK MEATBALLS

1 lb. ground meat
1 c. seasoned bread crumbs
½ c. Parmesan cheese
1 Tbsp. parsley, finely chopped
2 eggs, beaten
¼ c. onions, finely chopped
½ tsp. black pepper

1 tsp. salt
⅛ tsp. oregano
⅛ tsp. basil
¼ c. dry white wine
1 c. milk
½ stick margarine
2 c. Ragu sauce

Mix ingredients, using enough milk to moisten, so that the mixture will hold together. Take a small amount in your palm and form into meatballs. In a saucepan, melt margarine at 450°. Add meatballs and saute until golden brown. Remove and place in a shallow baking pan. Cover with Ragu sauce. Bake until meatballs are tender at 350°. Serves 24.

CHICKEN LIVER DIP

1 lb. chicken livers, chopped
½ c. dry wine
2 tsp. lemon juice
½ stick margarine
¼ c. onions, finely chopped

¼ c. sour cream
¼ tsp. white pepper
¼ tsp. red pepper
¼ tsp. oregano

In a saucepan, melt margarine at 400°. Add livers and saute until light brown. Add remaining ingredients, whisking in thoroughly. Chill, then place in a blender. Whip on a medium speed for 30 seconds. Serve with fresh vegetables and crackers. Serves 24.

MUSHROOM SQUARES

3 c. fresh mushrooms, chopped
    fine
1/4 c. onions, chopped fine
1 tsp. Worcestershire sauce
1 stick margarine

1/2 c. boiling water
6 oz. cream cheese
1/8 c. Parmesan cheese
2 c. Bisquick
1 Tbsp. butter

In a saucepan, melt 1 tablespoon butter at 350°. Add onions, mushrooms and Worcestershire sauce; saute until mushrooms are brown. In a bowl, combine margarine, boiling water and Bisquick. Remove and roll out to cover a 9x12 inch baking pan. Spread with cream cheese. Top with mushrooms, then Parmesan cheese. Bake for 30 minutes at 325°. Cool and cut into squares. Serves 24.

SHRIMP IN HOT LEMON SAUCE

2 lb. shrimp, peeled and
    deveined
1/2 stick margarine
Juice of 1 lemon
1 tsp. Tabasco sauce

1 tsp. Worcestershire sauce
1 Tbsp. dill pickle, finely
    chopped
1/4 tsp. garlic powder
1/4 c. sour cream

In a saucepan, melt margarine at 400°. Add shrimp and saute until deep pink. Reduce heat. Add remaining ingredients. Saute for 1 minute. Remove from heat. Serve in individual cups. Serves 24.

ST. FRANCIS SPICY NUTS

2 egg whites, beaten
1 tsp. water
1 c. roasted peanuts
1 c. whole almonds
1 c. pecan halves

1 c. brown sugar
1 Tbsp. pumpkin pie spice
1 tsp. salt
1 tsp. white pepper

Combine egg whites and water. Add nuts and coat thoroughly. In a separate bowl, combine sugar, pumpkin pie spice, salt, and white pepper. Add to nuts. Toss until well coated. Spread mixture on a lightly oiled baking dish. Bake at 325° for 20 minutes. Remove and break into clusters. Serves 12.

SHRIMP IN GRAPE LEAVES

2 doz. grape vine leaves
2 doz. large shrimp, peeled and
   deveined

   Rinse grape vine leaves in brine water and set aside. Split shrimp down the back, butterflying. Place shrimp butterfly side down on a grape leaf; fold in end of leaf. Arrange shrimp in a shallow baking dish with the fold side down.

   Marinade:

2 Tbsp. olive oil
4 Tbsp. wine vinegar
1/4 tsp. red pepper

1/4 tsp. white pepper
1 lemon, sliced thin

   Combine marinade sauce and pour over shrimp. Bake in a preheated oven at 350° for 30 minutes. Serve with lemon slices. Serves 12.

CHEESE TRIANGLES BY AN ITALIAN CAJUN

1 (3 oz.) pack cream cheese
1/2 lb. Feta cheese
1/2 lb. melted butter

1/2 lb. cottage cheese
3 eggs
1 lb. filo or pastry sheets

   In a bowl, combine the cheeses, mixing well. Add one egg at a time, blending well. Form 3 layers of filo sheets; paint with melted butter between each sheet. Cut sheets in 3 inch strips. Fill with cheese mixture and fold each strip in a triangular flag manner. Brush tops with melted butter. Bake at 325° until light brown. Serve. Serves 24.

CAJUN STYLE MEAT TRIANGLES

1 lb. ground meat
1/2 c. salad olives with pimentos,
   chopped
2 c. eggplant, cooked soft
1/4 c. onions, chopped fine
1/2 c. grated Italian cheese
2 eggs

1/2 lb. melted butter
1 lb. filo sheets
1/2 c. bread crumbs
1/2 tsp. white pepper
1 tsp. coarse ground black
   pepper
1/2 tsp. garlic powder

   In a saucepan, melt 1 tablespoon butter at 400°. Add onions and saute until golden brown. Add meat and saute until light brown. Stir in eggplant. Blend in olives. Remove from heat; blend in seasonings. Add remaining ingredients except filo sheets and butter. Form 3 layers of filo; paint each layer with melted butter. Cut into 3 inch strips. Add a tablespoon of filling and fold in a flag triangle motion. Brush top with melted butter. Bake at 325° until light brown. Serves 24.

CHEESE ASPARAGUS CRISPS

1 lb. cheese
2 Tbsp. mayonnaise
½ tsp. red pepper
¼ tsp. white pepper
1 tsp. horseradish

1 loaf thin sliced bread
1 large green pepper, chopped
    fine
1 large can asparagus

In a bowl, grate cheese and blend with mayonnaise. Add peppers and horseradish. Remove crust from bread and spread cheese mixture on each slice. Add finely chopped green peppers. Add asparagus stalks and roll bread, forming a bun. Fasten with toothpicks. Arrange on a flat baking dish and toast until brown. Serve. Serves 24.

GRAND CHEESE SPREAD

6 oz. cream cheese
2 Tbsp. sour cream
½ tsp. onion powder
1½ Tbsp. lemon juice
1 Tbsp. herbs, finely chopped
1 Tbsp. celery, finely chopped
1 c. salad olives, finely chopped

3 Tbsp. bacon, chopped
1 tsp. anchovy paste
½ c. almonds, chopped
1 Tbsp. horseradish
1½ Tbsp. parsley, chopped
1½ Tbsp. chives, finely chopped
½ tsp. red pepper

In a large bowl, combine ingredients thoroughly. This will require at least 3 to 5 minutes of whisking. Chill. Serve with a hard cracker. Serves 48.

SHRIMP PUFFS

2 doz. small shrimp, peeled
2 egg whites, whipped stiff
¼ tsp. paprika
¼ tsp. red pepper
½ c. mayonnaise
½ c. grated cheese

¼ tsp. white pepper
¼ tsp. black pepper
⅛ tsp. oregano
⅛ tsp. sweet basil
1 box saltine crackers

Combine ingredients except for shrimp. Blend well. Heap mixture on crackers and arrange on a flat baking dish. Press shrimp on top of mixture. Broil until shrimp are bright red. Serves 24.

CHICKEN FLIPS

2 boneless chicken breasts,
    ground
1 can cream of mushroom soup

3 sticks margarine
3 c. flour
10 oz. soft cream cheese

In a bowl, blend together cream cheese, flour and margarine. Chill. Roll thin and cut into 2 inch rounds. Place a tablespoon of chicken on each round and dab with mushroom soup. Press edges with a fork to seal. Sprinkle with paprika. Bake at 400° for 20 minutes. Serves 24.

CREOLE HUSHPUPPIES

1 c. corn meal
½ c. corn flour
½ c. all-purpose flour
1 Tbsp. baking powder
¼ c. green onions, chopped fine
2 tsp. minced garlic
2 eggs, beaten

1 c. milk
2 Tbsp. margarine
½ tsp. red pepper
½ tsp. black pepper
½ tsp. thyme
¼ tsp. white pepper
⅛ tsp. oregano
Corn oil

In a large bowl, combine dry ingredients thoroughly. Add garlic and green onions. Slowly add eggs, blending well. In a saucepan, melt margarine at 350°. Add milk and remove from heat. Combine with flour mixture, ¼ amount at a time. Stir well and chill. In a large skillet, heat enough corn oil at 350° to deep fat fry 1 tablespoon-sized hushpuppy at a time. Fry until golden brown. Drain on a paper towel. Serves 24.

HONEY GLAZED ONION RINGS

1 large sweet onion
2 tsp. honey

¼ c. brown sugar
2 Tbsp. margarine

Peel onion and slice into ⅛ inch thick rings. In a saucepan, melt margarine at 300°. Add onion rings and saute until light brown. Add sugar and honey. Reduce heat to 200°. Slowly cook onions, turning carefully, until well glazed. Serve. Serves 12.

"I don't care who you are. If that Cajun catches
you, he's gonna put you in that gumbo!"

Soups and Gumbos from the Bayou

CLOVICE'S CAJUN SOUP RECIPE
FOR DE BAYOU NATIONAL GUARD

4 alligator, peeled and chopped
3 rabbit, slightly skinned
2 of last night's coon, skinning
   optional
8 chicken, plucked and stuffed

6 duck, diced—plucking and gutting,
   optional
1 hamper
1 wheel barrow load of uncooked rice
1 bucket onion, diced
1 can lard

    Melt lard and saute everything until whatever. Add de vege'tables and cook
until absolutely maybe done. Add rice any ole'time. Can be served lukewarm, too
hot, partly cold, or frozen.

MORE KITCHEN WISDOM

When buying fresh fish always press the flesh, it should be firm and bounce back. Always make sure the fish you are buying hasn't been frozen. When fish has been allowed to thaw and remains in the grocery counter too long, it will lose its fresh flavor.

When frying chicken pieces in deep-fat watch for them to rise to the surface. This indicates that they're done. Wings are small and contain little meat. Don't brown them too much.

An easy way to toast sesame seeds is to put them in a skillet and shake them continuously until your desired color is attained. Baking them at 350 degrees in a shallow pan is suggested for the beginner until you get the hang of toasting them in a skillet.

30 medium oysters yield 1 pint. Oysters toughen quickly so they should rarely be cooked for more than 2 minutes.

If you must store ground meat, flatten it before putting it in the refrigerator so the cold will penetrate quickly. If meatballs are too small when are fried, they will become hard.

Chicken livers should have their membrane peeled off before frying. This keeps them from curling and helps in their grinding.

SOUPS AND GUMBOS FROM THE BAYOU

SHRIMP GUMBO CLAIBORNE

2 lb. peeled shrimp
2 c. dark red brown roux
3 c. okra, chopped
1 tsp. file (optional)
1 c. onions, chopped large
1 can tomatoes
2 qt. hot water

½ tsp. bay leaf
½ tsp. red pepper
½ tsp. black pepper
¼ tsp. sweet basil
3 cloves garlic, chopped
¼ tsp. oregano
¾ stick margarine

In a large deep saucepan, melt ¼ stick margarine at 300°. Saute vegetables, including okra, until soft. Slowly add roux. Add tomatoes. Blend well. Reduce heat to 250°. Add 2 quarts hot water and bring to a simmer. Add seasonings. In a separate saucepan, melt ½ stick margarine at 450°. Add shrimp and saute until pink. Add shrimp to mixture, blend well. Serves 6.

Warning: Do not add file until after the dish has been removed from the heat. Mix well. Simmer for 45 minutes until cooked. Two minutes before serving, stir in file.

RABBIT OR CHICKEN GUMBO POYDRAS

3 lb. chicken, chopped, or equal
   amount of rabbit
2 c. okra
1 can tomatoes
1 c. onions, chopped
2 c. brown roux
2 qt. hot water
1 heaping tsp. Creole seasoning

¼ c. green peppers, chopped
2 cloves garlic, chopped
¼ stick margarine
½ tsp. white pepper
¼ tsp. red pepper
¼ tsp. black pepper
¼ tsp. thyme
¼ tsp. basil

In a large saucepan, melt ¼ stick margarine at 400°. Add chicken and saute until light brown. Add onions, garlic and green peppers; saute until soft. Reduce heat to 250°. Add okra and tomatoes; saute for an additional 5 minutes. Reduce heat to 200° and add roux slowly, blending well. Add remaining ingredients, blending in thoroughly. At this point, it may be necessary to add additional hot water to reach your desired thickness. Simmer until chicken is tender. Serve with rice.

One technique from the bayou is to add the rice, ¾ cooked, directly to the dish. Remove from heat. Cover and allow the rice to cook within the meal. Serves 6.

CREOLE OYSTER GUMBO DELACROIX

2 doz. large oysters (retain
   water)
½ stick margarine
1 tsp. file (optional)
2 c. dark brown roux
3 qt. hot water
1 c. onions, chopped large
¼ c. green pepper, chopped
   large

3 cloves garlic, chopped
½ tsp. red pepper
½ tsp. black pepper
¼ tsp. thyme
¼ tsp. sweet basil
¼ tsp. tarragon

In a large saucepan, melt margarine at 400°. Saute vegetables until soft. Reduce heat to 300°. Add oysters and oyster water and saute for an additional 5 minutes. Slowly add roux; bring to a simmer. Blend in hot water to control thickness. Add remaining ingredients except for file. Simmer until gumbo thickens. Two minutes before serving, stir in file and remove from heat. Serve with rice. Serves 6.

File is a taste and a texture that some people enjoy and some don't. This dish is delicious either way.

SEAFOOD GUMBO BIG MAMOU

1 doz. oysters (retain water)
1 lb. shrimp, peeled
½ stick margarine
2 c. dark brown roux
3 qt. hot water
1 c. onions, chopped large
3 cloves garlic, chopped
¼ c. green pepper, chopped

¼ c. parsley, chopped
½ tsp. red pepper
½ tsp. white pepper
1 tsp. black pepper
¼ tsp. thyme
¼ tsp. basil
1 bay leaf

In a large saucepan, melt margarine at 400°. Saute shrimp and oysters until shrimp are pink and oysters are firm. Remove from pan and set aside. Add vegetables and saute until soft. Slowly add roux. Add oyster water. Add additional hot water to achieve desired thickness. Mix well and bring to a rapid simmer. Add seasonings, oysters and shrimp. Blend thoroughly. Cook for 20 minutes at a rapid simmer. Serves 6.

Optional: If you want to add 1 teaspoon file, mix in 2 minutes before serving.

CRAB GUMBO LITTLE MAMOU

6 blue crabs with shell removed
    and cleaned
1½ lb. peeled shrimp
2 c. dark red brown roux
1 can tomatoes
3 qt. hot water
¼ tsp. bay leaf
½ tsp. red pepper
½ tsp. black pepper

¼ tsp. thyme
¼ tsp. basil
3 cloves garlic, chopped
2 packs okra
2 c. onions, chopped large
¼ c. green pepper, chopped
3 Tbsp. parsley, chopped
½ stick margarine

In a large saucepan, melt margarine at 400°. Saute vegetables until soft. Add shrimp; continue to saute until pink. Slowly add roux, bringing to a simmer. Add tomatoes. Add hot water to achieve desired thickness, blending well. Bring to a brisk simmer. Break crabs in halves; remove large claws. Add crabs and seasonings; mix well. Cover and briskly simmer for 30 minutes. Serves 6.

CREOLE CHICKEN SOUP LAFAYETTE

2 lb. chicken (boneless), cut bite
    size
6 chicken bouillon cubes
2 qt. hot water
1 c. onions, chopped
¼ stick margarine

1 tsp. dark brown sugar
¼ c. Parmesan cheese
¼ tsp. black pepper
¼ tsp. red pepper
½ c. brown roux

Dissolve bouillon in 2 quarts hot water; set aside. In a large saucepan, melt margarine at 450°. Add chicken and saute until light brown. Remove from pan and set aside. Add onions and saute until light brown. Add bouillon liquid, bringing to a simmer. Slowly blend in roux. Add remaining ingredients, including chicken; mix well. Bring to a brisk simmer for 20 minutes. Sprinkle top of soup bowls with Parmesan cheese before serving. Try tempting this dish with 6 ounces of white rice. Serves 6.

DRIED SHRIMP GUMBO HOUMA

1 c. dried shrimp
6 hard-boiled eggs
2 cloves garlic, chopped
4 chicken bouillon cubes
2 qt. hot water
1 tsp. Tabasco sauce
1/4 tsp. black pepper
1/2 tsp. white pepper
1/4 tsp. red pepper

1/2 tsp. bay leaf
1/4 tsp. thyme
1/4 tsp. basil
1/4 tsp. oregano
3/4 c. green pepper, chopped
1/2 c. celery, chopped
1 c. onions, chopped
3 c. dark brown roux
1/4 stick margarine

Dissolve bouillon in 2 quarts hot water; set aside. In a large saucepan, add 1 cup of hot water. Bring to a simmer at 300°. Slowly add roux, maintaining a brisk simmer. Add vegetables. Add seasonings, blending well. In a separate saucepan, melt margarine at 400°. Blend in 1/4 cup hot water. Add shrimp and saute until pink. Add shrimp to main dish and bring to a simmer. Combine all ingredients, except for eggs, blending well. Simmer for 20 minutes. Cut eggs in halves; stir in 10 minutes before serving. Serve. Serves 8.

BEEF GUMBO DE QUINCY

3 lb. beef
1 c. celery, chopped
1/4 c. parsley, chopped
1 c. onions, chopped
1/2 tsp. black pepper
1/2 tsp. red pepper
1/4 tsp. basil
1/4 tsp. oregano

2 c. brown roux
1 pack okra
1 can tomatoes
1 Tbsp. dark brown sugar
4 beef bouillon cubes
3 qt. hot water
1/4 stick margarine
3 Tbsp. flour

Dissolve bouillon in 3 quarts hot water; set aside. In a large saucepan, melt margarine at 400°. Add flour; blend well until it gels. Saute vegetables until light brown. Add beef; saute until light brown. Do not overcook. Slowly add roux and bouillon liquid, blending well. Add remaining ingredients; simmer until beef is tender. Serve. Serves 9.

CHICKEN AND SMOKED SAUSAGE GUMBO PETTIBONE

3 lb. boneless chicken
1 lb. smoked sausage
¼ tsp. garlic powder
1 c. onions, chopped
1 c. celery, chopped
¼ tsp. black pepper
¼ tsp. basil
¼ tsp. thyme
¼ tsp. oregano

1 bay leaf
¼ tsp. red pepper
¼ tsp. white pepper
6 chicken bouillon cubes
2 qt. hot water
1½ c. flour
2 c. dark brown roux
1 stick margarine

Dissolve bouillon in 2 quarts hot water; set aside. In a bowl, combine seasonings; set aside. Rub chicken parts thoroughly with ½ seasoning mix. Combine flour and remaining seasonings in a large plate. Thoroughly pat chicken with flour mixture. In a large saucepan, melt margarine. Fry chicken at 400° until golden brown. Remove from pan; set aside. In the same pan, saute sausage until light brown. Slowly add roux and hot water to desired thickness. Add vegetables; saute until soft. Combine all ingredients; simmer for 30 minutes. Serve over rice. Serves 10.

BRIE SOUP WITH OYSTERS PONTCHARTRAIN

1 lb. Brie cheese, cut bite size
3 doz. oysters (including water)
2 c. brown roux
1 c. onions, chopped

½ c. celery, chopped
½ tsp. white pepper
¼ tsp. red pepper
2 c. sour cream
1 c. dry white wine
2 c. hot water

In a large saucepan, add 1 cup hot water at 350°. Slowly add roux and bring to a simmer. Add vegetables and seasonings; blend well. Add additional hot water to control thickness. Add oysters, including water. Stir in cream. Add cheese, blending well. Simmer until oysters are firm and cheese is blended. Five minutes before serving, blend in wine. Serve over pasta. Serves 10.

SEAFOOD AND SAUSAGE GUMBO SHREVEPORT

1 pt. oysters
1 lb. smoked sausage, chopped
1 lb. shrimp, peeled and
   deveined
2 c. dark brown roux
¼ tsp. red pepper
¼ tsp. white pepper
¼ tsp. black pepper

¼ tsp. basil
¼ tsp. thyme
¼ c. green pepper, chopped
3 cloves garlic, chopped
1 c. onions, chopped
3 chicken bouillon cubes
3 qt. hot water
¼ stick margarine

Dissolve bouillon in 3 quarts hot water; set aside. In a large saucepan, melt margarine at 350°. Saute vegetables until soft. Add oysters and shrimp; saute until shrimp are pink and oysters are firm. Add sausage; blend well. Slowly add roux until thoroughly blended. Add bouillon liquid. Add seasonings and mix well. Simmer for 20 minutes. Serve over rice. Serves 8.

Note: This is a dish that is often overcooked. Stay attentive to prevent this!

CREOLE OKRA GUMBO DESIRE

1½ lb. picnic ham
2 lb. chicken, cut up
2 packs okra, chopped
¼ stick margarine
1 can tomatoes
1 c. onions, chopped
3 Tbsp. parsley, chopped

3 Tbsp. green pepper, chopped
½ tsp. bay leaf
¼ tsp. thyme
1 tsp. Creole seasoning
2 c. brown roux
3 qt. hot water

In a large saucepan, melt margarine. Saute ham until light brown. Remove from pan, but allow drippings to remain; set aside. Lightly brown chicken in drippings, remove and set aside. Add vegetables; saute until light brown in remaining drippings. Add tomatoes; saute for 5 minutes. Slowly add roux and hot water to achieve desired thickness. Blend well. Add seasonings and remaining ingredients. Simmer until chicken is tender. Serve. Serves 8.

OYSTER STEW GRAND CHENIER

3 doz. oysters (including liquid)
1/4 c. green onions, chopped
1 qt. hot milk
1/4 c. celery, chopped
2 Tbsp. parsley, chopped

2 Tbsp. flour
2 Tbsp. margarine
6 cloves
1/4 tsp. red pepper
1/4 tsp. black pepper
1 Tbsp. Worcestershire sauce

In a large saucepan, melt margarine at 350°. Add flour, blending well until it gels and becomes light brown. Add oyster water and oysters; simmer until firm. Add vegetables; simmer until tender. Add hot milk. If necessary, reduce the heat. Do not boil. Add remaining ingredients; mix well. Simmer for 20 minutes or until roux thickens. Serve. Serves 6.

CAJUN VICHYSSOISE

2 c. potatoes, diced
1/2 c. onions, sliced
2 Tbsp. margarine
3 chicken bouillon cubes
2 c. hot water
1 tsp. white pepper
1/4 tsp. red pepper

1/4 tsp. sweet basil
2 c. milk
1 c. heavy cream
1 Tbsp. Worcestershire sauce
1 tsp. celery powder
1/2 tsp. hot sauce

Dissolve bouillon in 2 cups hot water; set aside. In a large saucepan, melt margarine at 350°. Add vegetables and saute until soft. Add bouillon liquid, potatoes and seasonings; blend well. Bring to a brisk simmer for 30 minutes. Mash potatoes; blend well. Add hot milk; blend with a whisk. Remove from heat. Combine together cream and Worcestershire sauce. Add to potato mixture. Serve cool. Serves 6.

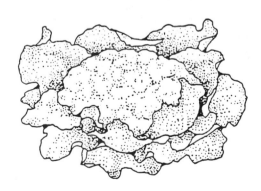

CAJUN VEGETABLE SOUP FRERET

2 lb. sirloin steak, cut in large
    chunks
½ lb. ham, chopped
1 onion, quartered
3 celery stalks, cut in fourths
3 carrots, chopped large
1 large turnip, chopped
1 small cabbage, quartered
1 can tomatoes
3 qt. hot water
2 potatoes, chopped large
3 Tbsp. parsley, chopped
½ tsp. white pepper
½ tsp. black pepper
¼ tsp. oregano
¼ tsp. tarragon
¼ c. uncooked macaroni (retain
    liquid)
1 c. dark brown roux
½ stick margarine
2 c. hot water

In a large saucepan, melt margarine at 400°. Saute meat and ham until light brown. Add vegetables except potatoes. Saute until soft. Reduce heat to 250°. Slowly add roux and 2 cups hot water drained from macaroni. Add remaining ingredients, except macaroni, one at a time; blend well. Simmer until contents are tender. Twenty minutes before serving, add macaroni. When tender, serve. Serves 10.

HAM AND SPLIT PEA SOUP BARONNE

2 c. ham, diced
1 lb. split peas
4 qt. hot water
1 c. light brown roux
1 onion, chopped
½ tsp. black pepper
¼ tsp. thyme
¼ tsp. oregano

In a large saucepan, bring 2 quarts water to a simmer. In a separate pan, saute ham until edges are brown. Add onion; saute until soft. Place the ham and onion in the simmering water. Add peas and remaining 2 quarts water. Bring to a rapid simmer; continue until peas soften. Reduce heat; add seasonings. Blend in roux and remaining ingredients. Continue to simmer until soup thickens. Serve. Serves 6.

This dish, when simmered slowly and brought to the consistency of a heavy sauce, is delicious over wild rice.

RED FISH OR GROUPER CHOWDER CONTI

2 lb. fish chunks
4 large potatoes, diced
1 c. celery, chopped
1 qt. hot milk
1/4 tsp. bay leaf
1/2 tsp. white pepper
1/2 tsp. black pepper
1/4 tsp. thyme

1/4 tsp. oregano
1 bay leaf
1/2 tsp. sweet paprika
1 c. onions, chopped
1/4 c. ham, finely chopped
1/2 stick margarine
1/4 c. white roux

In a large saucepan, melt 1/4 stick margarine at 350°. Add 2 cups of hot water. Add fish and simmer until tender, about 10 minutes. Warning: Make sure fish is firm, not falling apart. In a separate pan, melt remaining margarine at 450°. Add ham and saute until light brown. Add vegetables, except potatoes, to ham and saute until soft. Add potatoes and bring to a simmer until potatoes are tender. Combine this mixture with the fish. Ten minutes before serving, slowly add roux and milk. When chowder thickens, serve. Serves 8.

Note: I always tempt this dish with 6 ounces of good dry wine. Excellent over large slabs of baked fish.

SHRIMP BISQUE BAYOU BLACK

2 lb. shrimp, peeled and
    deveined
1/4 stick margarine
3 Tbsp. onion, finely chopped
1 c. sour cream
1/4 tsp. sweet paprika
1 tsp. salt
1/2 tsp. white pepper

1/2 tsp. black pepper
1/4 tsp. thyme
1/4 tsp. oregano
1 bay leaf
1/4 c. sherry
3 c. hot milk
2 Tbsp. chives
1/4 c. brown roux

Chop shrimp medium size. In a saucepan, melt margarine at 400°. Add shrimp and saute until pink. Caution: Do not overcook. Remove shrimp from pan and allow drippings to remain; set aside. In the same pan, add vegetables and saute until soft. Reduce heat to 175° and slowly add sour cream. Add 3 cups hot milk. Control the heat and do not allow to boil. Combine remaining ingredients, including shrimp. Simmer for 15 minutes. Serve with brown rice. Serves 6.

LOBSTER STEW SOUTH RAMPART

4 lobster tails, peeled and sliced
1/4 stick margarine
3 c. hot milk
1 c. sour cream

1/4 c. dark brown roux
Juice of 1/2 lemon
1 can lobster chowder soup
1/4 tsp. red pepper
1/2 tsp. salt

In a large saucepan, melt margarine at 400°. Add lobster and saute lobster for 1 minute. Reduce heat to 250° and saute for 5 minutes. Do not allow to brown. Add hot milk and sour cream. Slowly blend in roux. Add seasonings and chowder; blend well. Simmer until lobster is tender. Squeeze lemon over top and serve. Serves 6.

Note: If you simmer this dish until it thickens, it is excellent over a bed of steaming rice or mashed potatoes.

CREAM OF CAULIFLOWER SOUP NORTH RAMPART

2 packs frozen cauliflower or 1
    large fresh head
1 c. hot milk
1 c. sour cream
1/4 c. light brown roux
1/4 c. celery, chopped
1/4 c. onions, chopped

1/4 stick margarine
1 Tbsp. parsley, chopped
1/4 tsp. nutmeg
2 chicken bouillon cubes
2 c. hot water
1/8 tsp. garlic flakes

Dissolve bouillon in 2 cups hot water. In a saucepan, melt margarine at 400°. Add vegetables, except cauliflower, and saute until soft. Add bouillon liquid and bring to a simmer. Reduce heat to 200°. Add milk and sour cream; do not boil. Add roux slowly; maintain a brisk simmer. Add remaining seasonings and cauliflower. Blend well. Simmer until cauliflower is tender. Control thickness with additional hot water if needed. Serves 6.

Note: Melt a layer of American cheese on top and serve.

CREAMY AVOCADO SOUP GRETNA

1 c. avocado puree
1 c. avocado, cubed
2 cans cream of chicken soup
1/2 c. sour cream

1/4 c. light brown roux
1/4 tsp. white pepper
2 sprigs green onions, chopped
    fine

In a saucepan, bring soup to simmer. Add roux; blend well. Reduce heat to 150°. Add sour cream; blend in pureed avocado. Add remaining ingredients, including cubed avocado. Remove from heat and allow to set for 10 minutes.

This dish can be served warm or chilled. Garnish with parsley. Serves 6.

FRENCH ONION SOUP LOWERLINE

1 can cream of onion soup
1 can French onion soup
1 large onion, sliced into ¼ inch
    rounds
Grated rind of lemon
¼ tsp. nutmeg
½ c. sherry

1 pack toasted bread rounds
¼ tsp. garlic powder
¼ tsp. onion powder
½ c. Italian cheese
½ tsp. fresh ground black
    pepper
2 Tbsp. margarine

In a bowl, combine seasonings; set aside. In small saucepan, melt margarine at 400° and remove moisture. Stir in ½ seasoning mix. Remove from heat; place onion rounds in pan with melted margarine. Saute for 2 minutes. Try not to disturb onion rounds. In a separate saucepan, add soups and bring to a low simmer. Add remaining seasonings and bring to a simmer for 5 minutes. Add sherry. Remove from heat. Pour into 4 deep soup bowls. Sprinkle with lemon rind. Carefully float onion rounds on the surface. Top rounds with toasted bread rounds and sprinkle with cheese. Serves 4.

CAJUN CREAM OF CAULIFLOWER SOUP

2 packs frozen cauliflower
¼ c. onion, chopped
¼ c. celery, chopped
1 c. white roux
3 chicken bouillon cubes
3 c. hot water
2 c. hot milk

¼ tsp. nutmeg
½ tsp. white pepper
½ tsp. red pepper
¼ tsp. sweet basil
¼ tsp. oregano
½ c. grated cheese

In a large saucepan, add 3 cups hot water and bouillon cubes. Add cauliflower and cook until ¾ tender. Reduce heat to 200° and slowly add roux. Remove from heat and add milk. Blend carefully. Do not allow to curdle. Add remaining ingredients except cheese. Bring to a simmer until cauliflower begins to break apart. Five minutes before serving, sprinkle with cheese. Serves 4.

CHICKEN WITH RICE SOUP BAYOU BIENVILLE

2 c. leftover fried chicken breast,
    chopped
3 chicken bouillon cubes
3 c. hot water
½ c. celery, finely chopped
1½ c. cooked rice

1 c. light brown roux
2 Tbsp. parsley, chopped
½ tsp. red pepper
2 sprigs green onions, finely
    chopped
½ tsp. white pepper

In a large saucepan, bring 3 cups hot water to a low simmer. Add bouillon cubes. When cubes are dissolved, add roux. Blend in vegetables. Bring to a simmer. Add seasonings; continue to simmer for 5 minutes. Add remaining ingredients except rice. Blend well. Simmer for 10 minutes or until chicken is extremely tender. Add rice 5 minutes before serving. If additional moisture is needed, add hot water. Serves 6.

CREAM OF CREOLE ONION SOUP

¼ stick margarine
2 c. onions, chopped
2 c. brown roux
2 c. hot water
1 c. sour cream
4 egg yolks, beaten
¼ tsp. paprika

1 Tbsp. Worcestershire sauce
1 Tbsp. celery, chopped
¼ tsp. white pepper
¼ tsp. red pepper
1 small bay leaf
⅛ tsp. thyme

In a saucepan, melt margarine at 450°. Add onions and saute until golden brown. Add hot water; bring to a brisk simmer. Blend in roux. Reduce heat to 150° and add sour cream. Bring to simmer for 5 minutes. Remove from heat. Blend in egg yolks and remaining ingredients. Mix well. It may be necessary to add boiling water to control thickness. Simmer slowly for an additional 10 minutes. Serve with crackers. Serves 6.

CAJUN COUNTRY POTATO SOUP

2 large potatoes, peeled and
    chopped
¼ c. onion, chopped
¼ c. celery, chopped
2 Tbsp. margarine
½ tsp. red pepper
¼ tsp. thyme

⅛ tsp. basil
1 bay leaf
2 c. white roux
3 cubes chicken bouillon,
    crushed
1 tsp. Worcestershire sauce
½ tsp. white pepper

In a large saucepan, boil potatoes until tender. Remove from heat and drain. In a separate pan, melt margarine at 400°. Add onion and celery; saute until light brown. Add to potatoes along with crushed bouillon cubes and blend until smooth, using a hand blender. In a separate saucepan, bring 2 cups water to simmer. Blend in roux. Add remaining ingredients; mix well. Blend potato mixture with roux. Control thickness with hot milk. Simmer for 10 minutes. Do not allow to boil. Serves 4.

CREAM OF MUSHROOM SOUP PRYTANIA

1 large pack mushrooms, sliced
¼ stick margarine
3 chicken bouillon cubes
2 c. hot water
½ c. celery, chopped

⅓ c. onions, chopped
2 Tbsp. parsley, chopped
1 c. white roux
¼ tsp. white pepper
¼ tsp. red pepper

In a saucepan, melt margarine at 450°. Add vegetables, including mushrooms, and saute until light brown. In a separate pan, dissolve bouillon cubes in hot water; bring to simmer. Slowly blend in roux. Do not allow to boil. Add seasonings; mix well. Add vegetables and simmer at low heat for 20 minutes. Serve. Serves 4.

Note: Sprinkle lightly with fresh grated Parmesan cheese.

CRAWFISH BISQUE WITH MUSHROOMS MAGAZINE

1 pack fresh mushrooms, sliced
¼ stick margarine
1 c. creamy roux
2 c. hot water
2 c. crawfish tails, peeled and
  deveined

½ c. sour cream
¼ tsp. white pepper
¼ tsp. red pepper
⅛ tsp. bay leaf
⅛ tsp. thyme

In a saucepan, melt margarine at 400°. Add crawfish tails and saute for 3 minutes or until pink. Add mushrooms; saute until light brown. Add hot water and bring to simmer. Slowly add roux. Reduce heat to 150° and blend in sour cream. Add seasonings. Control thickness with additional hot water or warm milk. Mix well and serve. Serves 6.

Note: I tempt this dish with 2 ounces of strong brandy.

OYSTER BISQUE BAYOU FELICITY

2 pt. oysters (including liquid)
¼ stick margarine
2 Tbsp. minced onions
¼ tsp. garlic powder
1 c. cream of celery soup

1 c. hot milk
1 c. cream
¼ tsp. white pepper
⅛ tsp. paprika
3 egg yolks, beaten

In a saucepan, melt margarine at 400°. Add onions and saute until soft. Do not brown. Add oysters with liquid; bring to a simmer. Add milk; continue at a low simmer. Do not allow to boil. Add remaining ingredients except for egg yolks. Remove from heat. Allow to set until a light film forms on top. Slowly add egg yolks until thickened. Blend thoroughly. Sprinkle with chopped parsley. Serve. Serves 4.

Note: You may blend in ½ cup brown roux for a nutty flavor and added thickness. Serve over pasta or rice.

PEA SOUP CREOLE STYLE

1 can condensed consomme
  (your choice)
1 can cream of chicken soup
1 can peas (including liquid)
1 c. hot water
½ c. ham, finely diced
1 Tbsp. Worcestershire sauce

½ tsp. chili sauce
¼ tsp. white pepper
¼ tsp. red pepper
⅛ stick margarine
¼ c. light brown roux (optional)

In a large saucepan, melt margarine at 450°. Add ham and saute until light brown. Combine ham, chicken soup and consomme; bring to a simmer. Add hot water. Add peas. As peas soften, mash some for added thickness. Note: If using fresh garden peas, substitute light brown roux instead of mashed peas for thickness. Simmer for 10 minutes. Add remaining ingredients; simmer until peas are soft. Serve. Serves 4.

EASY SHRIMP SUPREME JACKSON SQUARE

1 can cream of mushroom soup
1 can asparagus soup
2 c. sour cream
1 c. shrimp, peeled, deveined
   and chopped fine
¼ c. dry sherry

¼ tsp. red pepper
2 sprigs parsley, chopped, for
   garnish
⅛ stick margarine
Dark brown roux for casserole
   base (optional)

In a saucepan, combine soups and bring to a simmer. Blend in sour cream. Do not allow to boil. In a separate pan, melt margarine. Add seasonings and shrimp and saute until rich pink. Add shrimp to soup mixture. Mix well. Simmer for 5 minutes. Add sherry. Control thickness with hot milk. Do not allow this dish to boil. Simmer for 10 minutes until blended well.

Note: Add ½ cup dark brown roux to use this dish as a casserole base for creamy vegetables. Garnish with sprigs of parsley.

CRAB SOUP COLISEUM STREET SUPREME

1 lb. cooked crabmeat
1 can cream of mushroom soup
1 can cream of chicken soup
1 c. white roux
1 c. hot water
¼ c. sherry

¼ tsp. white pepper
¼ tsp. red pepper
¼ tsp. Worcestershire sauce
¼ c. dry white wine
⅛ tsp. Louisiana hot sauce
¼ stick margarine

In a saucepan, melt margarine at 250°. Add seasonings and stir in crabmeat. Do not crush; carefully blend until crabmeat becomes light pink. Reduce heat to 250°. Add hot water, bringing to simmer. Add soups, stirring lightly. Blend in roux and wine. Combine all ingredients except sherry; allow to simmer for 20 minutes. Add sherry. Control thickness with additional hot water. Serve. Serves 6.

Note: The density of this dish will allow a variation from soup to sauce to casserole base.

CREOLE CHICKEN LEMON SOUP

6 chicken breasts (including
    skin), cut into quarters
3 qt. water
1 c. uncooked rice

1 tsp. salt
1/2 tsp. white pepper
1/4 tsp. ground red pepper
1/8 tsp. tarragon

In a large saucepan, add water, bringing to a simmer. Add salt and chicken and bring to a boil. Boil the chicken until tender, but not soft. Add rice and cook until rice is tender. Remove from the heat. Strain any moisture into a separate bowl and reserve. Remove chicken skin.

Sauce:

4 eggs

2 lemons

Beat eggs with a beater until they are light and frothy. Slowly add lemon juice and dilute the mixture with 2 to 4 cups of the hot broth. Beat constantly until well mixed. Add the egg lemon mixture to the rest of the broth, stirring constantly. Serve immediately. Serves 6.

BEEF VEGETABLE SOUP MORGAN CITY

2 lb. beef, cut into 1 inch
    squares
2 qt. cold water
1/2 c. carrots, diced
1/2 c. celery, diced
1/2 c. green peas
1/2 c. potatoes, diced
2 c. tomatoes, peeled
2 Tbsp. green pepper

1/2 c. onions, chopped
2 tsp. salt
1 Tbsp. parsley
1/4 tsp. tarragon
1/4 tsp. oregano
1/2 tsp. coarse ground black
    pepper
1/4 tsp. ground red pepper
1/4 c. dark red roux

In a large pot, add beef. Cover with water and bring to a boil. Reduce heat and simmer for 30 minutes. Add remaining ingredients and cook until tender. Serve. Serves 6.

FELICITY SPLIT PEA SOUP

1 c. smoked ham, diced
1 lb. split peas
2 boneless chicken breasts,
    chopped
3 qt. water
1/2 c. onions, chopped

1/2 c. carrots, diced
2 hard-boiled eggs, quartered
1 tsp. salt
1/2 tsp. ground red pepper
1/2 tsp. white pepper
1/2 stick margarine

In a large pot, add water, ham and peas. Bring to a boil until the peas are soft. Reduce the heat to 225°. Add seasonings. In a separate saucepan, melt 1/2 stick margarine at 450°. Add vegetables and saute until soft. Mash in hard-boiled egg yolks and remove from the heat immediately. Combine all ingredients into the soup. Stir well and simmer until soup thickens. Serves 6.

CAJUN STYLE GAZPACHO

6 tomatoes, peeled, seeded and
   chopped
¼ c. bell pepper, chopped fine
1 cucumber, peeled and diced
¼ c. onions, chopped
2 cloves garlic, chopped fine

¼ c. vinegar
¼ c. olive oil
1 tsp. salt
1 c. cold water
½ tsp. white pepper
¼ tsp. red pepper

In a blender, combine all ingredients on a medium speed until lique-fied. Chill 3 hours before serving. Garnish with parsley and serve. Serves 6.

IRISH CHANNEL BROCCOLI AND CHEESE SOUP

2 packs broccoli, chopped
1 lb. American cheese, cubed
6 chicken bouillon cubes
6 c. hot water
1 c. onions, chopped
¼ stick margarine

1 pack egg noodles
1 tsp. salt
1 tsp. white pepper
¼ tsp. red pepper
⅛ tsp. basil
¼ tsp. garlic powder

Dissolve bouillon cubes in 6 cups hot water; set aside. In a large saucepan, melt margarine at 400°. Add onions and saute until soft. Add bouillon liquid and bring to a boil. Slowly add egg noodles and salt. Cook for 5 minutes, stirring occasionally. Add broccoli and garlic powder. Cook for an additional 4 minutes. Reduce the heat to 300°. Add milk, cheese and seasonings. Cook until cheese is melted and the noodles are done. Serve. Serves 6.

CREOLE BEAN SOUP

½ lb. large lima beans
1 medium onion, chopped fine
1 c. tomato sauce
1 carrot, diced small
½ c. celery, chopped fine

¼ stick margarine
2 qt. water
½ tsp. black pepper
½ tsp. white pepper
1 tsp. salt

In a saucepan, melt the margarine at 400°. Add onion and saute until soft. Add tomato sauce, seasonings and water, blending well. Bring to a boil. Add limas, carrots and celery. Bring to a boil. Cover and cook until limas are tender. Serves 6.

COLD TOMATO SOUP LAKE BORGNE

4 ripe tomatoes, peeled and
    diced
1 medium onion, diced
2 Tbsp. olive oil
1 Tbsp. wine vinegar
1½ c. water
2 tsp. sugar
2 tsp. salt
1 cucumber, diced small
1 clove garlic, mashed
½ tsp. black pepper
¼ tsp. white pepper

In a food processor, combine all ingredients except for cucumbers. Process until well blended. Pour mixture into a salad bowl with a cover. Refrigerate overnight. Before serving, peel and dice cucumbers. Stir in well. Serve cold. Serves 6.

OKRA GUMBO LAKE CATHERINE SHORES

2 lb. shrimp, peeled and
    deveined
3 blue crabs, cleaned and
    quartered
1 (10 oz.) pack okra
1½ qt. water
2 bay leaves
½ c. bell pepper, chopped
1 (16 oz.) can tomatoes
¾ c. flour
1 c. onions, chopped large
6 strips thick sliced bacon
2 Tbsp. Worcestershire sauce
2 Tbsp. dry parsley
½ tsp. basil
1 tsp. Louisiana hot sauce
½ tsp. garlic flakes

In a large pot, add 1 quart of water and bring to a boil. Add bay leaves, lemon, salt, shrimp, and crabs. Bring to a boil until shrimp are deep pink. Remove from the heat. Reduce heat to 250°. Add okra, Worcestershire sauce, parsley, basil, and hot sauce. Allow to simmer while preparing gumbo roux.

Roux: In a saucepan, saute bacon until crisp. Remove from the drippings, crush and set aside. Blend in flour until light brown. Add onions, bell pepper and garlic. Slowly blend in 1 cup hot water. Combine roux mixture with the shrimp and crab mixture. Add tomatoes and liquid. Allow to simmer for 45 minutes and serve. Serves 8.

CREOLE SHRIMP AND SAUSAGE GUMBO

1 lb. Italian or Polish smoked
   sausage, cut into 1/2 inch
   rounds
1 lb. shrimp, peeled and
   deveined (retain the heads)
1 stick margarine
8 c. okra
3 c. cooked rice
1/2 c. green onions, chopped fine

2 c. onions, chopped
10 c. seafood stock
2 c. tomatoes, peeled and
   chopped
1 1/2 tsp. white pepper
1 1/2 tsp. black pepper
2 tsp. salt
1 tsp. garlic flakes
1 tsp. onion flakes
1/2 tsp. thyme
1/2 tsp. ground red pepper

In a bowl, add 10 cups hot water and 1 tablespoon crab boil. Bring to a boil. Add shrimp heads. Boil for 10 minutes and strain. Retain the stock and discard the heads. In a bowl, combine seasonings; set aside. In a large saucepan, melt margarine at 450° until a light smoke appears. Add 6 cups okra and saute for 3 minutes. Add 1/2 seasoning mix; continue to saute until okra is brown, stirring frequently. Add onions; saute until soft. Add 1 cup of stock and simmer for 5 minutes. Add tomatoes and 1 cup of stock. Saute for 5 minutes. Add remaining stock and remaining seasoning mix. Add sausage and simmer for 45 minutes. Add shrimp and green onions 5 minutes before serving. Serve with mounds of steaming rice. Serves 8.

FRENCH MARKET OYSTER GUMBO

3 doz. oysters (retain liquid)
1 c. small dried shrimp
1/4 stick margarine
2 c. heavy cream
1/2 c. onions, chopped
1/4 c. green onions, chopped

1/2 tsp. salt
1/4 tsp. white pepper
1/4 tsp. coarse ground black
   pepper
1 c. celery, chopped
1 c. water

In a large skillet, melt margarine at 450°. Add celery, peppers, 1 cup water, salt, and oyster liquid. Bring to a boil. Reduce the heat to 250°. Add shrimp. Stir in green onions. Slowly add cream, whisking constantly. Add oysters and cook until oysters curl. Remove from the heat. Ladle into bowls of steaming rice. Serves 6.

"The salad is served, Madam."
"Ohhh, that's so romantic."

Vegetables and Salads

A WORD FROM CLOVICE:

Vegetables was sometin' I was forced to eat wen I was a kid. And like most of us for'tunate men, what our momma's had given up on gettin' us to eat, our wives feel dey could accomplish. I'm a meat-eating car'nivorous animal and still hadn't gotten over de idea of takin' up space on my plate oc'cupied by a big T-bone steak to make room for dem string beans.

HOW TO'S IN THE KITCHEN

Dust your rolling pin and board with flour before rolling out the Bisquick mix; this will prevent any sticking.

Fillo are delicate pastry sheets and should be handled carefully. Do not attempt to handle fillo after it reaches room temperature; it will dry out quickly. Always brush butter between the layers.

The best wrapper for storing cheese in the refrigerator is aluminum foil. It keeps the odor in and prevents drying. All spreads with cheese should be blended at room temperature.

When grinding chicken never over-grind; it will become mushy. Use your largest grinder blade or tell the butcher to pass it through his grinder only once.

Hush puppies should be fried quickly to a golden brown. Overfrying will make the crust brittle. Frying too slow will cause them to soak up oil.

One must be careful glazing with brown sugar; too much heat will turn it black and gummy.

Never over-fry shrimp. Don't butterfly small shrimp before frying or they'll dry out. It's best to double-dip shrimp in batter to give them a good coating.

VEGETABLES AND SALADS

CREOLE RED BEANS AND RICE

1 lb. red beans
2 lb. boneless ham hock
1 c. onions, chopped
1 c. celery, chopped
1 c. green peppers, chopped
1 tsp. white pepper
1 tsp. Tabasco sauce
1/2 tsp. garlic powder

1/2 tsp. oregano
1/2 tsp. black pepper
1 tsp. thyme
1 tsp. bay leaf
1/4 tsp. margarine
1 c. red brown roux
1 tsp. salt

Pour beans in a microwave dish, cover with water and cook until 3/4 done. In a saucepan, melt the margarine at 450°. Chop ham hocks into bite-size pieces. Add and saute until light brown. Remove ham from pan and set aside. Add vegetables and saute until soft. Add red beans, including liquid. Add remaining ingredients except roux; blend well. Cover with water and bring to a boil. Add whatever water necessary to maintain a brisk boil for 20 minutes. Add roux, blending well. As beans soften, crush some to thicken the sauce. Simmer for 15 minutes. At this point, you should be aware of a sticking tendency. Stir frequently. Serve over a bed of rice. Serves 8.

CREOLE EGGPLANT ST. ANN

2 large eggplants
1/2 tsp. paprika
1/4 tsp. white pepper
1/4 tsp. black pepper
1/4 tsp. red pepper
1/2 tsp. onion powder
1/2 tsp. garlic powder

1/2 tsp. thyme
1/4 tsp. basil
1 c. all-purpose flour
1/2 c. seasoned bread crumbs
1/4 c. milk
3 eggs, beaten
1/2 c. Parmesan cheese

In a bowl, combine beaten eggs with milk. In a separate bowl, combine seasonings. Pour 1/2 seasoning mix into egg mixture. Add remaining seasonings with the flour; mix well. Add bread crumbs; mix thoroughly. Peel eggplants; cut in 1/2 inch rounds. Dip eggplants into egg mixture. Allow excess to drain. Pat thoroughly in flour mixture. Fry on both sides until golden brown. This should take about 3 minutes on each side. Sprinkle with Parmesan cheese. Serves 6.

CREOLE POTATO PATTIES IN CREAM SAUCE

2 lb. potatoes, peeled and diced
4 eggs, beaten
1/4 tsp. garlic powder
1/4 tsp. onion powder
1/4 c. flour
1/2 tsp. white pepper
1/4 tsp. black pepper
3 Tbsp. grated cheese
1 tsp. parsley, finely chopped
1/2 stick margarine

In a saucepan, boil potatoes; do not allow to become mushy. Mash, but do not whip potatoes. Add remaining ingredients except flour and margarine. Mix well. Shape into patties and dredge in flour. In a saucepan, melt margarine at 400°. Fry patties until golden brown on both sides. Place on a serving platter.

Sauce:

1 c. heavy cream
1/4 c. brown Creole mustard
1/2 c. grated American cheese
1/8 stick margarine

In a small saucepan, melt margarine at 200°. Add cream; blend in mustard. Remove from heat. Stir in cheese. Pour over top of potato patties. Serves 8.

CAJUN STYLE CRAB AND POTATOES CAKES

4 large Idaho potatoes, peeled
   and diced
1 lb. crabmeat
1/2 c. sour cream
1/4 c. onions, finely chopped
3 Tbsp. parsley, finely chopped
1 c. sharp yellow cheese
1/2 tsp. garlic powder
1/4 tsp. white pepper
1/8 tsp. red pepper
1/4 tsp. dry mustard
1/4 stick margarine

In a saucepan, boil potatoes until 3/4 cooked. In a saucepan, melt margarine at 400°. Add onions and parsley; saute until soft. Add crabmeat; saute for 3 minutes. Reduce heat to 250°. Blend in sour cream. Add seasonings; reduce heat to 200°. Fold in cheese and allow to melt. Drain potatoes and blend into mixture. If consistency is too thick to form cakes, add warm milk. Do not whip mixture, but allow to remain chunky. Lightly oil individual potato shells. Pour in mixture; sprinkle with paprika. Bake at 400° until top is light brown. Serves 8.

BAKED SWEET POTATOES CAMP STREET

8 sweet potatoes
1 tsp. vanilla
½ stick margarine
½ tsp. cinnamon
¼ tsp. nutmeg

Juice of 1 orange
1 small bag marshmallows
3 Tbsp. brown sugar
1 c. milk

In a saucepan, boil sweet potatoes until peeling is easily removed. Chop into small bits; do not whip. In a separate saucepan, bring milk to a low simmer. Do not boil. Add remaining ingredients to milk except marshmallows and margarine. Remove from heat. Fold this mixture into potatoes. Use half of margarine to oil casserole dish. Pour potato mixture into dish. Melt remaining margarine; cover over potatoes. Arrange marshmallows on top. Bake at 325° until marshmallows are golden brown. Serves 10.

SAUTEED MUSHROOMS CAJUN STYLE

1 large pack fresh mushrooms
½ c. onions, diced
½ c. celery, diced
2 Tbsp. parsley, finely chopped
1 tsp. salt

½ tsp. garlic powder
¼ tsp. white pepper
¼ tsp. black pepper
¼ tsp. oregano
½ stick margarine
4 c. cooked rice

Break stems from mushroom caps and chop fine. Slice caps in halves. In a saucepan, melt margarine at 400°. Add mushrooms and saute until light brown. Blend in remaining ingredients, except rice, stirring and shaking the pan continuously for 10 minutes. In a serving platter, arrange steaming rice in a long oval shape. Pour mushroom mixture down the center and serve immediately. Serves 4.

CAJUN CREAM STYLE MUSHROOMS

1 large pack fresh mushrooms
½ c. onions, diced
½ c. celery, diced
2 Tbsp. parsley, finely chopped
½ tsp. garlic powder
¼ tsp. white pepper

¼ tsp. black pepper
¼ tsp. oregano
½ stick margarine
1 can cream of mushroom soup
3 beef bouillon cubes
2 c. hot water
2 Tbsp. flour

Dissolve bouillon cubes in 2 cups hot water. Break stems from mushrooms and chop fine. Slice caps in halves. In a saucepan, melt margarine at 400°. Add vegetables and saute until soft. Add flour and blend until it gels and becomes a dark brown. Add seasonings, continuing to stir rapidly. Add bouillon liquid. Blend in mushroom soup. Allow mixture to thicken. Serve over rice or noodles. Serves 6.

CAJUN ONION CASSEROLE

6 large onions, cut in ¼ inch rounds (leave rounds intact)
1 lb. liver, chopped fine
1 Tbsp. Worcestershire sauce
¼ tsp. tarragon
½ tsp. oregano
1 Tbsp. parsley, finely chopped
¼ c. celery, finely chopped
¼ tsp. basil
¼ tsp. marjoram
¼ stick margarine
1 c. light brown roux
2 beef bouillon cubes
1 c. hot water
½ tsp. red pepper
1 tsp. coarse ground black pepper

Dissolve bouillon in 1 cup hot water; set aside. In a saucepan, melt margarine at 450°. Add liver and saute for 5 minutes. Add vegetables, except onions, and saute until soft. Add seasonings and Worcestershire sauce; saute for 2 minutes. Add roux and bouillon liquid; mix well. Simmer until mixture thickens. Remove from heat. In a lightly oiled casserole dish, pour in ¼ mixture. Arrange half of the onion rings. Add ¼ more of mixture. Arrange another layer of onion rings. Pour in remaining mixture. Bake for 30 minutes at 350° or until golden brown. Serves 6.

CHICKEN LIVER DIRTY RICE BURGUNDY

2 lb. rice, ¾ cooked
1½ c. onions, chopped
1 pack chicken livers
1 tsp. coarse ground black pepper
1 tsp. garlic powder
1 tsp. salt
¼ c. green onions, chopped
¼ c. parsley, finely chopped
½ stick margarine
2 chicken bouillon cubes
3 c. hot water

Dissolve bouillon cubes in 3 cups hot water; set aside. In a saucepan, melt margarine at 450°. Add livers and saute until light brown. Remove from the pan and chop. Allow drippings to remain. Add vegetables and saute until soft. Add seasonings; mix well. Add bouillon liquid; blend in well. Return chicken livers to the pan. Add rice and blend well. Simmer until liquid is absorbed and rice is tender. Serves 6.

CREOLE DIRTY RICE

2 c. cooked rice
1 c. leftover beef, cut in cubes
½ c. onions, chopped
½ stick margarine
¼ c. parsley, chopped
2 cloves garlic, finely chopped

3 Tbsp. green peppers, finely
  chopped
½ tsp. black pepper
¼ tsp. Tabasco sauce
3 Tbsp. Worcestershire sauce
¼ tsp. oregano
¼ tsp. basil

In a saucepan, melt ¼ stick margarine at 450°. Add vegetables and saute until light brown. Add seasonings; blend in well. Reduce the heat to 300°. Add Worcestershire sauce; blend well. Do not allow the Worcestershire sauce to mask the color. Add beef and remaining margarine; saute for 2 minutes. Reduce the heat to 250°. Add rice and saute until liquid is absorbed and rice turns a deep brown. Serves 4.

EGGPLANT CASSEROLE ROYAL STREET

2 large eggplants, peeled and
  cut into chunks
¼ stick margarine
1 c. light brown roux
½ c. milk
½ c. sharp yellow cheese or
  Parmesan cheese, grated

1 c. seasoned bread crumbs
½ tsp. salt
¼ tsp. red pepper
½ tsp. oregano
¼ tsp. basil
¼ c. onions, chopped
2 cloves garlic, chopped fine

In a saucepan, melt margarine at 450°. Add eggplants and saute until medium soft. Add vegetables and seasonings; blend well. Saute until vegetables and eggplants become soft. Slowly blend in roux. Reduce heat to 250°. Add milk and cheese, allowing cheese to melt. Remove pan from the heat. Fold in half of the bread crumbs. Blend well. Mixture should be very thick. In a lightly oiled casserole dish, pour in mixture. Cover with remaining bread crumbs. Bake at 350° until golden brown. Serves 8.

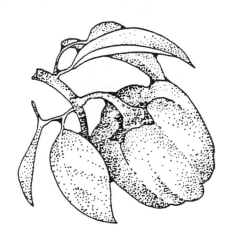

BAYOU EGGPLANT

2 large eggplants, peeled and
    cut into chunks
½ c. celery, chopped
½ c. onions, chopped
¼ c. green pepper, chopped
1 Tbsp. Worcestershire sauce
½ tsp. white pepper
½ tsp. black pepper

½ c. Italian cheese, grated
1 c. salad olives, chopped
1 c. bread crumbs
¼ tsp. oregano
¼ tsp. thyme
¼ tsp. bay leaf
½ stick margarine

In a saucepan, boil eggplants until soft, not mushy. Drain. In a separate saucepan, melt margarine at 450°. Add celery, onions and green pepper; saute until soft. Add eggplants and fold in; do not mash. Add seasonings, Worcestershire sauce and olives; blend well. Continue to saute for 5 minutes. Remove from heat. Fold in half of the bread crumbs and half of the cheese; blend well. In a lightly oiled casserole dish, pour in mixture. Cover with remaining bread crumbs and cheese. Bake at 375° for 30 minutes or until golden brown. Serves 8.

CABBAGE IN CREAM

1 large head cabbage
1 c. sour cream
½ c. grated sharp cheese
¼ tsp. garlic powder
¼ tsp. onion powder

¼ tsp. sweet basil
⅛ tsp. oregano
¼ tsp. white pepper
⅛ tsp. red pepper
1 tsp. salt

Cut cabbage into chunks. In a saucepan, add cabbage and boil until medium tender. Drain well. In a separate saucepan, heat sour cream to 250° until simmering. Blend in cheese and seasonings. Remove from heat immediately; it is not necessary for cheese to melt. In a lightly oiled casserole dish, arrange cabbage. Pour mixture over cabbage. Bake for 30 minutes at 350° or until golden brown. Serves 6.

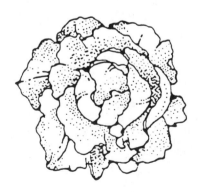

CREAMY BROCCOLI AND MUSHROOM CASEROLE TOULOUSE

4 packs broccoli
2 cans cream of mushroom soup
1/2 tsp. garlic salt
1/4 c. onions, chopped
1 can mushrooms
1/2 c. almonds, chopped

1/2 c. bread crumbs
1/4 tsp. white pepper
1/8 tsp. red pepper
1/4 tsp. oregano
Juice of 1/2 lemon
1/2 stick margarine

In a saucepan, boil broccoli until 3/4 done. It should remain crisp. Drain and set aside. In a saucepan, melt margarine at 450°. Add vegetables, except broccoli, and saute until soft. Add seasonings and soup, blending well. Add almonds and remove from heat. Add bread crumbs, blending well. In a lightly oiled casserole dish, pour half in 1/4 mixture. Arrange with half broccoli. Cover broccoli with an additional 1/4 mixture. Add remaining broccoli and cover with remaining mixture. Bake at 350° until broccoli is tender. Squeeze on lemon juice. Serves 10.

QUICK SPICY BROCCOLI

3 packs frozen broccoli
1/4 tsp. white pepper
1/4 tsp. black pepper
1/4 tsp. red pepper
1/8 tsp. sweet basil

Juice from 1/2 lemon
1 c. grated sharp Cheddar cheese
2 cans cream of chicken soup

In a bowl, combine seasonings; set aside. In a saucepan, boil broccoli until tender but crisp. In a lightly oiled casserole dish, arrange broccoli. Squeeze lemon juice over broccoli. In a saucepan, bring soup to a low simmer. Add cheese; remove from heat. Sprinkle half of the seasoning over broccoli. Pour soup mix over broccoli; sprinkle on remaining seasoning. Bake for 15 minutes at 350°. Serves 8.

BAKED CAULIFLOWER ATCHAFALAYA

1 large head fresh cauliflower
2 c. light brown roux
1 c. milk
1/4 tsp. black pepper
1/4 tsp. red pepper
1/2 tsp. white pepper

1 pimento, chopped fine
1/2 c. green onions, chopped fine
1/4 c. seasoned bread crumbs
1/4 c. grated sharp cheese
1/4 stick margarine

In a saucepan, boil cauliflower until tender but crisp. In a saucepan, melt margarine at 450°. Add seasonings, onions and pimento; saute until tender. Slowly blend in roux; bring to a simmer. Reduce the heat to 200°. Gradually add milk; blend well. Remove from the heat. Add cheese and bread crumbs, folding in well. In a lightly oiled casserole dish, pour in half mixture. Arrange cauliflower; add remaining mixture. Bake at 350° for 20 minutes or until light brown. Serves 6.

CAULIFLOWER IN CREAM SAUCE BAYOU BLACK

1 large fresh head cauliflower
1 c. light brown roux
1 c. milk
1 c. sharp grated cheese
½ tsp. white pepper
¼ tsp. garlic powder
¼ tsp. onion powder

Cook cauliflower until half done. Save liquid. Bring roux to a simmer. Add seasonings and milk; blend well. Reduce heat. Add cheese; blend well. Add cauliflower. Simmer at a low heat until mixture thickens and cauliflower is tender. Serves 6.

CAJUN ONIONS STUFFED WITH CELERY AND MUSHROOMS

6 large white onions
½ c. celery, chopped large
½ c. fresh mushrooms, sliced
1 c. bread crumbs
½ c. shredded Cheddar cheese
2 tsp. parsley, chopped fine
1 chicken bouillon cube
1 c. hot water
1 can cream of mushroom soup
¼ tsp. white pepper
¼ tsp. black pepper
1 tsp. salt
¼ stick margarine

Dissolve bouillon in 1 cup hot water; set aside. Peel onions and remove the outer layer. Slice the top off the onions, chop fine and set aside. Place onions in a saucepan. Cover with water and salt. Bring to a simmer at 225° for 25 minutes or until onions are tender. Remove from the pan, drain and allow to cool. Set aside. In a saucepan, melt margarine at 350°. Add bouillon liquid, onion tops, celery, and mushrooms; saute until the majority of the liquid has evaporated. Remove from heat and combine with bread crumbs, cheese and remaining ingredients. If filling is too soupy, add bread crumbs. Scoop out center portions of the onions, forming a shell. Fill with stuffing and bake in a casserole dish at 350° for 30 minutes. Serves 6.

LOUISIANA STUFFED LETTUCE

2 heads lettuce, sliced in halves
1 c. sour cream
3 Tbsp. flour
1 chicken bouillon cube
½ c. hot water
2 Tbsp. dry white wine
2 tsp. capers
½ tsp. white pepper
⅛ tsp. red pepper
3 Tbsp. margarine

Dissolve bouillon cube in ½ cup hot water; set aside. Remove center from the lettuce, forming a boat; set aside. Cut away the hard core of the lettuce and discard. Shred the remaining portions of the center; set aside. In a saucepan, melt margarine at 300°. Blend in flour and allow to gel. Add seasonings. Blend in bouillon liquid. Add sour cream and shredded lettuce. Mix well and allow to simmer for 5 minutes. Add wine and capers; simmer for an additional 10 minutes or until sauce becomes heavy. Remove from the heat and allow to cool. Spoon mixture into the lettuce boats. Place lettuce on a serving platter, chill and serve. Serves 4.

CREOLE MASHED POTATOES WITH CHEESE ROUX

4 large potatoes
2 Tbsp. flour
2 Tbsp. margarine
1/2 c. shredded American cheese
1/2 tsp. white pepper

1/2 tsp. salt
1/4 tsp. garlic powder
1/4 tsp. onion powder
1/2 c. sour cream
1/4 c. parsley leaves

Boil potatoes, peel and mash. In a bowl, combine seasonings; set aside. In a bowl, combine mashed potatoes, 1/2 seasoning mix and 1/4 cup sour cream. Blend well and spoon into individual soup bowls; set aside. In a saucepan, melt margarine at 450°. Add flour; blend well until a rich dark brown. Remove from the heat and blend in remaining sour cream, whisking rapidly. Blend in cheese, whisking continually to form a rich dark cream. Whisk in remaining seasoning and pour over top of potatoes. Bake at 300° for 15 minutes. Cover top generously with parsley leaves and serve. Serves 4.

FRENCH ONION RINGS, NEW ORLEANS STYLE

2 large onions
1 1/4 c. unsweetened pancake
  batter
1 c. milk

1 egg, beaten
1/4 tsp. red pepper
1/4 tsp. black pepper
2 c. corn oil

Peel onions and slice into 1/4 inch thickness. Separate slices into rings. In a flat dish, arrange rings and cover with milk. Let stand for 1 hour. Remove rings, drain and retain the milk. In a bowl, combine eggs, milk, seasonings, and pancake flour. Blend together well. In a large saucepan, heat corn oil to 400°. Fry onion rings until golden brown. Remove and place on a paper towel to drain. Serves 4.

CAJUN TURNIP GREENS

3 bunches turnip or mustard
  greens
1/2 c. onions, chopped
1/4 tsp. red pepper
1/4 tsp. white pepper
1/4 tsp. black pepper

1/4 c. ham, finely chopped
1/4 tsp. garlic powder
1/4 tsp. oregano
1/4 stick margarine
1/2 tsp. salt

In a saucepan, melt margarine at 450°. Add ham and saute until light brown. Add onions; saute until light brown. Add seasonings; blend in well. Remove from heat and set aside. In a pot, boil turnip greens until tender. Add ham and onion mixture. Simmer for an additional 10 minutes. Serve. Serves 6.

SPINACH IN SPICY SOUR CREAM SAUCE

2 packs frozen spinach	¼ tsp. red pepper
1 tsp. onion powder	½ tsp. white pepper
3 eggs, beaten	¼ tsp. black pepper
1 c. sour cream	¼ stick margarine
1 c. grated Parmesan or melted Cheddar	2 c. hot water
	½ tsp. salt

In a saucepan, melt margarine at 350°. Add 2 cups hot water and spinach; cook until ¾ done. Drain well. Add remaining ingredients; blend well. In a lightly oiled casserole dish, pour in mixture. Bake for 30 minutes at 350° until medium firm. Serves 6.

BROILED PARMESAN TOMATOES HOUMA

3 large tomatoes	1 tsp. salt
½ stick margarine	⅛ tsp. red pepper
½ c. bread crumbs	⅛ tsp. white pepper
¾ c. Parmesan cheese	⅛ tsp. sweet basil

In a bowl, combine seasonings; set aside. Peel tomatoes and slice into 1 inch thick rings. In a bowl, melt ¼ stick margarine at room temperature. Add ½ cup Parmesan cheese, bread crumbs and ½ seasoning mix; blend well. In a bowl, combine remaining margarine with remaining seasoning mix. Brush tomatoes with this mixture. Dip tomatoes into bread crumb mix; pat in well. Arrange tomatoes on a broiler rack, cover with aluminum foil and broil for 5 minutes until light brown. Turn tomatoes over and broil until brown. Sprinkle with remaining Parmesan cheese. Serve. Serves 4.

STUFFED EGGPLANT COLISEUM

1 large eggplant
2 eggs, beaten
2 Tbsp. flour

½ stick margarine
⅛ tsp. red pepper
⅛ tsp. white pepper

Slice eggplant in ½ inch rounds. In a bowl, combine eggs and seasonings; mix well. Pour flour into a large soup plate. Dip eggplant rounds into egg mixture, then dredge into the flour. In a saucepan, melt margarine at 350°. Fry eggplant until golden brown on both sides. Place eggplant in a lightly oiled casserole dish and set aside.

Stuffing:

2 lb. Ricotta cheese
¼ c. heavy cream
3 eggs, beaten
⅛ tsp. white pepper
¼ tsp. red pepper

½ lb. Mozzarella cheese, sliced
2 Tbsp. Romano cheese
1 c. tomato sauce

Stuffing: In a food processor, combine eggs, Ricotta and Romano cheese, seasonings and ¼ cup heavy cream. Whip until smooth. Pour over eggplant, cover with tomato sauce. Arrange Mozzarella cheese over the top. Bake at 350° for 30 minutes. Serves 4.

LOUISIANA STYLE ASPARAGUS

3 lb. fresh asparagus stalks
   (young and tender)
1 c. grated Italian cheese
2 eggs, beaten
½ c. dry white wine
1 c. seasoned bread crumbs

¼ tsp. garlic powder
¼ tsp. onion powder
1 tsp. white pepper
1 tsp. salt
1 c. flour
¼ stick margarine

In a bowl, combine seasonings; set aside. In a bowl, combine eggs, ¼ cup wine and ½ seasoning mix. In a flat plate, combine bread crumbs, flour and remaining seasoning. In a separate flat plate, spread cheese evenly. Trim asparagus well. Roll stalks in flour; shake off excess. Dip asparagus in the egg mixture, then roll into the cheese. In a saucepan, melt margarine at 300°. Add asparagus and saute until tender. Remove asparagus and place in a warm serving bowl. Add remaining wine to the saucepan, stirring briskly into the residue. Remove from the heat. Blend in remaining Italian cheese and pour over asparagus. Serve. Serves 6.

CREOLE LIMA BEANS

1 lb. fresh lima beans
¼ lb. bacon, chopped
2 cloves garlic, chopped fine
⅛ c. onions, chopped fine
1 c. firm tomatoes, diced

¼ c. parsley, chopped
½ tsp. black pepper
½ tsp. red pepper
½ tsp. salt

In a saucepan, boil lima beans until tender. Remove from the heat and set aside. Do not drain. In a separate saucepan, add bacon and saute until light brown. Add seasonings and vegetables; blend well. Saute until vegetables are soft. Add tomatoes and saute for 5 minutes. Combine this mixture to the lima beans; simmer until lima beans are tender. Serves 6.

STEWED EGGPLANT ANNUNCIATION

2 large eggplants
½ stick margarine
3 cloves garlic, chopped
½ c. onions, chopped
2 Tbsp. parsley, chopped
1 (12 oz.) can tomato sauce
½ c. Italian cheese

1 tsp. black pepper
½ tsp. oregano
⅛ tsp. sweet basil
⅛ tsp. thyme
3 Tbsp. flour
¼ c. dry white wine
1 c. hot water

Peel eggplant and cut into chunks. In a saucepan, melt margarine at 450°. Add eggplant and saute until medium soft. Remove from pan and arrange in a lightly oiled casserole dish. In the same pan, add flour; stir in until a rich brown. Add vegetables and saute until soft. Roux should be dark brown at this stage. Add hot water, whisking well. Add seasonings; blend well. Add tomato sauce and wine. Simmer sauce until thickened. Blend in ¼ cup cheese. Remove from heat. Pour mixture over eggplant. Sprinkle top with remaining cheese. Bake for 20 minutes at 350°. Serves 6.

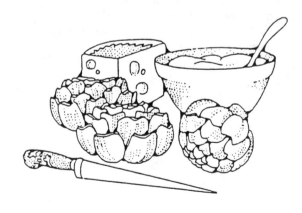

BASIN STREET BAKED MIRLITONS

3 mirlitons, peeled (vegetable
  pears)
1 lb. ground pork
½ c. Italian cheese, grated
3 medium onions, chopped
4 cloves garlic, pressed
¼ stick margarine

4 slices dry toast or stale bread
¼ tsp. red pepper
¼ tsp. white pepper
¼ tsp. black pepper
1 tsp. salt
1 c. hot water

Cut mirlitons in halves lengthwise; remove seed from the center. In a saucepan, boil mirlitons until tender. Scoop out inside, reserving shell for stuffing. In a separate pan, melt margarine at 450°; saute onions, garlic and pork until light brown. Add 1 cup of hot water; cook slowly. Add the drained and mashed mirlitons. Soak the toast or stale bread in water, then squeeze it out. Add to mirliton mix. Add seasonings; blend in well. Fill shells or pour into casserole dish. Cover with Italian cheese. Dot with margarine and bake at 350° until brown, about 25 minutes. Serves 6.

FRENCH FRIED GREEN TOMATOES

6 large green tomatoes
½ stick margarine
1 c. flour
½ tsp. white pepper
½ tsp. coarse ground black
  pepper

1 tsp. salt
¼ tsp. oregano
1 pack cheese slices (your
  choice)
2 eggs, beaten

In a bowl, combine seasonings; set aside. In a separate bowl, combine eggs and ½ seasoning mix. Combine flour with remaining seasonings. Dip tomatoes into egg mixture. Do not shake off excess. Pat well into seasoned flour. In a saucepan, melt margarine at 350°. Fry tomatoes on both sides until brown. When second side is brown, cover with cheese slices. Remove from heat, cover and let set until cheese is melted. Serve. Serves 8.

CAJUN BEETS IN CREAM SAUCE

2 cans sliced beets
1 c. sour cream
1 Tbsp. horseradish
3 tsp. chives, finely chopped
¼ tsp. garlic powder

¼ tsp. oregano
½ tsp. white pepper
½ tsp. salt
2 Tbsp. flour
¼ stick margarine

Place beets, including juice, in top of double boiler. Bring to a low simmer. In a saucepan, melt margarine at 300°. Add flour and seasonings, including horseradish and chives. Blend well until it gels. Reduce the heat to 200°. Blend in sour cream and simmer for 10 minutes. Pour over beets, blending in gently. Do not break up beets. Allow to simmer for an additional 10 minutes or until sauce thickens. Serve. Serves 4.

STUFFED MIRLITONS WITH SHRIMP BOURBON STREET

4 large mirlitons
3/4 lb. shrimp, peeled and
   deveined
1 large onion, chopped
1 clove garlic, minced
1/2 c. celery, chopped
3 Tbsp. margarine
3/4 c. grated sharp cheese

1/4 c. bread crumbs
1/4 tsp. red pepper
1/4 tsp. black pepper
1/4 tsp. white pepper
1/8 tsp. dry mustard
1/8 tsp. sweet basil
1 tsp. salt

In a bowl, combine seasonings; set aside. Parboil mirlitons until almost tender. Cut in halves. Remove the seed and discard. Scoop out meat. Mash and set aside. In a saucepan, melt the margarine at 450°. Add onion, celery and garlic; saute until soft. Add shrimp and 1/2 seasoning mix; saute until shrimp are pink. Blend in mashed mirlitons. Reduce the heat to 250°. Add 1/2 cup cheese, mixing well. Remove from heat. Place shells in a lightly oiled casserole dish. Fill with mixture; cover with remaining cheese and bread crumbs. Sprinkle top with remaining seasoning mix. Bake at 350° until crumbs are browned. Serves 4.

SPINACH UPPERLINE

2 pkg. frozen chopped spinach
4 Tbsp. margarine
2 Tbsp. flour
2 Tbsp. onion, chopped
1/2 c. evaporated milk
1 tsp. black pepper
1 tsp. red pepper

1/8 tsp. sweet basil
1/8 tsp. dry mustard
1/8 tsp. oregano
1 tsp. Worcestershire sauce
1 (6 oz.) roll jalapeno cheese,
   cut into small pieces
3/4 tsp. garlic salt
3/4 tsp. celery salt

Cook spinach according to directions on package. Drain and reserve 1/2 cup liquid. In a saucepan, melt margarine at 200°. Add onion; saute until soft. Add flour, stirring until blended and smooth, but not brown. Add spinach liquid slowly, stirring constantly, to avoid lumps. Add milk; blend well. Add Worcestershire sauce and simmer until smooth and thick; continue stirring. Add seasonings and cheese; stir continuously until cheese is melted. Combine with cooked spinach.

This may be served immediately or placed into a casserole dish and topped with bread crumbs. It is best when refrigerated overnight as a casserole and can also be frozen. Serves 6.

CANDIED YAMS RUSTON

2 lb. sweet potatoes
2 c. hot water
1 c. brown sugar
1 c. white sugar
1 orange
1 lemon

2 sticks cinnamon
1/2 tsp. ground mace
1 tsp. vanilla
4 sticks margarine
1 pack marshmallows

Peel sweet potatoes and cut into rounds; set aside. Slice the orange and lemon into rounds and remove the seeds; set aside. In a saucepan, melt margarine at 350°, bringing to a simmer. Add hot water. Add seasonings, blending well. Add orange and lemon rounds and allow to simmer for 10 minutes. Add sweet potatoes. Reduce heat to 250° and blend in sugars. Allow mixture to simmer until thickened or until sweet potatoes are tender. Remove from the heat. Pour into a lightly oiled casserole dish. Top with marshmallows. Braise under a broiler until marshmallows are brown. Serves 4.

STUFFED SQUASH CLAIBORNE

4 white summer squash
1 large onion, chopped fine
1 clove garlic, chopped fine
2 slices white bread
1 egg
4 Tbsp. tomato paste

1 c. cracker crumbs
2 Tbsp. parsley, chopped
4 Tbsp. margarine
1/2 tsp. white pepper
1/4 tsp. red pepper
1 tsp. salt

Boil squash in salted water until tender. In a saucepan, melt the margarine at 400°. Add onion, seasonings and garlic; saute until light brown. Dip bread in ice water, squeeze excess moisture and chop fine. Combine with onion and garlic mixture; cook for 5 minutes, stirring frequently. Scoop squash out of shells and chop fine. Add pulp to the onion mixture. Cook for an additional 3 minutes, stirring frequently. Reduce the heat to 200°. Beat the egg and blend in slowly. Add tomato paste; blend in well. Before removing from heat add chopped parsley.

This mixture can be either stuffed in shells or put into a casserole dish. Cover with cracker crumbs and dot with margarine. Bake at 350° until crumbs are brown. Serves 6.

BRABANT POTATOES ESPLANADE

4 large elongated Idaho potatoes
3 qt. hot water
1/8 tsp. cumin
1/4 tsp. ground red pepper
1/8 tsp. black pepper

1/4 tsp. onion powder
1/4 tsp. garlic powder
1/4 tsp. white pepper
2 tsp. salt
2 c. corn oil

Scrub potatoes thoroughly and cut into 1 inch cubes. In a large saucepan, add 3 quarts hot water and 1 teaspoon salt. Boil potatoes until fork tender. Remove from the pan and drain; set aside. In a small bowl, combine seasonings. Combine with potatoes, taking care when blending you do not smash the potatoes. In a large saucepan, heat corn oil to 350°. Fry potatoes until golden brown on both sides. Remove from the heat; place on a paper towel to drain excess oil. Serve. Serves 4.

CORN MAQUE CHOUX SAINT BERNARD

2 packs frozen corn kernels
1 c. onions, finely chopped
1/4 c. light brown sugar
1 stick margarine
1 tsp. white pepper
1/2 tsp. red pepper

1 tsp. salt
2 chicken bouillon cubes
2 c. hot water
1 c. evaporated milk
2 eggs, beaten

Dissolve bouillon cubes in 2 cups hot water; set aside. In a large skillet, melt 1/2 stick margarine at 400°. Add corn, onions, sugar, white pepper, salt, and red pepper. Saute until corn is tender and the starch begins to form a crust in the pan, about 10 minutes. Stir frequently. Add 1 cup bouillon slowly, so the crust will blend smoothly. Simmer for 5 minutes. Blend in remaining margarine, continuing to simmer for an additional 5 minutes. Reduce heat to 200°. Add remaining bouillon and simmer for an additional 20 minutes. Add 1/2 cup milk; blend in well. Remove from the heat. In a separate bowl, combine eggs and remaining milk. Whisk until foamy. Blend into corn mixture and serve. Serves 6.

CREOLE SCALLOPED POTATOES

4 large potatoes, cut in ¼ inch
  rounds
½ stick margarine
2 c. light brown roux
¼ c. celery, chopped
½ c. onions, chopped
3 cloves garlic, chopped
1 tsp. black pepper
½ tsp. red pepper

1 tsp. salt
¼ tsp. thyme
¼ tsp. bay leaf
¼ tsp. oregano
½ tsp. curry powder
2 chicken bouillon cubes
1 c. hot water
½ c. grated cheese (your choice)

Dissolve bouillon cubes in 2 cups hot water; set aside. In a saucepan, melt margarine at 450° until a light smoke appears. Singe potatoes on both sides. Remove from pan and set aside. In the same saucepan, add vegetables; saute until soft. Add seasonings; saute for 1 minute. Slowly add bouillon liquid, bringing to a rapid simmer. Add roux; blend well. Reduce the heat to 300° and allow to simmer for 10 minutes. In a lightly oiled casserole dish, pour half of mixture into dish. Arrange potatoes in an overlapping fashion. Cover with remaining mixture. Sprinkle with cheese. Bake at 350° for 30 minutes or until potatoes are tender. Serves 6.

CREOLE STIR-FRY VEGETABLES, CONTI

1 c. onions, chopped large
½ c. green pepper, chopped
  large
1 pack frozen Italian vegetables
1 c. bean sprouts

2 chicken bouillon cubes
2 c. hot water
2 Tbsp. soy sauce
¼ stick margarine
1 tsp. white pepper

Dissolve bouillon cubes in 2 cups hot water; set aside. In a large skillet, melt margarine at 400°. Add onions and green pepper; saute until soft. Add Italian vegetables; stir in well. Simmer for 3 minutes. Add 1 cup bouillon liquid and simmer for an additional 5 minutes. Add seasoning and remaining bouillon. Add bean sprouts and soy sauce. Reduce the heat and simmer until the majority of the moisture is removed and vegetables are tender. Serves 4.

STUFFED ARTICHOKES HAMMOND

4 artichokes
½ c. bread crumbs
½ c. Romano cheese
1 tsp. garlic powder
½ tsp. onion pepper

¼ tsp. red pepper
¼ tsp. white pepper
1 Tbsp. parsley, finely chopped
¼ stick margarine

Cut bottoms of artichokes off to allow them to stand easy. Place in a large skillet with a cover. Add ½ inch water. Bring to a simmer. Remove pan from the heat immediately and set aside while preparing stuffing. In a bowl, combine all ingredients except margarine and artichokes. Blend well. Remove artichokes from the water and allow to drain. Press top of artichoke down firmly to allow leaves to spread. In a saucepan, melt margarine and remove from heat. Spread leaves gently; dab with melted margarine. Fill open leaf sections with mixture. Steam in a covered pan for 45 minutes or until leaves pull away. Serves 4.

SHRIMP SALAD CREOLE

1 lb. shrimp, peeled and
  deveined
⅓ tsp. garlic powder
¼ c. celery, chopped
2 hard-boiled eggs, finely
  chopped
¼ c. dill pickle, finely chopped

½ tsp. white pepper
¼ tsp. ground red pepper
1 tsp. salt
Juice of ½ lemon
3 Tbsp. mayonnaise
1 Tbsp. Cajun shrimp boil
2 c. hot water

In a saucepan, add 2 cups hot water and bring to a brisk simmer. Add shrimp boil, simmering for 3 minutes. Add shrimp and cook until a deep pink. Remove shrimp. Drain and set aside. Discard boil mix. In a separate bowl, combine all ingredients except mayonnaise. Blend together well. Fold in mayonnaise. Do not beat. Chop shrimp into fourths. Add to mixture, blending well. Allow to chill. Serve on a bed of shredded lettuce, garnished with parsley. Serves 6.

CRABMEAT AND ARTICHOKE SALAD

1 lb. crabmeat (chunky)
2 c. artichoke parts, chopped
¼ c. salad olives, chopped
1 Tbsp. mayonnaise
¼ stick margarine

¼ tsp. red pepper
¼ tsp. white pepper
1 tsp. salt
Juice of ½ lemon

In a saucepan, melt margarine at 350°. Add crabmeat and carefully stir for 5 minutes. Do not break up chunks. Reduce heat to 200°. Allow pan to cool before adding artichoke hearts. Stir in artichokes for 1 minute and remove from the heat. Blend in seasonings and salad olives. Remove from the pan and place contents in a bowl. Allow to cool, then add mayonnaise and lemon juice. Chill. Serve with crackers. Serves 4.

SHRIMP IN CAJUN POTATO SALAD

1 lb. shrimp, peeled and
    deveined
4 large Idaho potatoes, peeled
    and diced
6 hard-boiled eggs
½ c. mayonnaise
Juice of 1 lemon
¼ tsp. oregano
¼ tsp. white pepper
1 tsp. salt

1 tsp. red pepper
2 tsp. prepared mustard
1 Tbsp. parsley, finely chopped
¼ c. green pepper, finely
    chopped
¼ c. onions, finely chopped
¼ c. celery, finely chopped
¼ stick margarine

In a saucepan, melt margarine at 350°. Add shrimp and saute until pink. Remove from heat. Set aside and allow to cool. Boil potatoes until fork tender. Remove from heat. Drain well and set aside. In a large bowl, combine remaining ingredients. Chop shrimp into quarters and blend into seasoned mixture. Add potatoes and mayonnaise, blending well. Avoid crushing potatoes. Place in the refrigerator and chill. Serves 6. *Delicious served hot or cold.*

POTATO FLAKE IN ONION SALAD CAMERON

1 head lettuce
2 Idaho potatoes
1 c. onions, chopped fine
1 c. celery, chopped fine
1 can English peas

¼ lb. bacon
1 c. Parmesan cheese
1 c. mayonnaise
2 Tbsp. sugar

Boil potatoes until fork tender. Remove from heat and drain well. Cut in halves lengthwise, then slice into flakes; set aside. Cut lettuce into 1 inch chunks, toss and separate. In a saucepan, fry bacon until crisp at 450°. Remove from the pan and crush. In a lightly oiled casserole dish, make consecutive layers of potatoes, lettuce, onions, celery, and peas. Spread mayonnaise in an even layer over the top. Sprinkle on sugar, then Parmesan cheese. Top with crumbled bacon. Wrap casserole dish tightly with aluminum foil and place in the refrigerator overnight. Serve as a chilled salad. Serves 4.

CRABMEAT SALAD DUFRECHE

4 c. crabmeat (chunky)
3 Tbsp. gelatin
2/3 c. cold water
1 Tbsp. sugar
3 Tbsp. flour
1 Tbsp. dry mustard
3 egg yolks, beaten
1 whole egg, beaten
2¼ c. milk

¾ c. green onion, chopped
½ c. pimento, diced
3 c. celery, diced
3 Tbsp. margarine
½ c. tarragon vinegar
1 tsp. Worcestershire sauce
1 tsp. salt
½ tsp. red pepper
½ tsp. white pepper

Dissolve gelatin in cold water. In double boiler, cook the following until thick: Sugar, flour, mustard, egg yolks, whole egg, milk, vinegar, and margarine. Add gelatin and remaining ingredients except crabmeat. Carefully fold in crabmeat; avoid breaking up chunks. Chill and serve on a bed of lettuce with a dab of mayonnaise. Serves 8.

CREOLE TOMATO SALAD

4 large Creole tomatoes,
    chopped
2 cucumbers, sliced
1 onion, sliced thin
¼ c. celery, chopped fine
¼ tsp. prepared mustard
¼ tsp. white pepper
¼ tsp. red pepper

2 mild jalapeno peppers,
    chopped
1 c. dry cheese, chopped (we
    like Feta)
3 Tbsp. salad oil
3 Tbsp. vinegar
1 tsp. salt

Combine oil, vinegar and seasonings. Whisk well until creamy. Combine remaining ingredients. Cover with seasoned oil. Toss lightly and serve. Serves 6.

TART TUNA SALAD THIBODEAUX IN CREAM SAUCE

1 large can tuna
2 hard-boiled eggs, chopped
½ c. salad olives, chopped
1 Tbsp. chives, finely chopped
½ c. mayonnaise
¼ tsp. white pepper

¼ tsp. red pepper
1 tsp. salad oil
2 Tbsp. flour
2 Tbsp. margarine
½ c. sour cream
1 tsp. salt

In a saucepan, melt margarine at 400°. Add flour; blend until it gels. Immediately remove from heat, place in a large bowl and allow to cool. Whisk in sour cream and seasonings. Chill for 10 minutes in the refrigerator. Blend in olives and chives. Blend in, one at a time, the following: Mayonnaise, salad oil and eggs. Fold in tuna; avoid breaking up chunks. Chill until firm. Serves 6.

CAESAR SALAD

2 heads romaine lettuce
1 c. seasoned croutons
½ tsp. garlic powder
½ c. olive oil
1½ tsp. seasoned salt
¼ tsp. dry mustard
⅓ tsp. coarse black pepper

6 anchovy fillets
½ tsp. Worcestershire sauce
1 egg
Juice of 1 lemon
3 Tbsp. Parmesan cheese
4 Tbsp. very dry white wine

In a bowl, combine olive oil with garlic powder. Add seasonings and Worcestershire sauce; blend well. Mash anchovies into a paste and combine with mixture. Add lemon juice and wine; blend well. In a salad bowl, drop an egg. Add seasoned oil mix; combine thoroughly. Add lettuce leaves; toss generously. Add Parmesan cheese and croutons. Toss lightly and serve. Serves 6.

CREOLE COLE SLAW

1 medium head cabbage
Juice of 1 lemon
1 c. wine vinegar
2 Tbsp. parsley, finely chopped
2 Tbsp. chives, finely chopped
¾ c. sour cream or plain yogurt

½ tsp. celery seed
½ tsp. dark brown sugar
½ tsp. white pepper
½ tsp. red pepper
1 tsp. salt
½ c. almonds, finely chopped

Cut cabbage head in quarters. Remove the hard inner core and discard. Shred cabbage thin and place in a large bowl. Cover with 1 cup vinegar; toss thoroughly. Cover with aluminum foil and place in refrigerator, allowing to chill for 1 hour. After removing from refrigerator, drain well. If necessary, blot with paper towel. Combine remaining ingredients, except almonds, and toss thoroughly into cabbage. Allow to chill. Top with almonds and serve. Serves 6.

FRESH CREOLE SPINACH SALAD

1 lb. fresh spinach
1 Tbsp. olive oil
2 Tbsp. lemon juice
1 egg
1 tsp. sugar
1 tsp. white pepper
½ tsp. red pepper
1 tsp. salt

¼ tsp. paprika
¼ tsp. prepared mustard
½ tsp. garlic powder
¼ c. catsup
1 c. olive oil
¼ c. wine vinegar
⅓ c. warm water
1 Tbsp. Worcestershire sauce

Wash the spinach and drain well. Cut into strips. Place in a large bowl. Sprinkle with olive oil and lemon juice and chill. Place eggs, salt, paprika, peppers, mustard, Worcestershire sauce, garlic, catsup, and sugar in a blender and whip for 10 seconds. Add olive oil alternately with vinegar, blending constantly. Blend until mixture thickens. Add warm water, blending constantly. Place spinach in a bowl. Pour enough of the sauce over the spinach to coat well, then toss lightly. Garnish with tomato wedges. Serves 6.

CREOLE FRIED CHICKEN SALAD

1 lb. boneless chicken, cut into
   1 inch squares
3 c. all-purpose flour
2 eggs, beaten
1 c. milk
1 c. corn oil
1 stick margarine
1 tsp. garlic flakes
1/4 c. parsley, chopped fine
2 heads lettuce, torn into bits
1 c. celery, chopped
1 c. zucchini, cut into half rings

1 c. green peppers, chopped
1 c. red cabbage, chopped
1 c. carrots, chopped
1 romaine lettuce
2 Creole tomatoes, cut into
   wedges
1/2 tsp. white pepper
1/2 tsp. red pepper
1/2 tsp. onion powder
1/2 tsp. black pepper
1/2 tsp. sweet paprika
2 tsp. salt

In a small bowl, combine seasonings; set aside. In a bowl, combine 1/2 seasoning mix with chicken, coating well. In a separate bowl, add flour and remaining seasoning mix; mix well. In another bowl, blend together eggs and milk until fluffy. In a large saucepan, heat corn oil to 350°. Dredge chicken into seasoned flour, then into the egg mixture, coating thoroughly. Drop chicken pieces separately into the flour, coating well. Place into the hot oil and fry until golden brown. Remove from pan and set aside. Place on a paper towel to drain, then into a bowl.

In a separate skillet, melt margarine at 450° until moisture is removed. Stir in garlic flakes and parsley for 1 minute and remove from the heat and pour over chicken. In a large salad bowl, toss together lettuce pieces, zucchini, green pepper, celery, red cabbage, and carrots. Add chicken. Line individual salad bowls with romaine leaves. Add chicken salad and surround with tomato wedges.

Salad Dressing:

4 jalapeno peppers, chopped
1/4 tsp. white pepper

6 Tbsp. white vinegar
1 c. hot water

Place ingredients in a blender. Whip for 2 seconds and strain into a cup. Pour over salad. Surround with tomato wedges. Serves 6.

SPANISH ONION SALAD DELGADO

1 large onion
1/4 head lettuce
1 large Creole tomato, cut into
    wedges

1 ripe avocado, diced
1 Tbsp. parsley, chopped

Slice onion into 1/4 inch rings and separate. Shred lettuce and line serving platter. Arrange tomato wedges, avocado and onion rings in a circular pattern. Sprinkle with chopped parsley.

Chili Dressing:

2 Tbsp. lemon juice
2 Tbsp. vinegar
1 c. salad oil
1/2 tsp. red ground pepper

2 tsp. brown sugar
1 tsp. chili powder
1/4 tsp. oregano
1/2 tsp. salt

Combine all dressing ingredients in a bowl. Whisk together vigorously for 1 minute. Pour over salad. Chill and serve. Serves 4.

CRAWFISH AND AVOCADO SALAD DES ALLEMANDES

1 lb. crawfish, peeled and
    deveined
2 Creole tomatoes
1 large onion
1 ripe avocado

1 c. Greek olives
1/2 c. parsley, chopped
1 Tbsp. crawfish boil
2 c. hot water

In a saucepan, bring 2 cups hot water to a boil with crawfish boil. Add crawfish, boil for 3 minutes and remove from pan. Drain and dice. Slice tomato into wedges. Slice onion into 1/4 inch rings and separate. Peel and cut avocado into 1 inch squares. In a salad bowl, combine all ingredients and toss well.

Dressing:

Juice of 1 lemon
3 Tbsp. white wine
6 Tbsp. olive oil
1/2 tsp. salt

1 tsp. coarse ground black
    pepper
1/2 tsp. garlic flakes

In a bowl, combine dressing ingredients. Whisk together well for 3 minutes. Pour over salad and serve. Serves 4.

CRABMEAT SALAD DANIA

1 lb. crabmeat, cooked
1 c. onions, chopped fine
4 oz. salad oil
¼ c. cider vinegar
¼ c. ice water
½ tsp. salt
½ tsp. white pepper

Place ½ onions in a salad bowl. Add ½ crabmeat; add remaining onions. Top with remaining crabmeat. Sprinkle vinegar and salad oil over the salad, followed by the ice water. Add seasonings. Toss lightly. Cover and refrigerate for 6 hours. Drain well and serve on a bed of lettuce. Serves 4.

PASTA SALAD LECOMPTE

2 c. macaroni
½ c. salad olives, chopped
¼ c. sour cream
1 tsp. salt
½ tsp. coarse black pepper
¼ tsp. oregano
¼ tsp. celery seed
1 c. celery, diced
3 Tbsp. green onion tops,
    chopped
1 Tbsp. onion, chopped
2 Tbsp. very dry wine or wine
    vinegar
Juice of ½ lemon
1 Tbsp. olive oil
Hot water
1 head romaine lettuce leaves

In a saucepan, bring water to a boil. Add ½ teaspoon salt and macaroni; cook until tender. Remove from heat and drain. Place in a bowl and stir in 1 teaspoon olive oil. Allow to chill. In a large salad bowl, combine remaining ingredients thoroughly. Add macaroni; stir in well. In separate bowls, form a bed with romaine lettuce leaves. Spoon in pasta salad. Chill. Serve with tomato slices. Serves 6.

BRANDY WALDORF SALAD

1 c. apples, diced
1 c. seedless grapes
½ c. pecans, chopped
½ c. mayonnaise
1 c. celery, diced
¼ c. seedless raisins
½ c. brandy

In a bowl, combine apples, grapes and brandy. Toss together thoroughly and marinate for 1 hour, stirring frequently. Blend in remaining ingredients thoroughly. Set aside for 15 minutes. Toss and serve. Serves 6.

CHICKEN AND RICE SALAD KENNER

2 boneless chicken breasts,
    boiled and diced
1 c. rice
1 tsp. Creole mustard
2 tsp. dry red wine
¼ c. olive oil
½ c. Swiss cheese, diced
½ c. black olives, pitted and
    diced

2 Tbsp. salad olives
¼ c. green peppers, chopped
3 Tbsp. gherkins, diced
2 qt. hot water
2 tsp. salt
¼ c. vinegar

Bring 2 quarts water to a boil. Add 1 teaspoon salt and rice. Boil for 10 minutes; remove from the heat. Cover and set aside for 5 minutes. Rinse rice in cold water and drain thoroughly. In a bowl, add mustard, remaining salt and vinegar; blend together well. Add oil and rice; toss into the dressing. Add remaining ingredients. Toss together well and chill. Serves 4.

SPICY ORANGE CHICKEN SALAD

6 pieces boneless chicken
    breast
1 bed watercress
4 oranges, peeled and sliced
2 Tbsp. brandy
2 Tbsp. olive oil

1 tsp. brown sugar
¼ tsp. cayenne pepper
¼ tsp. tarragon
1 tsp. white pepper
Juice of ½ lemon
½ stick margarine

In a saucepan, melt margarine at 450° until a light smoke appears. Add chicken and saute until golden brown on both sides. Remove from the pan and dice. Return to the heat and saute for 2 minutes. Remove and drain well. In a salad bowl, combine remaining ingredients except watercress. Add chicken, tossing in well. Chill and serve over a bed of watercress. Serves 8.

HOT CHICKEN SALAD IN BECHAMEL SAUCE BURAS

1 lb. cooked chicken, chopped
1 c. celery, chopped
¼ c. thick light brown roux
¼ tsp. tarragon

½ c. toasted almonds, chopped
Juice of 1 lemon
½ c. mayonnaise
¼ stick margarine

In a saucepan, melt margarine at 450°. Add chicken and saute until brown. Reduce the heat to 200°. Blend in roux well and remove from the heat. Blend in remaining ingredients except for mayonnaise. Allow to cool. Fold in mayonnaise. Line the bottom of a serving dish with romaine lettuce; top with chicken salad.

Sauce:

2 Tbsp. margarine
2 Tbsp. flour
1 chicken bouillon cube
1 c. hot water
1 small onion, diced
3 Tbsp. sliced carrots

1 tsp. coarse ground black
   pepper
⅛ tsp. bay leaf
¼ c. sour cream
½ tsp. salt

Dissolve bouillon cube in 1 cup hot water; set aside. In a saucepan, melt margarine at 350°. Stir in flour until it gels. Add chicken bouillon and remaining ingredients except for sour cream. Remove from heat and allow to cool. Blend in sour cream. Pour over top of salad and serve. Serves 6.

SCALLOP POTATO SALAD IN FRENCH DRESSING COVINGTON

2 c. cooked scallops, diced
4 potatoes, peeled, boiled and
   chopped
2 Tbsp. parsley, chopped
2 Tbsp. green onion, chopped

½ tsp. red pepper
½ tsp. white pepper
⅛ tsp. basil
⅛ tsp. tarragon

In a large salad bowl, combine together all salad ingredients. Toss well.

Dressing:

1 c. salad oil
½ c. olive
1 tsp. Worcestershire
½ tsp. salt
2 Tbsp. sugar

1 tsp. garlic flakes
1 tsp. brown mustard
¼ c. green onions, chopped fine
⅛ c. parsley, chopped fine

In a blender, combine together all ingredients. Whip for 10 seconds. Pour over top of salad; toss vigorously. Chill and serve. Top with croutons. Serves 6.

SHRIMP STUFFED ONION OPELOUSAS

1 lb. shrimp, peeled and
    deveined
6 large onions
1 c. cream cheese
3 strips bacon

1 tsp. dry mustard
1 Tbsp. pimento, chopped
½ tsp. salt
¼ tsp. red pepper
¼ tsp. white pepper

    Peel onions and remove centers with an apple corer, leaving the cores approximately 3 inches thick. Retain centers. In a saucepan, saute bacon at 450° until brown. Remove and crush. Add shrimp to drippings; saute until a deep pink. Remove and chop. Chop onion centers fine; saute until soft. Remove from pan. In a bowl, combine all ingredients thoroughly. Arrange onions in a serving dish; stuff the cores. Chill for 1 hour and serve. Serves 6.

SHRIMP ASPARAGUS SALAD ST. JOSEPH

1 lb. cooked shrimp, chopped
2 cans asparagus, well drained
4 Tbsp. mayonnaise
Juice of ½ lemon
1 small can artichoke hearts,
    quartered

½ tsp. white pepper
¼ tsp. sweet basil
⅛ tsp. dry mustard
2 hard-boiled eggs, sliced

    In a deep salad bowl, arrange asparagus upright surrounding the edge. Place artichoke hearts on the bottom of the bowl to keep asparagus upright. In a separate bowl, combine remaining ingredients thoroughly except eggs and shrimp. Blend well and set aside. Cover artichoke hearts with shrimp. Arrange eggs in the outer edge in a circular pattern. Pour seasoning mix over the salad. Chill and serve. Serves 6.

CREOLE CRAWFISH TOMATO SALAD

1 lb. crawfish tails, cooked
4 Creole tomatoes, cut in 8
    wedges
1 c. onions, sliced

1 avocado, diced
¾ c. Greek olives, pitted and
    halved
½ c. parsley, chopped

    In a large salad bowl, combine salad ingredients and toss well.

    Dressing:

2 Tbsp. wine vinegar
Juice from ½ lemon
6 Tbsp. olive oil
1 clove garlic, minced

¼ tsp. white pepper
¼ tsp. red pepper
¼ tsp. sweet basil

    In a separate bowl, combine dressing ingredients; mix well. Pour into a blender. Whip for 2 seconds. Remove and pour over salad. Toss in well. Allow to chill and toss again before serving. Serves 6.

HEART OF ARTICHOKE AND SHRIMP SALAD

2 c. hearts of artichoke,
  quartered
1 lb. shrimp, peeled and
  deveined
1/4 c. salad olives, chopped
1 green pepper, sliced thin
1/4 c. parsley, chopped

1 tsp. paprika
1/2 c. mayonnaise or plain yogurt
1 Tbsp. flour
2 Tbsp. margarine
1/2 c. hot water

In a saucepan, melt margarine at 400°. Add shrimp and saute until pink. Remove from pan. Set aside and chop. Add flour; stir in until it gels. Return shrimp. Stir for 1 minute. Blend in 1/2 cup hot water for 1 minute and remove from heat. Allow to cool.

In a salad bowl, combine remaining ingredients except mayonnaise and shrimp. Toss well. In a separate bowl, blend mayonnaise and shrimp together and spread over top of salad. Chill and serve. Serves 4.

HOT ONION AND TOMATO SALAD DELACROIX

6 ripe Creole tomatoes
6 medium size white onions
2 lb. green peppers, cleaned
  with seeds removed
4 Tbsp. olive oil
1 (7 oz.) jar whole red pimentos

1/2 tsp. white pepper
1/4 tsp. red pepper
1/4 tsp. sweet paprika
1/4 tsp. oregano

Peel and cut onions in thin slices. Cut green peppers in halves lengthwise, then slice into strips. In a saucepan, add olive oil and heat to 250°. Add peppers and onions for 5 minutes or until soft; set aside. Cut tomatoes into slices. Drain pimentos and cut into 1/2 inch strips. Add tomatoes and pimentos to the pepper and onion mixture. Add seasonings. Return salad to the saucepan. Saute at 250° until tomatoes are soft. Serves 6.

This salad can be served hot or cold.

CREOLE RED ONION AND CABBAGE SALAD

1 medium size head red cabbage
1 large Vidalia onion
1/2 c. sugar
1 c. mayonnaise
1 c. red wine vinegar

1/4 c. vinegar
2 tsp. horseradish
1/4 tsp. white pepper
1/2 tsp. red pepper
1 tsp. salt

Cut cabbage in half; remove the hard core and discard. Shred and place in a large bowl. Peel and slice onion into thin rings. Add to the cabbage. Add red wine vinegar and toss well. Cover and chill for 1 hour.

In a small bowl, combine mayonnaise, vinegar and horseradish; blend well. Remove cabbage from refrigerator; drain well. Discard wine vinegar. Place cabbage in a salad bowl. Add mayonnaise mixture; toss well. Add seasonings and sugar; toss well. Cover, chill and serve. Serves 6.

GREEK SALAD, THE CREOLE WAY

4 ripe Creole tomatoes,
   quartered
2 cucumbers, sliced
½ head lettuce, broken
1 onion, sliced and quartered
3 Tbsp. salad oil
3 Tbsp. wine vinegar
½ tsp. oregano
½ tsp. coarse ground black
   pepper
¼ tsp. white pepper
¼ c. Salonica peppers
½ c. Feta cheese, crumbled
½ c. Greek olives, pitted

Arrange cucumbers, onion, lettuce, olives, and tomatoes in a salad bowl. Combine vinegar, oil, oregano, and seasonings. Pour over salad. Add remaining ingredients. Toss and serve. Serves 6.

LOUISIANA STRAWBERRY SALAD

1 pack frozen strawberries
1 (6 oz.) pkg. strawberry jello
1 Tbsp. Knox gelatine
2 c. boiling liquid
1 c. cottage cheese
1 can fruit cocktail
1 can crushed pineapple
1 can mandarin oranges
1 c. pecans, chopped
1 c. mayonnaise
¼ c. light brown sugar

Combine and drain juices from the canned fruit. If necessary, add enough water to form 2 cups. In a saucepan, bring fruit juices to a brisk simmer; set aside. In a bowl, combine gelatins and add fruit juices. Stir well and allow to cool. In a blender, add mayonnaise, sugar and cottage cheese; blend until smooth. To the gelatin, add mayonnaise mixture; fold in fruits and nuts. Place in a fruit mold. Chill and serve. Serves 6.

CREOLE SHRIMP TOMATO ASPIC

1½ env. gelatin
¼ c. cold water
2 c. tomato juice
1 tsp. Worcestershire sauce
¼ tsp. Louisiana hot sauce
1 Tbsp. parsley, minced
¼ c. celery, chopped fine
2 carrots, grated
1½ c. shrimp, cut in pieces
2 hard cooked eggs, sliced
1 bay leaf
1 rib celery
¼ onion
½ tsp. white pepper
¼ tsp. red pepper
1 tsp. salt
Juice of ½ lemon

Dissolve gelatin in cold water. In a saucepan, combine the tomato juice, bay leaf, celery rib, and onion. Bring to boil at 300°. Simmer slowly for 5 minutes. Remove onion, bay leaf and celery and add dissolved gelatin. Mix well. Add salt, peppers, lemon juice, Worcestershire sauce, and hot sauce. Add minced parsley, chopped celery, carrots, and shrimp. Pour a small portion into a large mold or individual molds and arrange slices of hard cooked eggs in bottom. Allow to gel; pour in remaining mixture. Place in refrigerator until firm. Turn mold out on lettuce leaves and top with a dab of mayonnaise. Serves 4.

CAJUN JAMBALAYA SALAD

1 c. shrimp, cleaned, peeled and
    sliced
1 c. cooked chicken, diced
1 c. ham, diced
¼ stick margarine
½ tsp. salt
½ tsp. white pepper
½ tsp. red pepper
4 Tbsp. soy sauce

1 Tbsp. brown sugar
1 clove garlic, chopped fine
1 c. canned peas
2 carrots, grated
1 green pepper, sliced thin
1 c. cooked cauliflower
1 c. cooked asparagus spears
¼ c. parsley, chopped

In a saucepan, melt margarine at 400°. Add shrimp, salt, peppers, sugar, garlic, and 2 tablespoons soy sauce. Saute for 3 minutes. Add ham and chicken; saute for 1 minute. Remove from the heat.

Rice Mixture:

1½ c. rice
½ tsp. garlic powder
1 tsp. sugar

2 tsp. corn oil
1 chicken bouillon cube
3 c. hot water

In a saucepan, add 3 cups hot water, bouillon and remaining ingredients. Cook rice until done, but crispy. Remove from the heat and drain well. In a large bowl, combine all remaining ingredients, tossing well. Chill and serve. Serves 8.

COTTAGE COMPOTE

1 (12 oz.) box dry cottage
    cheese
1 large can evaporated milk
1 tsp. almond flavoring
2 env. gelatin
2 cans fruit cocktail

½ c. celery, chopped
½ c. pecans, chopped
1 (4 oz.) bottle maraschino
    cherries, chopped
½ c. brandy

Place cottage cheese in mixing bowl, gradually adding milk, beating at medium speed. Add almond flavoring. Drain liquid from cans of fruit cocktail. Dissolve gelatin in ½ of liquid. In a saucepan, bring balance of liquid to boil and add gelatin. Remove from heat and add gelatin to the cottage cheese mixture. Beat at a high speed until fluffy. Pour into a bowl and combine all ingredients. Pour into a mold. Chill until firm. Serve in squares on a bed of lettuce. Garnish with green grapes and top with a dab of whipped cream. Serves 6.

CREOLE EGG SALAD DRESSING

5 hard-boiled eggs
¼ c. lemon juice
¼ tsp. sweet basil
¼ tsp. sweet paprika

½ tsp. salt
⅛ tsp. white pepper
⅛ tsp. red pepper
¼ c. mayonnaise or plain yogurt

Chop eggs fine. Combine all ingredients; mix well. Chill. Serve over lettuce wedges.

MUSTARD CREAM DRESSING MONROE

1 pt. sour cream
1 tsp. dry mustard
2 tsp. Creole mustard
Juice of 1 lemon
¼ tsp. salt

¼ tsp. red pepper
2 tsp. all-purpose flour
2 tsp. margarine
½ c. hot water

In a saucepan, melt margarine at 300°. Add flour; blend until it gels. Remove from heat and blend in hot water. Whisk in well. Add seasonings; whisk well. Whisk in thoroughly dry mustard. Add lemon juice and blend in sour cream and Creole mustard. Combine thoroughly. Chill and serve.

PIQUANT MAYONNAISE DUPRE

2 egg yolks or 1 whole egg
1 pt. salad oil
½ tsp. Worcestershire sauce
¼ tsp. Louisiana hot sauce
¼ tsp. red pepper

½ tsp. black pepper
1 tsp. mustard
2 Tbsp. vinegar
3 Tbsp. boiling water

Put egg yolks or whole egg into a small mixing bowl; add all other ingredients except oil and water. Beat on medium speed until thoroughly mixed. Increase speed to medium high; slowly add salad oil, a small amount at a time, until mayonnaise begins to thicken. Oil can then be added faster. When all oil is used, add boiling water and mix thoroughly. (Boiling water does away with oily appearance.)

Grated onion can be added if mayonnaise is to be used for sandwiches and potato salad.

CREAMY CREOLE DRESSING

2 c. mayonnaise
2 Tbsp. dark brown sugar
½ c. dry wine
2 Tbsp. ketchup
1 tsp. paprika
¼ tsp. dry mustard

1 tsp. onion powder
1 egg white, beaten stiff
½ tsp. garlic powder
¼ tsp. red pepper
½ tsp. salt

Combine ingredients thoroughly. Chill and serve.

SESAME HONEY SALAD DRESSING

1 egg
½ c. onions, chopped
¾ c. sesame seeds, toasted
1 c. wild honey
1½ c. dark roasted pecans

½ c. jalapeno peppers, chopped
¼ tsp. red pepper
¼ c. white vinegar
1 c. hot water

In a food processor, combine pecans, sesame seeds, onions, and egg. Blend well. Add jalapeno peppers. Pour into a bowl. Combine remaining ingredients, except for honey and hot water, stirring well. In a separate bowl, combine honey and hot water; blend well. Add to pecan mixture and blend well. Chill and serve.

SPICY THOUSAND ISLAND DRESSING

1 c. sweet relish
½ tsp. red pepper
1 tsp. white pepper
1 tsp. salt
1 raw egg

1 c. firm tomatoes, peeled and
    chopped
2 hard-boiled eggs, chopped
1 c. vegetable oil
¼ c. onions, chopped

In a food processor, combine egg and onions; beat for 10 seconds. Immediately add oil in a slow stream. Add tomatoes. Add hard- boiled eggs and seasonings. Blend for 10 seconds. Take a spatula and make sure all ingredients are at the bottom of the processor. Process for another 10 seconds. Transfer to a mixing bowl. Blend in relish. Chill and serve.

SPICY BLEU CHEESE DRESSING

½ lb. Bleu cheese
½ c. buttermilk
½ c. onions, chopped
1 tsp. garlic, minced
2 c. vegetable oil

1 egg
2 tsp. white pepper
½ tsp. red pepper
1 tsp. salt

In a food processor, combine garlic, egg and onions; process for 5 seconds. Immediately add oil in a thin stream. Add buttermilk and blend for 5 seconds. Add seasonings and blend for an additional 5 seconds. Transfer mixture to a large bowl and add Bleu cheese. Whisk in thoroughly, breaking up large lumps. Chill and serve.

CREOLE SHRIMP MAYONNAISE

3 Tbsp. onions, chopped fine
2 Tbsp. celery, chopped fine
1 c. shrimp
1 egg

Seasonings:

1/4 tsp. oregano
1/4 tsp. thyme
1/4 tsp. sweet basil
1 bay leaf

1 1/4 c. salad oil
Juice of 1/2 lemon
2 tsp. white vinegar
2 Tbsp. margarine

1/2 tsp. salt
1/2 tsp. dry mustard
1/2 tsp. red pepper
1/4 tsp. white pepper

Combine seasonings and set aside. In a saucepan, melt margarine at 350°. Add celery and onions; saute for 2 minutes. Stir continuously. Reduce the heat to 250°. Blend in seasoning mix. Add shrimp; saute until tender. Remove from heat and discard bay leaf; allow to cool. In a food processor, add egg, beating well for 30 seconds. Add shrimp mixture. With machine still running, gradually add oil in a steady stream. Add vinegar and lemon juice. Make sure there is no residue left on side of processor. Blend for an additional 10 seconds. Chill before serving.

CREOLE VINEGAR CREAM DRESSING

2 tsp. flour
2 eggs, beaten
1 Tbsp. dark brown sugar
1/2 tsp. paprika
1 tsp. Creole mustard

1 c. milk
1/2 c. vinegar
1/2 tsp. white pepper
1/4 tsp. sweet basil
1/2 stick margarine

In a bowl, combine egg and milk; set aside. Melt margarine in top of double boiler. Add seasonings, mustard and sugar. Heat to a low simmer. Add egg and milk slowly, whisking all the time. Add flour; continue to whisk. Add vinegar in the same manner, whisking until contents thicken. Serve.

TIPSY CREOLE FRUIT SALAD DRESSING

1/2 c. pineapple juice
Juice of 1 orange
Juice of 1 lemon
1/2 c. brown sugar

1/8 tsp. salt
3 eggs
1 tsp. grated lemon rind
1/4 c. peach brandy

In a small bowl, combine lemon juice, orange juice and pineapple juice. If this does not form 1 cup, add additional juice. Place in top of a double boiler. Blend in sugar, eggs, salt, and grated lemon rind. Blend thoroughly. Bring to a simmer and cook until mixture thickens. Remove and chill. Blend in brandy. Serve over a fruit salad.

1 pound of peas in the pod will yield 1 cup of peas. When buying peas look for plump pods with a velvety feel. Avoid any yellowish pods. Separate frozen peas by tapping the box on a table.

One pound of peanut butter will yield 2 cups. Store-bought peanut butter is homogenized and contains fats. Store upside-down in your cabinet. Fresh-ground peanuts contain no fats or additives.

Most market tomatoes are picked green, then gas-ripened. Buy tomatoes that are marked "vine-ripened". They have a far better flavor. Do not refrigerate your tomatoes, this diminishes their taste.

1 pound of raw potatoes will yield 2 cups, mashed. Always add a little butter or margarine when boiling potatoes, it will keep a scum ring from forming and sticking to the potatoes. Boil the potatoes with the skin on, they will peel easily when hot.

Do not use bacon in clam chowder; use salt pork to make the real thing. As long as a clam shell is tightly closed, it is alive and fresh.

Before mashing potatoes dry them well, this will make them creamier. Do not add cold milk to potatoes, this will cause them to mat down.

> "You think you got problems!
> That darn Cajun thinks I'm a shrimp!"

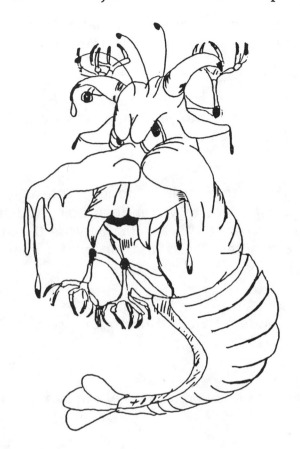

Shrimp in its Many Moods and Tastes

A WORD FROM THE AUTHOR:

The mood of shrimp changes like the color of the moon on the surface of my beloved bayou country. My wife and I have trawled Lake Pontchartrain for shrimp at night, during the early mornings and late evenings. As the moods of the bays and estuaries change, so can the delicious variety of dishes from appetizers, salads, etouffe's, and gumbos. I'm getting hungry just writing this and I just received a honey-do from my wife requesting that we have Cajun fried butterfly shrimp tonight for dinner.

Shrimp are pure in their form. You must search diligently to find a fat content. Their calorie value is one of the lowest foods we can consume. There's no such thing, believe me, as eating too much shrimp. Cook lots at one time and let the leftovers satisfy tomorrow's taste requests.

A GUIDE IN FOOD PREPARATION #2

Always soak canned crabmeat in ice water for 10 minutes before using. Crabmeat rinsed this way will return to its fresh taste.

The best cheese for soups are Swiss, Parmesan, Romano, Cheddar, or Gruyere. Grate your cheese fresh; pre-grated cheese will make your soup cloudy.

Four medium tomatoes yield 1 pound. The easy way to peel tomatoes: Bring a pot of water to a boil. Add the tomatoes. Remove the pot from the heat. Remove the tomatoes from the water after 2 minutes. Pierce the top with a knife and peel the skin down in strips.

Gumbo is a wonderful way of using leftovers and is subject to infinite variations.

Gumbo is best served over mounds of hot rice in a large flat soup bowl.

Sprinkle a little nutmeg over a bowl of oyster stew before you serve it.

Don't cook cauliflower in an aluminum pot; it will darken the vegetable.

SHRIMP IN ITS MANY MOODS AND TASTES

SHRIMP ETOUFFE'S LAKE PONTCHARTRAIN

4 lb. shrimp, peeled and
   deveined
½ tsp. thyme
½ tsp. sweet basil
1 c. onion, chopped
½ c. celery, chopped
½ c. green pepper, chopped
1 stick margarine
½ c. green onions, chopped
¼ tsp. ground red pepper or
   cayenne

1 tsp. paprika
½ tsp. white pepper
¼ tsp. black pepper
1 tsp. fresh garlic or flakes
3 Tbsp. Worcestershire sauce
4 c. hot water
1 c. dark brown roux
Salt to taste

In a large saucepan or Dutch oven, melt margarine at 400°. When margarine is hot and moisture is removed, add shrimp and seasonings. Saute for 5 minutes or until shrimp are deep pink. Remove shrimp from pan, allowing a majority of the margarine to remain. Add vegetables and Worcestershire sauce. Saute for 10 minutes or until vegetables are soft. Add 2 cups hot water; blend in 1 cup of basic dark brown roux. Return shrimp to mixture; bring to simmer. Add remaining 2 cups of hot water to control thickness or to your desired consistency. Simmer for 30 minutes.

Serve over hot cooked rice or combine rice to dish. Remove from heat and let stand for 5 minutes. Garnish generously with parsley. Serves 8.

SAUTEED SHRIMP ST. CHARLES PARISH

2 lb. shrimp, peeled and
   deveined
1 stick margarine
1 c. green onion, chopped
1 tsp. garlic salt
1 c. hot water
1 tsp. Tabasco sauce

½ tsp. dry mustard
½ tsp. sweet basil
¼ tsp. black pepper
¼ tsp. white pepper
¼ c. dark red brown roux
Salt to taste

In a large saucepan, melt margarine at 400°. Add green onion and saute until light brown. Reduce heat to 200° and add seasonings. Add hot water, bring to a boil and add roux. Add remaining ingredients, including shrimp. Simmer until shrimp are tender. Serves 6.

CHARTRES STREET SHRIMP STUFFED TOMATOES

6 large tomatoes
2 lb. boiled shrimp, peeled and
deveined
4 Tbsp. onion, chopped
4 Tbsp. celery, chopped
¼ c. salad olives, chopped
½ c. mayonnaise

Juice of ½ lemon
3 hard-boiled eggs, chopped
fine
⅛ tsp. white pepper
⅛ tsp. garlic powder
Salt to taste

Hollow out tomatoes and set aside. Retain the centers and chop. Mix all ingredients thoroughly. By the way, friends, if shrimp are large, cut into quarters. Stuff tomatoes. If you have any excess ingredients, save for a delicious sandwich or snack later. Serve on a bed of lettuce. Garnish with a little parsley and a wedge of lemon on the side. Serves 6.

SHRIMP WITH EGGS CONSTANCE

1 lb. shrimp, peeled and
deveined
½ stick margarine
½ green pepper, chopped fine
½ c. milk
8 eggs
1 medium onion, chopped fine

4 green onion tops, chopped
fine
¼ tsp. garlic salt
¼ tsp. white pepper
⅛ tsp. paprika

In a bowl, combine eggs and milk at room temperature. Whisk until blended and set aside. In a saucepan, melt margarine at 450°. Add remaining ingredients, including shrimp. Saute for 2 minutes. Reduce the heat to 300° and saute for an additional 3 minutes. Remove from heat and allow to cool at room temperature. Add milk and egg mixture. Return to heat and simmer until ingredients have reached a thick rich consistency. Serve as a main dish for brunch. Serves 6.

BOILED SHRIMP CABILDO

4 lb. shrimp
4 Tbsp. crab boil
2 Tbsp. margarine
¼ c. wine vinegar
1 onion, chopped

2 stalks celery, chopped
½ green pepper, chopped
¼ tsp. red pepper
½ tsp. Louisiana hot sauce

In a deep pan, combine ingredients; cover with water. Bring to a brisk boil. Continue to boil for 3 to 6 minutes according to size of shrimp. Cover and set aside for 20 minutes. Serves 6.

The vegetables and shrimp are delicious together.

BARBECUE SHRIMP ST. JOHN PARISH

3 lb. large shrimp, peeled and
    deveined
1 stick margarine
½ tsp. thyme
¼ tsp. oregano

⅛ tsp. white pepper
⅛ tsp. red pepper
½ tsp. garlic salt
½ tsp. salt

In a wide flat pan, melt margarine at 200°. Add shrimp while moisture still remains. Add remaining ingredients; continue to saute at 400° for 1 minute. Mix together briskly. Reduce heat to 250°. Arrange shrimp in a neat order on one side and saute to a bright red color. Turn them over and saute opposite side to a bright red color. Remove from heat immediately. Serve over toasted Italian, French or Greek bread. Serves 6.

FRIED SHRIMP ST. JAMES

3 lb. shrimp, peeled and
    deveined
2 c. flour
2 Tbsp. baking powder
4 eggs
1 c. milk
¼ tsp. red pepper

⅛ tsp. thyme
¼ tsp. basil
¼ tsp. sweet paprika
⅛ tsp. garlic powder
⅛ tsp. onion powder
1 tsp. salt

Split back of shrimp and butterfly. In a large bowl, combine milk, eggs, baking powder, and seasonings at room temperature. Add shrimp, folding in well. Allow to marinate for ½ hour, or time permitting, marinate for 2 hours in refrigerator. Pour flour in a large flat dish. Remove shrimp, one at a time, and dip into flour. Dip shrimp again into marinade and then again in flour. Shake off lightly. Deep-fry with enough oil to allow shrimp to float at 400°. Fry until shrimp float to the top and turn brown. Serves 6.

SHRIMP COCKTAIL

3 lb. boiled shrimp (medium to
    large)
1 medium onion

2 stalks celery
¼ green pepper

Add 4 quarts water to a large saucepan. Add vegetables and bring to a boil. Add 3 tablespoons Creole shrimp boil. Add shrimp and boil until deep pink. Cover and set aside. Drain shrimp thoroughly. Discard the water. Chop vegetables fine after boiling. Add 1½ cups of Creole cocktail sauce. Add shrimp. Saute together for about 5 minutes or until well heated. Remove from heat. Allow to thoroughly chill. Place the lettuce leaf on the bottom of a glass bowl and add a generous dip. Serves 8.

SHRIMP CREOLE RACELAND

3 lb. shrimp, peeled and
   deveined
2 stalks celery, chopped
2 medium onions, chopped
½ green pepper, chopped
4 cloves garlic, chopped
½ tsp. thyme

¼ tsp. basil
¼ tsp. bay leaf
½ tsp. Tabasco
1 stick margarine
1 c. basil red brown roux
2 c. hot water
Salt to taste

In a large saucepan, melt margarine at 400°. Add vegetables and saute for 5 minutes at 400°. Reduce heat to 200° and add red brown roux. Stir briskly. Add shrimp and hot water. Add seasonings. At this point, it may be necessary to add additional hot water to control thickness. Simmer briskly for 40 minutes. Serves 6.

Note: Avoid boiling. Don't leave this dish unattended; it must be stirred frequently. It may be necessary to add additional water. I like this dish to arrive at the consistency of a thick syrup. Serve in a bowl. Tempt with 6 ounces of dry white wine. This recipe may be used to create a pasta casserole.

SHRIMP PIE CREOLE DUPLESSIS

4 lb. shrimp, peeled and
   deveined
1 stick margarine
1½ c. sour cream
½ c. green pepper, chopped
⅓ c. onion, chopped
⅓ c. celery, chopped
½ tsp. dry basil
¼ tsp. thyme
½ tsp. fresh garlic or flakes
½ tsp. dry mustard

½ tsp. onion powder
½ tsp. black pepper
½ tsp. white pepper
1 tsp. paprika
1 c. basic brown roux
2 c. hot water
8 aluminum pot pie shells
1 tsp. salt
1 can dairy case croissant
   dough or biscuits

In a large saucepan, melt ½ stick margarine at 200°. Before moisture is removed, add vegetables. Saute until soft at 250°. Slowly blend in 1 cup of basic brown roux. Add 1 cup of hot water, blending with a whisk. Keep mixture in constant movement. In a separate pan, melt ½ stick margarine at 300°. Add seasonings and shrimp; saute until deep pink. Combine with vegetables. Add additional cup of hot water; blend well. Watch closely, friends. We want this dish to arrive at a fairly thick consistency. It will have a tendency to stick when thickness occurs. Remove from heat. Blend in sour cream. While mixture is hot, fill pie shells ¾ full. Cover the top of the pot pie with unrolled croissant dough. Tuck around the edges. If you prefer, rolled out biscuit dough will do the same. Bake at 350° until crust browns. Serves 8.

SHRIMP VERMILION BAY

3 lb. shrimp, peeled and
deveined
2 c. medium size mushrooms,
sliced
1 c. dry white wine
1 tsp. garlic salt
1 tsp. onion powder
1 tsp. white pepper
1 tsp. garlic powder
1 tsp. curry powder

½ tsp. thyme
¼ tsp. red pepper
¼ tsp. black pepper
1 bay leaf
1 tsp. salt
1 c. sour cream
Juice of 1 lemon
1 c. green onion, chopped
¼ c. parsley, chopped
1 stick margarine

In a saucepan, melt margarine at 300°. Add seasonings and vegetables except parsley. Saute at 300° until vegetables are soft. Add wine slowly. Bring to simmer for 5 minutes. Add lemon juice. Add shrimp and saute until bright pink. Reduce heat to 200° and blend in sour cream. Simmer until thickened. Remove from heat. Sprinkle with parsley leaves. Serve over rice or top with croutons. Serves 8.

FRIED SHRIMP LECOMPTE

3 lb. shrimp, peeled and
deveined
Polyunsaturated corn oil
(enough to float shrimp)
½ tsp. garlic powder
1 tsp. Tabasco sauce
4 Tbsp. Worcestershire sauce

½ tsp. onion powder
6 eggs
¼ c. wine vinegar
2 c. Creole corn meal fish fry
½ c. milk
Salt to taste

In a large bowl, combine seasonings, eggs and milk at room temperature. Blend in wine vinegar and whisk thoroughly. Place shrimp in egg mixture and marinate for 40 minutes. Stir occasionally. In a large flat plate, spread the fish fry. In a large frying pan, add enough corn oil to allow shrimp to float while frying at 400°. If you like splitting the back of your shrimp and butterflying, please do so. While the oil is heating, remove shrimp, one at a time, from marinade and pat thoroughly into the corn meal mix. Shake gently and drop shrimp individually into the hot oil. When they reach a crisp, golden brown, remove from pan. Serve with a cocktail sauce of your choice. Serves 6.

SHRIMP DIRTY RICE ST. PETER

2 c. small shrimp, peeled and
  deveined
1 stick margarine
Juice of ½ lemon
4 Tbsp. Worcestershire sauce
2 c. cooked rice

½ tsp. garlic powder
½ tsp. onion powder
¼ tsp. oregano
¼ tsp. thyme
½ tsp. black pepper
Salt to taste

In a saucepan, melt margarine at 300°. Add shrimp and saute until pink. Quickly add seasonings. Keep shrimp moving at all times. Add well drained, cooked rice. Please make sure rice is not been overcooked or dish will be mushy. Do not reduce heat; continue to saute until rice and shrimp are thoroughly coated. At first signs of rice sticking, remove from heat and serve. Serves 4.

DIRTY RICE DE LAFAYETTE

2 c. small shrimp, peeled and
  deveined
4 Tbsp. soy sauce
4 c. cooked, well drained wild
  rice
2 eggs, lightly beaten
6 oz. mushrooms (canned or
  fresh)

1 c. green onion, chopped
1 stick margarine
¼ tsp. garlic powder
⅛ tsp. white pepper
½ tsp. Tabasco
⅓ tsp. curry powder
1 oz. dry white wine
Salt to taste

In a saucepan, melt margarine at 300°. Add shrimp and saute until pink. Add seasonings, including mushrooms and green onion. Continue stirring until well coated and blended. Add dry white wine. Remove from heat and add eggs, blending well. Add rice and continue stirring until all ingredients are well blended, about 5 minutes. Serve as a main entree. Serves 6.

Note: Shrimp may be substituted with pork, ham, chicken, or scallops.

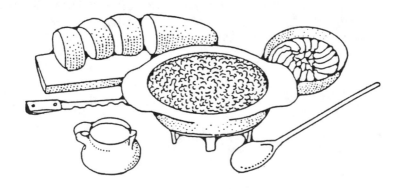

SHRIMP EGGPLANT JAMBALAYA BOGALUSA

2 lb. shrimp, peeled and
   deveined
2 large eggplant, peeled and
   diced
1 stick margarine
1 can whole tomatoes
1 c. celery, chopped
1/2 c. green pepper, chopped
1 c. onion, chopped
3 cloves garlic, chopped
1/8 tsp. white pepper

1/8 tsp. red pepper
1/8 tsp. black pepper
1/4 tsp. thyme
1/8 tsp. powdered bay leaf
1 c. hot water
2 c. rice or 1 c. seasoned bread
   crumbs or 1/4 c. light brown
   roux with tomato puree
   (optional)
Salt to taste

In a large saucepan, melt margarine at 300°. Add shrimp and saute until pink; remove from pan. Add eggplant, onion, celery, green pepper, and garlic. Saute until soft. Add tomatoes, including water from the can. If you intend to use rice, add uncooked. If you intend to use bread crumbs, save until later. Return shrimp and add seasonings. Add 1 cup hot water, stirring slowly. Cook at 250° for about 40 minutes or until rice is cooked. If you intend to use seasoned bread crumbs as a substitute for rice, add 10 minutes before dish is cooked. Blend in bread crumbs and cook slowly until moisture is removed. Serves 6.

This dish will stick if too much heat is applied. If you decide to use neither bread crumbs or rice, add 1/4 cup of light brown roux or tomato puree to enhance texture and consistency of the dish.

CAJUN JAMBALAYA TCHOUPITOULAS
(Shrimp, Chicken, Rabbit)

2 lb. small shrimp, peeled and deveined
2 doz. oysters
1 c. boneless chicken breast, diced
1/2 c. any good smoked sausage, diced
1/2 c. tasso, chopped, or a good smoked ham
2/3 tsp. bay leaf
1 tsp. dry oregano leaves
1/2 tsp. thyme
2 c. onion, chopped
1/2 c. green pepper, chopped
1 1/2 c. celery, chopped
6 cloves garlic, chopped fine
2 cans whole tomatoes
6 oz. tomato sauce
1/2 c. green onion, chopped
2 c. uncooked rice
1/2 tsp. red cayenne pepper
1/2 tsp. white pepper
1/2 tsp. black pepper
1/2 stick margarine
1 c. brown roux
2 c. hot water
Salt to taste

In a bowl, combine all seasonings; mix well. Set aside. In a saucepan, melt 1/2 stick margarine at 350°. Add sausage and saute for about 5 minutes. Add green pepper, celery, onion, and garlic; saute until soft. Add chicken; saute until white. Do not overcook. By all means, nice people, keep this dish moving. Add seasonings; stir constantly. Cook for about 2 minutes. Add tomatoes, including water from the can. Add tomato sauce; blend well. Cook until chicken becomes tender. Keep it moving. Slowly add roux; add 2 cups hot water. Bring to a boil for about 5 minutes. Reduce heat to 250°. Add rice, shrimp and oysters. Stir until boiling. Add hot water to control thickness.

At this point, you have the choice of simmering this dish until it gets to a dense thickness or placing it in a casserole dish. Bake at 350° for 25 minutes. Serves 8 as an entree or 12 as an appetizer.

FLAMING SHRIMP FAUBOURG ST. MARY

2 lb. large shrimp, peeled and deveined
2 c. mushrooms
1/2 lb. lowfat turkey ham, diced 1/2 inch
1 c. brandy
Salt to taste

Place on skewers in alternating series: One large shrimp, one large mushroom and one piece of turkey ham. Barbecue over grill for 10 minutes. Rotate frequently so the shrimp cook on all sides. Place brandy in a flat pan, warming on side of the grill. When barbecue is cooked, dip skewers in brandy, making sure all sides are totally saturated. Next, touch skewers over grill so they burst into flame. Serve flaming for a dramatic effect. Serves 6.

CAJUN SHRIMP JEAN LaFITTE

3 c. shrimp, peeled and
   deveined
4 tomatoes, cut into large
   chunks
1½ c. sour cream
2 Tbsp. soy sauce
6 Tbsp. all-purpose flour
¼ stick margarine

2 green peppers, cut into large
   pieces
Juice of a lemon
⅛ tsp. black pepper
⅛ tsp. white pepper
⅛ tsp. garlic powder
1 tsp. onion powder
Salt to taste

In a saucepan, melt margarine. Add green peppers and seasonings; saute until soft at 300°. Reduce temperature and remove green peppers. Stir flour into margarine. Add sour cream, stirring briskly. Add chunks of tomatoes. Return green peppers to pan; add shrimp and remaining ingredients. Cook over a low heat, stirring frequently, for 10 to 15 minutes. Serve over hot rice. Serves 8.

SHRIMP AND OYSTERS IN GARLIC PASTA MAGAZINE

1 lb. shrimp, peeled and
   deveined
1 stick margarine
1 lb. spaghetti, cooked
1 tsp. garlic powder
6 to 8 oz. oysters
1 can oyster stew
½ c. green onions, chopped

½ tsp. thyme
¼ tsp. white pepper
½ tsp. paprika
½ tsp. black pepper
½ tsp. onion powder
½ c. fresh, grated Parmesan
   cheese
Salt to taste

After spaghetti is cooked and properly drained, stir 2 tablespoons melted margarine and set aside. In a separate bowl, combine seasonings; mix well. Set aside. In a saucepan, melt remaining margarine at 300°. Add shrimp, green onions and seasonings. Saute until shrimp turn pink. Again, keep this dish moving. Add oysters and oyster stew. Cook until oysters begin to curl or become firm. Add spaghetti and cook until dish is thoroughly heated, approximately 2 to 3 minutes. Sprinkle on Parmesan cheese. Serve. Serves 6.

SHRIMP IN CREAM SAUCE GAIGNET

2 lb. boiled shrimp, peeled and
   deveined
3 c. hot milk
¼ c. celery, diced
¼ c. onions, diced
¼ green pepper, diced
1 tsp. white pepper
1 bay leaf

¼ tsp. oregano
¼ stick margarine
8 Tbsp. all-purpose flour
3 eggs, well beaten
¼ tsp. garlic powder
⅛ tsp. thyme
¼ c. parsley, chopped
Salt to taste

In a saucepan, melt margarine at 350° until moisture is removed. Add flour, stirring in slowly until it gels. Reduce temperature to 200°. Add celery, green pepper, onion, parsley, and seasonings. Saute for about 2 minutes. Slowly add milk, bringing to a simmer. Blend well. This should produce a cream sauce texture. Reduce heat to 250°. Add eggs; continue to blend well. Add shrimp and cook until tender, about 10 minutes. Serves 6.

SHRIMP AMANDINE CREOLE

2 lb. shrimp, peeled and
   deveined
½ stick margarine
½ tsp. garlic powder
⅛ tsp. thyme

¾ c. almonds, chopped
1 tsp. Tabasco sauce
¼ c. dry vermouth
Juice of 1 lemon
Salt to taste

In a bowl, marinate shrimp in lemon juice, Tabasco sauce, garlic, and thyme for ½ hour. In a saucepan, melt ¼ stick margarine at 300°. Add shrimp and marinade; saute until pink. Remove and place on a hot platter. Melt remaining margarine. Add almonds and vermouth. Bring to simmer for 4 minutes. Pour over top of shrimp. Serve over rice. Serves 6.

SHRIMP IN WHITE WINE BEAUREGARD

4 lb. shrimp, peeled and
   deveined
4 tsp. flour
1 c. sour cream
1 stick margarine
¼ tsp. white pepper
¼ tsp. red pepper

½ tsp. curry powder
½ c. green onions
¼ green pepper, chopped fine
1½ c. dry white wine
½ c. seasoned bread crumbs
Salt to taste

In a saucepan, melt ½ stick margarine at 200°. While moisture remains, blend in flour. Add sour cream and blend slowly, bringing mixture to slow simmer. Add seasonings. Cook slowly for 15 minutes. In a separate saucepan, melt remaining margarine at 300°. Add shrimp; saute until pink. Add green onions and shrimp to cream sauce. Add white wine. Bring mixture to simmer and saute for 15 minutes. Add seasoned bread crumbs. Reduce heat and stir frequently for 2 minutes. Serve. Serves 8.

DEVILED SHRIMP, CAJUN STYLE

2 lb. shrimp, diced
¼ c. minced onions
⅛ c. green pepper, chopped fine
½ stick margarine
1 tsp. dry mustard
6 Tbsp. flour

1 c. sour cream
2 oz. sherry
1 c. bread crumbs
⅛ tsp. white pepper
¼ tsp. red pepper
Salt to taste

In a saucepan, melt margarine at 300°. Add shrimp and saute until pink. Add seasonings and vegetables. Add flour and continue to stir while simmering for 2 minutes. Reduce heat and add sour cream. Bring to slow simmer. Don't give up on the stirring. Add sherry and remove from heat. At this point, fold in ½ cup bread crumbs and place in a lightly greased casserole dish. Sprinkle with remaining bread crumbs. Bake at 350° for 25 minutes. Serves 6.

QUICK SHRIMP CREOLE MUSHROOM ANNUNCIATION

2 lb. shrimp, peeled and
  deveined
2 cans mushrooms
4 eggs, deviled
½ stick margarine
2 c. milk
¼ c. flour

1 c. grated American cheese
½ tsp. red pepper
½ tsp. black pepper
⅛ tsp. oregano
⅛ tsp. sweet basil
Salt to taste

In a saucepan, melt margarine. Add shrimp and saute until pink at 300°. Remove shrimp; set aside. Retain drippings. Add flour slowly to the margarine. Reduce heat to 150°. Add milk, stirring in slowly. Add 1 cup of cheese; bring to simmer. Continue to stir; this dish will stick easy. Add seasonings, blending well. Add mushrooms. Remove from heat. Fold in deviled eggs. Arrange the shrimp in the bottom of a lightly oiled casserole dish. Sprinkle ½ cup cheese over shrimp. Pour mixture over shrimp. Sprinkle remaining cheese on top. Bake at 350° for 20 minutes. Serves 6.

SHRIMP AND POTATO AU GRATIN LAFAYETTE

2 large Irish potatoes, baked
2 lb. shrimp, peeled and
   deveined
½ c. fresh crabmeat
1 tsp. onion powder
¼ c. parsley, chopped
¾ c. grated cheese (your choice)
2 oz. sherry
1 tsp. white pepper

¼ tsp. red pepper
¼ tsp. sweet basil
1 Tbsp. Worcestershire sauce
¼ c. sour cream
1 tsp. prepared Creole mustard
¼ stick margarine
¼ c. milk if necessary
½ tsp. white pepper
Salt to taste

In a saucepan, melt margarine. Add shrimp; saute until pink at 300°. Reduce heat to 200°. Add sour cream and remaining ingredients except ½ grated cheese and potatoes. Blend well. Bring to a simmer for 5 minutes or until cheese is thoroughly melted. Place ½ of mixture in a casserole dish. Slice potatoes in ½ inch thickness. Place on top of ingredients in casserole dish. Pour remaining mixture over potatoes. Sprinkle generously with grated cheese. Bake at 350° for 20 minutes. Serves 6.

CREOLE SCAMPI RAMPART

1 doz. large shrimp, peeled and
   deveined
1 Tbsp. green onions
½ tsp. saffron
¼ tsp. sweet basil
1 can cream of shrimp soup or
   chowder

1 Tbsp. Hollandaise sauce
⅛ stick margarine
¼ tsp. garlic powder
½ c. dry vermouth
½ tsp. white pepper
¼ tsp. red pepper
Salt to taste

In a saucepan, melt margarine at 200°. Add the green onions and shrimp; saute for 4 minutes at 300°. Add the vermouth and seasonings; simmer for 10 minutes. Remove the shrimp from the mixture. Add the rest of the ingredients, blending well. Simmer until it thickens. Place shrimp under broiler and lightly brown. Arrange shrimp on bed of rice and cover with sauce. Serves 4.

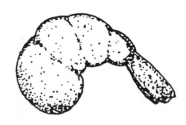

SHRIMP VIEUX CARRE

5 lb. shrimp
4 boiled potatoes
1½ sticks margarine
2 tsp. all-purpose flour
1 c. heavy cream
½ c. light cream
½ tsp. white pepper

¼ tsp. red pepper
1 c. green onions, minced
¼ c. green pepper, minced
1 c. dry white wine
¼ tsp. garlic flakes
Salt to taste

Wash, peel, devein, and quarter shrimp; set aside. Prepare cream sauce as follows: Melt ½ stick margarine in a double boiler. Add flour slowly and blend well until gels. Add creams and seasonings. Simmer for about 20 minutes, stirring consistently, until cream sauce thickens. Remove from heat. In a separate saucepan, melt remaining margarine at 300°. Add shrimp and saute until pink. Add green onions and green pepper, then slowly add cream sauce. Simmer for 15 minutes. Do not allow to boil. Add 1 cup white wine and allow mixture to steep.

To serve, lightly oil individual ramekins lightly with margarine. Make a ruffle of cream potatoes around the edge of each dish. Spoon in the center a portion of shrimp mixture. Sprinkle cream potatoes lightly with grated yellow cheese. Place under broiler until cheese is melted and potatoes are light brown.

BARBECUE STUFFED SHRIMP DELACROIX

1 c. fresh crabmeat
3 doz. large shrimp
2 Tbsp. margarine
3 Tbsp. onion, chopped
3 Tbsp. celery, chopped
2 Tbsp. green pepper, chopped
2 Tbsp. flour

½ c. milk
½ c. bread crumbs or crackers
1 tsp. parsley, chopped
Salt to taste
¼ tsp. coarse black pepper
1 tsp. Worcestershire sauce
1 c. barbecue sauce

In a saucepan, melt margarine at 300°. Add onion, celery and green pepper; saute until soft. Stir in flour; slowly add milk. Stir ingredients until it thickens. Add bread crumbs, crabmeat, Worcestershire sauce, parsley, salt, and pepper. Mix well. Reduce heat to 200° and simmer for 1 minute, stirring well. Remove from heat. Peel and devein shrimp, leaving the edge of the tails on. Split back of the shrimp and spread. Stuff back of shrimp with crab stuffing. Hold together with toothpicks. Arrange shrimp in a broiler pan. Place in broiler, approximately 5 inches away from heat. Baste occasionally with barbecue sauce of your choice, approximately 5 minutes on each side. Serves 6.

SHRIMP IN EGGPLANT BATTER ST. JOHN

2 lb. shrimp, peeled and
  deveined
3/4 c. beer
4 tsp. margarine
1/4 c. corn meal
3/4 c. flour
1/2 c. corn flour
2 eggs
1/2 c. heavy cream
1/2 tsp. red pepper
1 tsp. onion powder
1/4 tsp. salt
1/2 tsp. white pepper
1/2 tsp. garlic powder

3 Tbsp. margarine
3 Tbsp. corn oil
6 c. eggplant, peeled and
  chopped
1 c. onion, chopped fine
2 tsp. garlic, minced
1 tsp. thyme
1 tsp. sweet basil
1/2 tsp. black pepper
1/4 tsp. oregano
2 tsp. brown sugar
1/2 c. green onions, chopped fine

Place beer and margarine in a small saucepan. Heat at 200° until margarine melts. Remove from heat and pour into a large mixing bowl. Add corn meal. Beat well with a whisk and allow to stand for 5 minutes. Stir in 1/4 cup flour and corn flour. Add eggs, then cream. Mix well after each addition. Add 1/2 teaspoon red pepper, 1/4 teaspoon salt, onion powder, 1/4 teaspoon white pepper, and garlic powder. Mix well and set aside.

Place 3 tablespoons margarine with 3 tablespoons corn oil in a large pan. Add eggplant and saute at 200° until light brown, about 10 minutes. Stir occasionally. Add onion and continue to cook for 5 to 10 minutes, stirring occasionally. Add minced garlic, thyme, basil, black pepper, oregano, 1/2 teaspoon salt, and remaining red pepper. At this point, stir well, scraping bottom of pan. Lower heat and continue cooking for 5 minutes. Stir in sugar. Add green onions and cook for an additional 5 minutes. Add eggplant mixture to the bowl of corn meal mixture; beat thoroughly. Set aside.

Shrimp Seasoning:

2 tsp. red pepper
2 tsp. dried thyme leaves
2 tsp. dried basil
3/4 tsp. salt
1 tsp. white pepper

1/2 tsp. black pepper
1/2 tsp. oregano
5 doz. large shrimp, peeled with
  tip of tail remaining
Corn oil

Combine Shrimp Seasoning mix in a small bowl. In a separate bowl, combine 1 teaspoon seasoning mix with 1/2 cup of flour. Pour remaining seasoning mix over shrimp. In a deep skillet, heat 4 inches of corn oil to 375°. Dip shrimp in seasoned flour; shake off excess lightly. Coat shrimp well with batter and fry until golden brown.

CAJUN SHRIMP AND OYSTER GUMBO

2 lb. shrimp, peeled and
    deveined
2 doz. raw oysters
1/2 stick margarine
1 medium size can whole
    tomatoes
1 c. onions, chopped
6 cloves garlic, chopped
1 c. red brown roux
1/4 c. parsley, chopped
1 oz. Worcestershire sauce

Juice from 1 lemon
1/2 tsp. thyme
1/2 tsp. bay leaf
1/4 tsp. red pepper
1/4 tsp. white pepper
1/4 tsp. black pepper
2 cans chicken soup
3 cubes chicken bouillon
1/2 c. green pepper, chopped
3 c. 3/4 cooked rice
Salt to taste

In a large saucepan, melt margarine. Add the green pepper and onions; stir in well. Add garlic and saute until soft at 300°. Add chicken soup and bouillon. Stir frequently; bring to simmer. Add the bay leaf, thyme and peppers; blend well. Add tomatoes with their own juice. Reduce heat to 200° and slowly add roux. Stir well. Bring to a low boil for 20 minutes. Add the shrimp and oysters, including oyster water. Continue at a low simmer for 5 more minutes. Add the parsley, lemon juice and Worcestershire sauce; continue at a low boil for 5 additional minutes. At this point, add 3 cups of cooked rice or serve over cooked rice. Remove entire contents from heat. Cover and set aside for an additional 10 minutes and serve.

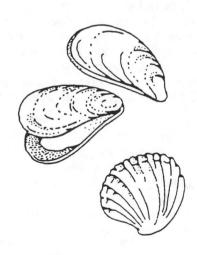

SHRIMP STUFFED EGGPLANT WITH OYSTER SAUCE LAKE CHARLES

Seasoning Mix:

2 bay leaves
1 tsp. salt
3/4 tsp. red pepper
1/2 tsp. black pepper
1/2 tsp. dried thyme
1/2 tsp. white pepper
4 large eggplants
2 sticks margarine
1 c. onions, chopped
2/3 c. celery, chopped
1/2 c. green pepper, chopped
1 lb. peeled small shrimp or
    crawfish tails
1 c. fish soup
1/2 c. hot water
1/2 c. onions, chopped fine

1 tsp. salt
1/2 tsp. white pepper
1/4 tsp. red pepper
1/2 tsp. dried basil
1/4 tsp. nutmeg
1 tsp. lemon juice
1 tsp. minced garlic
1 1/2 c. all-purpose flour
1 c. heavy cream
3 doz. large oysters (save liquid)
1/2 c. green onion, chopped fine
1 1/2 c. bread crumbs
1 c. milk
2 eggs

Second Seasoning Mix:

2 tsp. salt
1 tsp. white pepper
1 tsp. dried mustard
1/2 tsp. red pepper

1 tsp. paprika
1 tsp. onion powder
1 tsp. garlic powder
Corn oil

In a medium bowl, combine (first seasoning mix) ingredients and set aside. Peel eggplants and cut in halves crosswise. Carve out the center meat to form a shell. Place pulp in a saucepan with 1 stick of margarine, 1 cup onions, celery, and green peppers. Cook at 350° for about 3 minutes, stirring occasionally. Add the first seasoning mix; stir well. Continue cooking for 3 minutes. Scrape bottom of pan. Add shrimp or crawfish; cook for 3 minutes. Add 1/2 cup of oyster water and cook for an additional 3 minutes. Remove from heat; set aside.

In a saucepan, melt the remaining stick of margarine at 200°. Add the chopped onions, salt, white pepper, red pepper, basil, nutmeg, lemon juice, and garlic. Saute for 4 minutes; blend well. Stir in 1/3 cup flour until well blended, then stir in remaining 1 cup stock. Increase heat to 400°; bring to a boil. Continue cooking until mixture thickens. Add cream and reduce heat. Stir in oysters, green onions and cook for 5 minutes. In 3 separate pans, add milk and eggs; blend well. In a small bowl, combine with second seasonings. Add 2 teaspoons seasonings to flour, 1 teaspoon to bread crumbs. Sprinkle remaining seasoning on eggplants. Fry eggplants thoroughly until golden brown. Combine ingredients and serve.

SHRIMP PIE NAPOLEONVILLE

1 lb. shrimp, peeled and
    deveined
4 tsp. margarine
4 tsp. flour
2 c. hot milk
2 tsp. margarine

½ lb. fresh mushrooms
1 tsp. dry sherry
½ tsp. mace
½ tsp. black pepper
2 c. corn flakes
Salt to taste

In a saucepan, melt 4 teaspoons margarine at 300°. Add flour until gels. Slowly add hot milk, blending well. Remove from heat and set aside. In a separate pan, melt 2 teaspoons margarine at 400°. Add shrimp and mushrooms. Saute until shrimp turn pink. Reduce heat and add sherry. Blend in seasonings. Remove from heat. Lightly oil a casserole dish and arrange shrimp. Top with cream sauce and cover generously with corn flakes. Bake at 375° for 20 minutes. Serves 6.

SHRIMP CURRY ST. MARY'S PARISH

1 lb. cooked shrimp, peeled and
    deveined
1 c. white roux
1 can cream of chicken soup
3 sprigs parsley
2 stalks celery, chopped large
1 onion, chopped large

2 Tbsp. lemon juice
2 Tbsp. curry powder
1 c. white wine
1 c. seasoned bread crumbs
¼ stick margarine
Salt to taste

Place cream of chicken soup in a saucepan and bring to a low simmer. Add white wine, stirring well. In a separate saucepan, melt margarine and saute vegetables until soft. Slowly add roux; blend well. Add seasonings and combine with cream of chicken mixture. Mix well. Bring to low boil. Add shrimp, continuing at a low boil. Remove from heat and pour mixture into a lightly oiled baking dish. Cover with seasoned bread crumbs. Bake, uncovered, at 350° for 25 minutes. Serves 6.

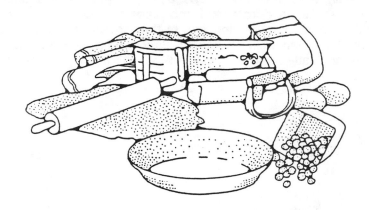

SHRIMP MUSHROOM PIE WESTWEGO

1 lb. shrimp, peeled and
   deveined
½ stick margarine
1 c. mushrooms
1 can cream of mushroom soup
8 oz. mixed frozen vegetables
⅛ tsp. oregano

⅛ tsp. sweet basil
⅛ tsp. red pepper
⅛ tsp. white pepper
⅛ tsp. thyme
2 oz. dry white wine
1 can dairy biscuits or Bisquick
Salt to taste

In a saucepan, melt margarine and add shrimp. Saute shrimp for 5 minutes or until pink at 300°. Add all ingredients, including soup, vegetables, wine, and seasonings. Cook until mixture is well blended and begins to simmer. If it's too thick, additional wine or hot water can be added. Continue to simmer for 20 minutes.

Meanwhile, use canned biscuits of your choice or Bisquick. Dust a light amount of flour on a cutting board. Roll biscuits flat; try to make as few passes with your roller as possible. Pour mixture into aluminum pie shell. If you like the crust at the bottom, then make 2 crusts. (Lightly brown bottom crust before adding mixture.) Place flattened biscuits over the pie shell. Bake for 20 minutes at 325° until top crust is brown. Serves 6.

SHRIMP STUFFED WITH MUSHROOMS LAKE BORGNE

12 to 16 large mushrooms
1 lb. medium to small peeled
   shrimp
⅓ c. seasoned bread crumbs
2 Tbsp. lemon juice
½ tsp. onion powder

¼ tsp. garlic powder
¼ stick margarine
2 oz. sour cream
1 egg, beaten
Salt to taste

Wash mushrooms and remove the stems. Set tops aside, face up; chop the stems fine. In a flat saucepan, melt margarine. Add the shrimp and saute at 300° until pink. Remove shrimp from margarine; set aside. Allow juices to remain. Place mushroom tops face up in margarine and saute for 2 minutes at 300°. Remove from heat and place tops down in a lightly oiled, shallow baking pan. Combine the rest of the ingredients, including shrimp with the margarine. Mix well. Stuff into mushroom caps. Bake at 375° for 20 minutes or until lightly browned. Serves 6.

SHRIMP LAKE CATHERINE

2 lb. shrimp, peeled and
   deveined
¼ stick margarine
2 c. sour cream
6 oz. dry white wine
¼ c. green onions, chopped
¼ tsp. garlic powder

⅛ tsp. red pepper
⅛ tsp. white pepper
¼ c. flour
2 (8 oz.) frozen spinach
Parmesan cheese
Salt to taste

After thawing spinach properly, drain and arrange in a lightly oiled 10 inch pie pan. In a saucepan, saute shrimp in melted margarine until pink at 300°. Remove shrimp and arrange in layers over spinach. Save drippings. Return pan at 200°; slowly stir in sour cream. Add the wine and the rest of the ingredients. Mix well. This is one of those keep-it-moving type dishes. When the sauce thickens, pour over the shrimp and spinach. Sprinkle with Parmesan cheese. Bake at 350° for 30 minutes. Serves 6.

SHRIMP BALLS BAYOU TOULOUSE

2 lb. shrimp, peeled and
   deveined
1 c. seasoned bread crumbs
1 c. all-purpose flour
2 large eggs, beaten
1 c. onion, chopped
4 cloves garlic, chopped

1 tsp. Worcestershire sauce
3 sprigs parsley, chopped
3 sprigs green onions, chopped
   fine
¼ tsp. red pepper
¼ tsp. black pepper
Salt to taste

In a food processor, add onions, garlic and shrimp. Lightly grind. Place in a large mixing bowl and add remaining ingredients. Mix well with your hands and shape into balls. Roll balls in flour and fry until golden brown. Set aside.

Sauce:

¼ stick margarine
1½ c. brown roux
½ c. onions, chopped fine
1 green pepper, chopped fine
1 qt. hot water
1 can tomato paste

3 bay leaves
¼ tsp. basil
¼ tsp. white pepper
¼ tsp. black pepper
Salt to taste

Melt margarine at 300° and add 1 quart of hot water. Bring to simmer. Blend in roux; add onions, green pepper and remaining ingredients. Bring to simmer. Add shrimp balls and simmer at a low heat for 45 minutes. Serves 6.

SHRIMP STEW BAYOU BLACK

2 lb. medium shrimp, peeled and deveined
1 doz. oysters
2 onions, chopped
4 stalks celery, chopped large
½ green pepper, chopped large
6 cloves garlic, chopped fine
2 c. basic dark red roux
2 cans onion soup

½ stick margarine
½ tsp. oregano
½ tsp. thyme
¼ tsp. bay leaf
¼ tsp. red pepper
¼ tsp. white pepper
¼ tsp. black pepper
1 (8 oz.) frozen okra
Salt to taste

In a large saucepan, melt ¼ stick margarine; saute okra for 3 minutes at 300°. Remove from pan; set aside. Add remaining margarine and allow to melt until moisture is removed. Add all vegetables and seasonings except okra. Blend well. Saute until soft, but not brown. Reduce heat to 200° and add soup; bring to a simmer. Stir occasionally. Blend in roux slowly and continue simmering. Add shrimp, oysters and okra. Simmer for 40 minutes. Serve over rice. Serves 8.

SHRIMP CASSEROLE BAYOU BLUE

1 lb. shrimp, peeled and deveined
5 slices white bread or crackers
1 stick margarine
2 c. American cheese, grated

3 eggs, beaten lightly
2 c. hot milk
½ tsp. red pepper
½ tsp. white pepper
1 tsp. salt

Rinse shrimp and pat dry; set aside. Remove crust from bread. Spread bread generously with margarine and cut into ½ inch cubes. Alternate layers of bread, shrimp and cheese in an 8 inch casserole dish. In a bowl, combine slightly beaten eggs with milk, salt and pepper. Pour contents into a lightly oiled casserole dish. Set casserole in a pan of hot water and bake at 350° for 1 hour. Serves 4.

THYME

SHRIMP WITH ASPARAGUS AND ARTICHOKE HEARTS TERREBONE

1 lb. shrimp, peeled and
  deveined
1 can artichoke hearts,
  quartered
¼ c. mayonnaise
Juice of 1 lemon
2 hard-boiled eggs, chopped
4 sprigs parsley, chopped

⅛ tsp. white pepper
1 can asparagus, drained and
  halved
1 Tbsp. mayonnaise
¼ stick margarine
1 Tbsp. Creole mustard
Salt to taste

In a small saucepan, melt margarine at 300°. Add pepper and shrimp and saute until deep red. In a mixing bowl, combine eggs, parsley, ¼ cup mayonnaise, and lemon juice. In another salad bowl, combine the artichoke hearts, asparagus and shrimp; mix gently to avoid damaging ingredients. Pour mayonnaise dressing over the top; mix gently. Combine Creole mustard and 1 tablespoon mayonnaise. Serve over a leaf of lettuce, surrounded with tomato wedges. Top with mayonnaise mustard mixture. Serves 4.

SHRIMP WITH CHINESE VEGETABLES, CAJUN STYLE

2 lb. shrimp, peeled and
  deveined
1 (16 oz.) frozen Chinese
  vegetables
½ lemon, sliced with skin
¼ tsp. white pepper
¼ tsp. red pepper

¼ tsp. black pepper
1 c. sour cream
¼ tsp. sweet basil
½ stick margarine
2 oz. teriyaki sauce
Salt to taste

Melt margarine in electric wok at 250°. Add the peppers, seasonings and lemon. Saute for 2 minutes. Add shrimp; saute for 3 minutes or until pink. Add the vegetables and raise heat to maximum. Keep this dish moving. Add the remaining ingredients; stir well. Reduce heat to 200°. Cover and stir frequently until vegetables are cooked and very crisp. Serve over a bed of rice and top with fresh grated Parmesan cheese. Serves 8.

SHRIMP STEW ESPLANADE

2 lb. shrimp, peeled and
  deveined
1 stick margarine
3 Tbsp. all-purpose flour
2 medium onions, diced
1 medium green pepper, diced
2 celery stalks, diced
1 clove garlic, minced

1 Tbsp. Worcestershire sauce
1 Tbsp. green onion tops,
  chopped
1/2 tsp. black pepper
1/4 tsp. red pepper
1/4 tsp. white pepper
1 bay leaf
1/4 tsp. thyme

In a saucepan, melt margarine at 400°. Add flour slowly; continue to stir until flour reaches a chocolate brown. Remove from heat and add vegetables, stirring in briskly. Add Worcestershire sauce; stir briskly until mixture ceases to sizzle. Add shrimp; stir in lightly. Return to heat. Blend in enough hot water to bring mixture to a syrup consistency. Let simmer at 200° for an hour. Serve with cooked rice; garnish with onion tops. Serves 6.

SHRIMP FONTAINBLEAU

3 lb. large shrimp, peeled and
  deveined
1/2 c. dry sherry
2 Tbsp. sweet sauce

1 c. soy sauce
1 head lettuce, shredded
Juice of 1 lemon
Salt to taste

Combine soy sauce, sweet sauce and sherry; bring to a boil. Pour into a shallow pan and lightly simmer on a barbecue pit. Place 5 shrimp per skewer. Place skewered shrimp in sauce mixture, allowing to simmer for 1 minute. Remove skewer from sauce and place over coals and grill until a rich pink. While shrimp are barbecuing, brush frequently with sauce.

Footnote: If you prefer not using a skewer, place shrimp directly in sauce, turning frequently, so they are well coated. This will allow the shrimp to lay in the boiling action of the sauce.

In a separate bowl, combine shredded lettuce and lemon juice. Arrange on plates, lay one skewer on each plate and serve. Rice is an excellent bed for this dish. Serves 6.

SHRIMP IN GARLIC SAUCE WITH FRIED RICE BAUDUC

1½ lb. shrimp, peeled
¼ stick margarine
1 tsp. garlic powder
½ tsp. onion powder
¼ tsp. white pepper

¼ tsp. red pepper
Juice from 1 lemon
⅛ tsp. thyme
Salt to taste

Melt margarine in electric wok at 400°. When moisture is removed, add the seasonings. Bring to a quick simmer. Add shrimp and saute to a rich pink. Add lemon juice and saute for 1 minute. Set aside.

Fried Rice:

2 c. small shrimp, cooked and
   chopped
2 tsp. soy sauce
4 c. brown rice, cooked
½ stick margarine
2 eggs, lightly beaten

1 large pack fresh mushrooms,
   chopped
½ tsp. black pepper
½ c. green onions, chopped
Salt to taste

Melt margarine in a saucepan at 400°. Add shrimp; stir in briskly. Remove from heat when shrimp are pink. Add eggs, mushrooms, salt, and pepper. Return to heat at 200° for 5 minutes. Add cooked rice and soy sauce; stir briskly for 5 minutes. Add green onions. Place rice as a bed on a large platter. Top with garlic shrimp. Serves 4.

QUICK BARBECUE SHRIMP CROWLEY

2 lb. shrimp, peeled and
   deveined
1 c. barbecue sauce
¼ c. red dry wine

4 Tbsp. creamy peanut butter
¼ stick margarine
¼ tsp. red pepper
Salt to taste

In a saucepan, melt margarine at 300°. Slowly add peanut butter and blend well. When peanut butter is totally melted, reduce temperature to 200° or at a slow simmer. Add red wine, one ounce at a time, and allow mixture to gel. If mixture gels too quickly, remove from heat. Remove from heat and slowly add barbecue sauce and red pepper. Return to heat. Skewer shrimp and barbecue over coals until a deep pink. Dab frequently into peanut butter barbecue sauce. When the shrimp becomes heavily coated with barbecue sauce, serve over a bed of cooked rice. Serves 4.

SHRIMP GUEYDAN

2 lb. shrimp, peeled and
   deveined
1 stick margarine
1 large pack fresh mushrooms,
   halved
1/3 c. green onions, finely
   chopped
1 tsp. garlic, finely chopped
1/4 tsp. red pepper
1/4 tsp. white pepper
1/4 tsp. black pepper
1/8 tsp. oregano
1/4 tsp. thyme
1/4 tsp. basil
1/4 c. parsley, chopped fine
1/2 c. brown roux (optional)
Salt to taste

In a saucepan, melt 1/2 stick margarine until moisture is removed at 300°. Add shrimp and seasonings; saute until pink. Remove from heat; set aside. In a separate saucepan, melt remaining ingredients at 250°. Add mushrooms and vegetables except parsley; saute until soft. Return shrimp and saute for 5 minutes. Serve over a bed of rice; garnish with parsley. Serves 6.

Note: Add 1/2 cup brown roux slowly with water and simmer for 10 minutes for a delightful variation to this dish.

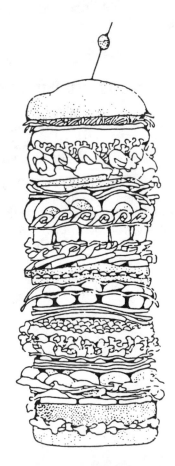

FISH ON THE LINE

BLACKENED REDFISH JACMEL

5 (6 oz.) fish fillets (redfish,
    tilefish or pompano)
1/4 tsp. white pepper
1/4 tsp. red pepper
1/4 tsp. black pepper
1/2 tsp. thyme

1/2 tsp. oregano
1 tsp. onion powder
1 tsp. garlic powder
1 tsp. paprika
2 tsp. Worcestershire sauce
1 stick margarine

In a saucepan, melt 1/4 stick margarine at 225°. Combine thoroughly all powdered seasonings and add to margarine. Blend well. Add the Worcestershire sauce and remaining seasonings to the margarine; stir well. Dip the fish fillets into this mixture. When both sides are coated well, remove from heat; set aside. In a large flat skillet, melt remaining margarine until moisture is removed and a light smoke appears at 400°. Do not allow to burn. Place the fish fillets in the hot margarine.

Be careful, because the dish may flame. If the temperature is proper, it should take no more than 2 minutes cooking time on each side. This will create a delicious blackened taste. Serve over a bed of rice. Serves 5.

STUFFED FISH WITH SHRIMP PETIT

1 large redfish, grouper or red
    snapper
1/2 c. green pepper, chopped
3 cloves garlic, chopped
1/2 stick margarine
1 c. small shrimp, peeled and
    deveined

1 medium onion, chopped
1 c. chunky crabmeat
1 egg, beaten
3/4 c. seasoned bread crumbs
1/8 tsp. white pepper
1/8 tsp. red pepper
1/8 tsp. thyme

In a saucepan, melt 1/4 stick margarine at 250°. Add vegetables and saute until soft. Remove from heat and set aside. In a separate saucepan, melt remaining margarine at 400°. Stir in seasonings briskly; reduce heat to 200°. Add shrimp and saute until bright pink. Gently fold in crabmeat and saute for 3 minutes. Add vegetable mixture; stir in egg. Remove from heat. Gently fold in bread crumbs. Clean redfish thoroughly, allowing head to remain. Place in a lightly oiled baking pan. Stuff mixture into the whole fish of your choice and bake for 45 minutes at 350°. Serves 5.

FLOUNDER IN WINE SAUCE PERSAC

6 (6 oz.) flounder fillets
1 small onion, sliced (creating
   rings)
⅛ stick margarine
3 Tbsp. flour
½ tsp. coarse ground black
   pepper

½ tsp. bay leaf
⅛ tsp. thyme
2 large egg yolks
Juice of 1 lemon
½ c. dry white wine
1 c. hot water

Lightly oil a casserole dish large enough to accommodate fish. Place the onion rings at the bottom; arrange in a manner to support the fish. Arrange fish over the onions. Combine the wine, lemon juice and seasonings, mixing well. Pour this over the fish. Bake for 20 minutes at 325°. Carefully remove the fish fillets, allowing sauce to remain. In a separate saucepan, melt the margarine at 200°. Add the flour. Stir, using a whisk, and allow to gel. Slowly add 1 cup of hot water. When mixture thickens, remove from heat and add the egg yolks. Add the remaining sauce to this mixture, stirring well for 5 minutes on a low simmer. Replace the fillets in casserole dish; pour sauce over the fish. Bake at 250° for 15 minutes. Serves 6.

POMPANO IN MUSHROOM SAUCE HOLMWOOD

2 large pompano or 4 medium
   orange roughy
1 pack fresh mushrooms
1 can cream of mushroom soup
1 c. small shrimp, peeled and
   deveined
2 c. hot water
1 bay leaf

¼ stick margarine
¼ c. green onion, chopped
⅛ tsp. white pepper
⅛ tsp. red pepper
⅛ tsp. basil
⅛ tsp. oregano
¼ c. cream colored roux
Juice of ½ lemon

Place the lemon juice and 1 cup water in a skillet. Bring to a simmer. Add the pompano and poach for 4 to 6 minutes until tender. Carefully remove the pompano and discard the water. In a separate saucepan, melt ¼ stick margarine at 250°. Add shrimp and mushrooms; saute until shrimp are pink. Add cream of mushroom; bring to simmer. Add onion and seasonings; mix well. Add 1 cup hot water and slowly add the roux. This will cause sauce to thicken to a paste consistency. Remove from heat and add additional hot water if necessary. Pour half the sauce in a lightly oiled casserole dish; add the fish. Add remaining sauce on top. Cover with a lid, place in oven and bake at 300° for 20 minutes. Serve with pasta or creamed potatoes. Serves 4.

STUFFED FLOUNDER CREOLE STYLE

3 flounder
1 c. crabmeat
1 c. celery, chopped
1 c. green onions, chopped
½ c. parsley, chopped
¼ tsp. sweet basil
1 bay leaf
1 oz. lemon juice

¼ c. green pepper, chopped
1 medium onion
¼ stick margarine
1 c. bread crumbs
⅛ tsp. white pepper
⅛ tsp. red pepper
⅛ tsp. oregano

Clean flounder thoroughly, allowing head to remain. Split and form a pocket on top of the flounder to receive stuffing. Lightly oil inside of pocket and sprinkle with seasonings. In a saucepan, melt the margarine at 250°. Add the vegetables except whole onion; saute until soft. Add crabmeat and saute for 3 minutes. Carefully add the bread crumbs, stirring and folding. Set aside. Slice onion into thin rings and line bottom of lightly oiled shallow baking pan. Place flounder on top of onions. Stuff the pockets of the flounder with this mixture. In a separate bowl, combine lemon juice with seasonings; mix well. Pour over flounder. Add 1 pat of margarine to each flounder; bake at 350° for 40 minutes. Serves 4.

REDFISH SUPREME LEGRAND

1 (4 to 5 lb.) redfish
1 c. hot water
½ c. corn oil
1¼ sticks margarine
8 Tbsp. flour
¼ c. green onion, chopped
2 Birds Eye green peppers, chopped
¼ tsp. red pepper
1 c. celery, chopped
1 c. parsley, chopped

1 lb. shrimp, peeled and deveined
2 doz. oysters
1 pack fresh mushrooms
½ c. grated American cheese
¾ c. bread crumbs
½ tsp. black pepper
⅛ tsp. basil
⅛ tsp. oregano
1 tsp. salt

Clean and dress redfish; combine salt, red and black pepper and oil. Rub fish inside and out with mixture. Place fish on a rack in a roasting pan and add water. Do not allow fish to touch water. Cover and bake at 350° for 40 minutes. Save drippings.

Sauce: While fish is cooking, melt ½ of the margarine in a large saucepan. Add flour and stir consistently until golden brown. Add remaining seasonings, chopped onions, celery, parsley, and Birds Eye peppers. Simmer for 5 minutes.

In a separate pan, melt remaining margarine. Add oysters, shrimp and mushrooms; saute until shrimp are pink. Add drippings from the roaster. Place fish in a lightly oiled flat baking dish. Cover with first mixture, then cover with second mixture. Sprinkle with a layer of grated cheese, then bread crumbs. Bake at 400° for 15 minutes. Serves 6.

ALMOND CURRY TUNA JACQUES

2 (6½ oz.) cans tuna
½ c. blanched almonds, chopped
¾ tsp. curry powder
½ stick margarine
½ tsp. garlic powder
1 tsp. Worcestershire sauce
2 c. milk

6 Tbsp. flour
¼ tsp. sweet basil
2 medium tomatoes, chopped coarsely
1 c. cooked rice
⅛ tsp. red pepper
⅛ tsp. white pepper
⅛ tsp. oregano

Melt ⅔ margarine in an electric skillet at 300°. Add tomatoes, curry powder, garlic powder, Worcestershire sauce, and seasonings. Blend well and simmer for 3 minutes. Add remaining seasonings, then slowly add flour, blending well. Reduce heat to 200° and stir in milk until mixture thickens. Add tuna fish; simmer for 10 minutes. As this proceeds, melt remaining margarine in a pan. Add the almonds and rice; mix well. Serve curry tuna over the almond rice. Serves 6.

BAKED SNAPPER IN RED WINE LOYOLA

1 large red snapper (6 to 8 lb.)
1/4 c. green pepper, chopped
1/4 c. green onion, chopped
1/4 c. parsley, chopped
1/4 c. onions, chopped
1/4 stick margarine
1 tsp. tarragon

6 oz. red wine
6 strips bacon
1 (No. 2) can tomatoes
1/8 tsp. white pepper
1/8 tsp. red pepper
1 tsp. lemon juice
3/4 tsp. minced garlic
2 c. 3/4 cooked rice

In a saucepan, melt margarine; saute the green pepper, garlic and onion until soft at 300°. Reduce heat to 200° and add parsley, lemon juice and seasonings. Simmer for 3 minutes. Add tomatoes, including water, and simmer for an additional 3 minutes. Add wine; simmer briskly for 5 minutes. Remove from heat; set aside.

Clean fish thoroughly, allowing head to remain. Place fish in an oiled casserole dish and top with strips of bacon. Pour mixture over the fish and bake at 350° for 45 minutes. Baste regularly. Drain 3/4 cooked rice thoroughly and spoon around fish. Remove from oven, cover for 10 minutes and serve. Serves 6.

GLAZED FLOUNDER FRANCOIS ENOUL

2 large flounder
1 tsp. oregano
1/8 tsp. black pepper
1/4 tsp. red pepper
1/2 tsp. thyme
1/2 tsp. basil
1/2 tsp. garlic powder

3 Tbsp. lemon juice
4 Tbsp. mayonnaise
4 Tbsp. prepared mustard
1 1/2 Tbsp. capers, chopped
1 Tbsp. parsley, chopped
3/4 c. beer

Lightly oil baking dish, placing flounder fleshy side up. Add beer. Mix together oregano and peppers; sprinkle over top of flounder. Broil at a medium heat for 15 minutes.

To Prepare Sauce: In a bowl, mix mustard and mayonnaise; blend thoroughly. Add seasonings, making sure they are blended well. Add remaining ingredients. Remove fish from broiler and spread sauce evenly but generously. Return to broiler for 7 to 8 minutes. Serves 4.

STUFFED FLOUNDER KENNER

4 (6 oz.) flounder fillets
1 c. small shrimp, peeled and
   deveined
1 c. oysters
Juice from 1 lemon
1 tsp. Tabasco sauce
½ stick margarine

2 eggs
1 c. crushed saltine crackers
2 Tbsp. Worcestershire sauce
¼ tsp. thyme
⅛ tsp. dried sweet basil
1 tsp. dark brown sugar

Lightly oil a baking pan and place flounder fleshy side up. Split flounder, making a pocket. Combine basil and brown sugar; rub inside of pocket. In a saucepan, melt margarine at 200°. Add shrimp and oysters; saute for 3 minutes or until oysters are firm. Add remaining seasonings, lemon juice and eggs, stirring well. Fold in cracker crumbs. Remove from heat and carefully stuff flounder. Bake at 350° for 20 minutes. Place individual flounders on a large platter, surrounded with Cajun fried rice. Serves 4.

FLOUNDER CASSEROLE LULING

3 lb. flounder fillets
½ c. bread crumbs
1 (7 oz.) can tuna
6 oz. shrimp, peeled and
   deveined
½ stick margarine
1 medium onion, chopped

1 can cream of Cheddar soup
1 can cream of mushroom soup
⅛ tsp. white pepper
⅛ tsp. red pepper
⅛ tsp. basil
⅛ tsp. oregano

Preheat oven to 350°. In a saucepan, melt ¼ stick margarine over a low heat (200°). Add shrimp; saute until pink. Add tuna and saute for an additional 3 minutes. Remove from pan and set aside. Save drippings. Add flounder to pan and saute on each side for 2 minutes at 300°. Remove and set aside. Saute onion and remaining seasonings until soft. Reduce heat to 200° and add soups slowly, blending well. Return shrimp and tuna; mix well. Pour ½ mixture in bottom of baking pan. Arrange flounder on top of sauce and cover with remaining mixture. Sprinkle with bread crumbs. Bake for 25 minutes at 325° or until tender and flaky. Serves 8.

SNAPPER WITH CORN BREAD STUFFING PRYTANIA

1 (4 to 5 lb.) red snapper
6 bacon strips
½ stick margarine
1 lemon
½ tsp. black pepper

¼ tsp. oregano
¼ tsp. sweet basil
¼ tsp. sweet paprika
⅛ tsp. red pepper
⅛ tsp. white pepper

Preheat oven to 350°. Lightly oil a baking dish. Make small slits on sides of fish and arrange in baking dish. Remove fat from bacon, arranging the bacon in the slits on the side of the fish. Combine melted margarine, lemon juice and seasonings; mix well. Coat fish generously with this mixture. Place fish in oven and bake for 20 minutes at 300°.

Corn Bread Stuffing:

2 c. corn bread, crumbled
1 medium onion, chopped
½ c. celery, chopped
2 hard-boiled eggs, chopped

¼ stick margarine
⅛ tsp. white pepper
⅛ tsp. black pepper
Hot water

In a saucepan, melt margarine. Add onion, celery and seasonings; saute until soft. Combine with corn bread and eggs. Add hot water until stuffing is moist. Remove fish from oven and stuff. Return to oven and bake at 350° for 30 minutes. Serves 8.

STUFFED RED SNAPPER WITH CREOLE CRABMEAT

1 (4 to 6 lb.) red snapper or
  other like fish (dress up
  weight)
1 lb. crabmeat
½ c. bread crumbs
½ c. green pepper, chopped
1 medium onion, chopped
½ c. green onion, chopped
½ c. parsley, chopped

½ stick margarine
¼ tsp. sweet paprika
1 lemon, sliced
½ tsp. black coarse pepper
1 can cream of mushroom soup
½ tsp. white pepper
⅛ tsp. basil
⅛ tsp. oregano

In a bowl, combine seasonings; set aside. Lightly oil a baking dish. Take 1 teaspoon of seasoning mix and rub fish inside and out. Place in baking dish. In a saucepan, melt margarine; saute vegetables for 5 minutes or until soft at 200°. Combine bread crumbs and soup in a separate bowl. Add crabmeat; mix well. Add this mixture to sauteed vegetables, blending well. Add remaining seasoning mix. Stir over low heat at 175° for 15 minutes.

You should determine at this time if stuffing is too moist; if so, add additional bread crumbs. Fill fish with stuffing, arrange lemon slices over the top and sprinkle with paprika. Bake for 40 minutes at 350°. If the fish shows a tendency towards dryness, baste with a small amount of margarine and lemon juice. Serves 8.

MULLET IN ROUX GRAVY MARIGNY

2 lb. mullet
2 lb. white potatoes, quartered
¾ c. onions, chopped
½ stick margarine
¼ c. green onion, chopped

1 c. white roux
¼ tsp. thyme
¼ tsp. red pepper
½ tsp. black pepper
¼ tsp. oregano
Salt to taste

Boil potatoes ¾ cooked in 2 cups of water; set aside. In a saucepan, melt margarine at 400° and remove moisture. Fry mullet strips for 2 minutes on each side. Remove from heat. Add onions and seasonings; saute until soft. Reduce heat to 200°. Slowly blend in roux, stirring frequently. Add 1 cup hot water or enough until roux reaches cream consistency. Add potatoes, including water; simmer for 15 minutes or until mixture thickens. Arrange mullets in a lightly oiled casserole dish and cover with sauce. Bake at 350° for 15 minutes. Serve with mashed potatoes. Serves 6.

CAJUN SHARK STEW

2 lb. shark meat, cut bite size
½ stick margarine
1 c. onions, chopped
2 c. brown roux
1 c. hot water
½ c. green pepper, chopped
¼ c. green onions, chopped
3 cloves garlic, chopped
2 cans tomato sauce

¼ tsp. red pepper
¼ tsp. black pepper
⅓ tsp. thyme
½ tsp. bay leaf
3 Tbsp. Worcestershire sauce
¼ tsp. sweet basil
½ tsp. celery seed
¼ tsp. chervil
¼ tsp. oregano

In a large saucepan, melt ¼ stick margarine at 400°. Add vegetables and saute until light brown. Reduce heat to 200°. Add 1 cup hot water; bring mixture to simmer. Slowly blend in roux. Add tomato sauce and remaining ingredients except red and black pepper. Blend well. In a separate saucepan, melt remaining margarine at 400°. Blend in red and black pepper. Add shark bites and saute for 3 minutes. Remove from heat and combine with sauce. It may be necessary to control liquid with hot water. Keep at a brisk simmer for 45 minutes. Serve over a bed of rice. Serves 6.

CREOLE FRIED SHARK

2 lb. shark fillets
1 c. Bisquick flour
½ tsp. thyme
½ tsp. sweet basil
1 tsp. white pepper

1 tsp. black pepper
½ tsp. oregano
1 c. cream
2 eggs, beaten

In a bowl, combine seasonings with Bisquick flour. Blend well. In a separate bowl, combine beaten eggs with cream. Dip fillets in cream and allow to marinate for 20 minutes. Drain off excess liquid; pat well into flour. Fry until golden brown. Serve with lemon quarters. Serves 4.

SHARK BORDELAISE

2 lb. shark steak, cut bite size
¾ stick margarine
½ c. green onions, chopped fine
1½ c. red burgundy wine
1 tsp. garlic flakes
1 bay leaf
1 tsp. black pepper
¼ c. onions, chopped
¼ c. carrots, chopped

¼ c. celery, chopped
¼ c. leeks, chopped
2 Tbsp. tomato paste
½ c. dark brown roux
2 chicken bouillon cubes
2 c. hot water
2 tsp. red currant jelly
1 pack fresh mushrooms, quartered

In a saucepan, melt ¼ stick margarine at 200°. Add ½ cup green onions; saute until soft. Add burgundy wine, garlic, bay leaf, and black pepper. Simmer for 15 minutes, stirring frequently. In a separate saucepan, melt ½ stick margarine at 300°. Add onions, carrots, celery, and leeks. Saute until golden brown. Blend in tomato paste and roux. Dissolve bouillon cubes in 2 cups of hot water and add to roux mixture. Simmer for 15 minutes. Add mushrooms, jelly and shark; continue simmering until shark is tender. Serve over a heaping bed of brown rice. Serves 6.

TROUT IN CREAM OF ROSE WINE SAULET

2 lb. trout fillet
½ stick margarine
1 c. rose wine
1 c. sour cream
¼ c. green peppers, chopped
½ c. green onion, chopped

½ tsp. garlic powder
¼ tsp. white pepper
½ tsp. Tabasco sauce
¼ tsp. black pepper
½ tsp. thyme
¼ tsp. basil

In a saucepan, melt margarine at 400° until moisture is removed. In a bowl, combine garlic powder, peppers and remaining seasoning except Tabasco. Sprinkle trout generously with seasoning mix. Saute trout on each side for 1 minute and remove from pan; save drippings. Reduce heat to 250°. Add green peppers and onion; saute until soft. Add wine and bring to simmer. Stir in sour cream. Reduce to a low simmer, stirring until mixture thickens. Add trout and simmer for 10 minutes or until tender.

If mixture is too thick before adding the trout, additional wine can be used. Serve with mashed potatoes or French fries. Serves 6.

TROUT VERSAILLES

2 lb. trout fillets
½ stick margarine
Juice of 1 lemon
½ c. green onions, chopped
3 sprigs parsley
¼ c. celery, chopped
1 c. dry white wine
1 c. hot water

1 tsp. salt
3 Tbsp. flour
1 c. light cream
1 can seedless grapes
2 Tbsp. whipped cream
¼ tsp. white pepper
¼ tsp. red pepper

In a saucepan, melt ¼ stick margarine at 200°. Add green onions, parsley, celery, wine, and water. In a small bowl, combine salt and peppers in a small bowl. Rub fish thoroughly. Place fish into mixture and simmer slowly for about 10 minutes. Remove fish and place in a baking serving dish; save drippings. In a separate saucepan, melt remaining margarine at 200°. Add flour and drippings; blend well. Bring to a simmer. Add light cream and whipped cream and set aside. Arrange grapes around the fish. Pour sauce over fish. Brown under a broiler for 5 minutes. Squeeze with lemon juice. Garnish with parsley and serve with steaming rice. Serves 6.

SCALLOPS ST. MARIE

2 lb. scallops
¼ stick margarine
2 c. white wine
¼ c. onions, chopped fine
2 c. Bechamel Sauce (see recipe)
1 c. bread crumbs

2 tsp. Creole mustard
½ tsp. white pepper
¼ tsp. red pepper
¼ tsp. oregano
1 tsp. salt
1 large pie shell

In a saucepan, melt margarine at 200°. Add onions and saute until soft. Add scallops, seasonings and wine; bring to simmer for 10 minutes. Remove scallops and continue to simmer the liquid. Add Bechamel Sauce, blending well. Add mustard. Slice scallops in halves and add to sauce. Heat and spoon into pie shell. Sprinkle top with bread crumbs. Place pie shell under broiler until bread crumbs are brown. Serve. Serves 6.

CREOLE FISH SOULE

3 lb. fish fillets (at least 1 inch thick)
Juice of 1 lemon
¼ stick margarine
4 oz. flour
1 large cauliflower, ¾ cooked
1 Tbsp. parsley, chopped
1 large onion, chopped
1½ Tbsp. curry powder

½ tsp. salt
¼ tsp. white pepper
¼ tsp. red pepper
¼ tsp. onion powder
¼ tsp. black pepper
¼ tsp. basil
⅛ tsp. garlic powder
1 c. hot water

Cut fish into chunks. In a saucepan, melt margarine at 400°. After moisture is removed, add seasonings. Add fish chunks and fry on both sides for 2 minutes. Remove fish from pan; set aside. Save drippings. Reduce heat to 200°. Add parsley, lemon juice and onion; saute for 2 minutes. Remove from heat. Add curry powder and flour; blend well. Gradually add hot water while stirring. After blending, return to heat and cook for 5 minutes. In a lightly oiled casserole dish, arrange cauliflower in a neat row down the center. Arrange fish on both sides; cover with sauce. Cook for an additional 10 minutes. Garnish with parsley and serve. Serves 6.

BAKED SHEEPSHEAD IN SHRIMP AND OYSTER SAUCE
SEELAS

1 (3 to 5 lb.) sheepshead
2 doz. shrimp, peeled, deveined
   and chopped
1 c. small oysters
1 c. mushrooms, sliced
1/2 c. croutons, crushed
1/4 c. parsley, chopped
8 oz. white wine
1 can tomatoes

1/2 tsp. thyme
1/2 tsp. bay leaf
1/2 stick margarine
1 large onion, chopped
3 Tbsp. flour
1/4 tsp. red pepper
1/4 tsp. white pepper
1/2 tsp. curry powder

In a saucepan, melt 1/4 stick margarine at 300°. Add shrimp and oysters; saute for 3 minutes. Remove from heat. In another saucepan, melt remaining margarine; saute all vegetables until soft. Add flour; blend in well. Add white wine and bring to a brisk simmer. Add tomatoes and seasoning; bring to a boil. Reduce heat to 200°. Add shrimp, oysters and remaining ingredients. Saute for 5 minutes. Arrange fish in a lightly oiled baking dish and cover with mixture. Bake until tender; it will be necessary to turn fish over twice.

Throughout the baking of this dish, keep an eye on the moisture content. If needed, add white wine. Cover with croutons. Serves 6.

BAKED TUNA WITH MUSHROOMS THIBERGE

1 (6 1/2 oz.) can tuna fish
1 large pack fresh mushrooms,
   halved
1 can cream of mushroom soup
2 oz. bread crumbs

3 sprigs parsley
1/4 stick margarine
1/8 tsp. white pepper
1/8 tsp. red pepper
Juice of 1/2 lemon
1/8 tsp. sweet basil

In a saucepan, melt margarine at 300°. Add mushrooms and saute for 3 minutes. In a separate pan, add soup and bring to simmer. Blend in tuna for 3 minutes. Pour into lightly oiled baking dish. In a separate bowl, combine seasonings and lemon juice. Sprinkle with bread crumbs and add layer of mushrooms. Bake for 5 minutes at 350°. Garnish with parsley. Serves 4.

BAKED MACKEREL CAMERON PARISH

1 large Spanish mackerel (5 to 6 lb.)
½ c. flour
½ stick margarine
1 c. onions, chopped
2 c. celery, chopped
¼ c. green pepper, chopped
3 c. canned tomatoes

1 tsp. chili powder
1 lemon, sliced
2 small bay leaves
1 Tbsp. garlic, minced
½ tsp. red pepper
1 tsp. salt
Parsley sprigs
1 Tbsp. Worcestershire sauce

In a bowl, combine seasonings with flour. Dredge fish thoroughly inside and out. Place in a lightly oiled baking dish. In a saucepan, melt margarine at 300°. Saute onions, celery and green pepper until tender. Place tomatoes, Worcestershire sauce, chili powder, ½ lemon slices, bay leaves, garlic, salt, and red pepper in a food processor. Grind slightly. Add to sauteed ingredients. Pour sauce around fish. Bake in a moderate oven at 350° for 45 minutes. Baste frequently. Garnish with lemon slices and parsley. Serve with steaming hot rice. Serves 6.

CAJUN FISH CAKES

2 c. chopped fish, cooked
1 tsp. onion powder
2 c. mashed potatoes
¼ tsp. sweet paprika
¼ tsp. sweet basil
⅛ tsp. thyme

⅛ tsp. red pepper
⅛ tsp. white pepper
⅛ tsp. black pepper
1 egg, beaten
¼ stick margarine
1 c. flour

In a saucepan, melt margarine at 300°. Add fish and saute for 3 minutes. Remove from heat and allow to cool. In a bowl, combine seasonings. Add mashed potatoes and blend well. Add fish; blend well. Form into patties. Dip patties in beaten egg, then into flour. Fry until golden brown. Serves 4.

This is excellent for leftover fish.

TROUT AMANDINE DELACROIX ISLAND

4 medium size trout
1 c. flour
1 stick margarine
1 c. toasted slivered almonds
1 lemon, sliced thin
½ c. heavy cream
½ tsp. red pepper

½ tsp. thyme
½ tsp. basil
½ tsp. salt
¼ tsp. white pepper
¼ tsp. black pepper
¼ tsp. oregano

In a bowl, combine seasonings with flour. Pat fish thoroughly, coating heavily. In a saucepan, melt margarine at 300°. Add trout and fry for 3 minutes on each side. When trout is a golden brown, remove from heat and place carefully on a heated serving platter. Add cream to pan and mix rapidly. Add almonds and carefully stir in, making sure they are fully coated. Bring to simmer. Pour over trout and arrange rounds of lemon. Serve with French fries. Serves 6.

TROUT AMANDINE MAGAZINE

4 (8 oz.) trout fillets
¼ c. corn oil
1 c. sliced almonds
1 lemon, sliced
4 sprigs parsley, chopped

½ stick margarine
⅛ tsp. white pepper
⅛ tsp. red pepper
2 eggs, beaten
1 c. flour

In a bowl, blend pepper seasonings with beaten eggs. Dip trout in eggs; let excess drain. Coat with flour. In a saucepan, add oil and bring to 350°. Add trout and fry until golden brown. Remove from pan; discard corn oil. Melt margarine at 300°; add almonds and brown. Arrange trout on platter; cover with almonds. Serve; garnish with lemon and parsley. Serves 6.

FLOUNDER ORLEANS IN SAUCE MEUNIERE

2 (2 lb.) flounder fillets
¼ stick margarine
1 tsp. allspice
½ tsp. thyme
4 sprigs parsley, chopped

¼ tsp. sweet basil
1 can mushrooms
1 c. white roux
¼ tsp. white pepper
½ c. hot water

In a bowl, blend together seasonings. In a saucepan, melt ¼ stick margarine at 200°. Add vegetables; saute until soft. Add seasonings; blend well. Saute for 1 minute. Slowly add roux and ½ cup hot water. Blend well. Remove from heat. Pour ½ ingredients in a lightly oiled baking pan and arrange flounder. Pour remainder over flounder. Bake at 350° until done. Serves 4.

Sauce:

¼ c. margarine
1 Tbsp. celery, chopped
1 Tbsp. green onion, chopped
2 Tbsp. lemon juice

½ tsp. salt
¼ tsp. black pepper
¼ tsp. red pepper
1 tsp. Worcestershire sauce

Mix ingredients in order presented. Simmer briefly and serve over fish.

SEAFOOD PASTA, CAJUN STYLE

1 (8 oz.) pkg. spaghetti
2 c. tomato juice
1 lb. shrimp, peeled and
    deveined
1½ lb. scallops
2 tsp. salt
1 tsp. caraway seeds
2 Tbsp. vinegar

¼ stick margarine
3 oz. flour
2 c. hot milk
½ c. sherry
¼ tsp. red pepper
¼ tsp. white pepper
¼ tsp. oregano
2 c. hot water

In a saucepan, cook spaghetti until tender and drain. Add tomato juice and simmer for 30 minutes. Stir frequently. In a separate saucepan, add 1 cup hot water, caraway seeds, oregano, white pepper, and red pepper. Add 1 cup hot water, vinegar and salt. Add scallops and shrimp; simmer for 20 minutes. In a separate saucepan, melt margarine at 200°. Stir in flour until it gels. Reduce heat to 150°. Add milk; blend well. Remove seafood from heat and drain. Add seafood to sauce. Add sherry; blend well. Add spaghetti tomato mixture. Lightly oil a baking dish and pour in mixture. Place under a broiler approximately 4 inches from flame. Broil until light brown. Serves 6.

SPICY TUNA PIE OLIVIER

1 large can chunky tuna fish
1 Tbsp. lemon juice
1/2 c. green onions, chopped
1 small onion, chopped
1/4 stick margarine
3 Tbsp. flour

1/8 tsp. red pepper
1/8 tsp. white pepper
1/8 tsp. thyme
1/4 c. grated cheese of your
  choice
2 c. hot water

In a saucepan, melt margarine at 300°. Add onions and saute until light brown. Add flour; blend well until light brown. Slowly add 2 cups hot water and simmer for 2 minutes. Add tuna and remaining ingredients except cheese. Place mixture in a lightly oiled casserole dish; sprinkle with cheese. Bake at 400° for 40 minutes. Serve over mounds of steaming rice. Serves 4.

FISH AND SCALLOP PILIE

2 lb. fish fillets
1 lb. scallops
1/4 c. onions, chopped fine
1 Tbsp. chicken bouillon
1 c. croutons
2 c. hot water

1 c. white roux
1/2 stick margarine
1/4 c. salad olives, chopped
1/8 tsp. red pepper
1/8 tsp. white pepper
1/4 tsp. thyme

Dissolve bouillon in 2 cups hot water; set aside. In a deep saucepan, melt 1/4 stick margarine at 300°. Blend 1/2 cup roux. Add 1 cup hot water; mix well. Remove from heat. In a separate saucepan, melt 1/4 stick margarine at 300°. Add onions and saute until soft. Add scallops; saute for 3 minutes. Add the seasonings and chicken bouillon, which has been dissolved in 1 cup hot water. Add remaining roux; stir well. If this mixture is too thick, add hot water sparingly. Arrange fish in a lightly oiled casserole dish. Pour mixture over fish; sprinkle with olives and croutons. Bake at 350° for 40 minutes. Serves 6.

SPICY CAJUN SQUID

2 doz. medium size squid,
  prepared and cleaned
1 c. flour
1 tsp. red pepper
1 tsp. thyme
1 tsp. basil
1 1/2 tsp. salt

1/2 tsp. white pepper
1/2 tsp. black pepper
1/2 tsp. oregano
Corn oil (enough to float squid
  while frying)
4 eggs, well beaten

Keep in mind while preparing this dish, the most important is not to overfry the squid; if it becomes tough, the taste is destroyed. In a bowl, beat eggs well at room temperature. Add oregano, peppers, thyme, salt, and basil; blend well. Cut the body of the squid in 1/2 inch circles. Separate the tentacles into bite size. Dip the squid in seasoned egg mix. Coat well with flour; shake off excess. Fry at 400° for 4 to 6 minutes or until golden brown. Serves 6.

WHITE PERCH CALCASIEU

6 white perch
1/8 tsp. dry mustard
4 oz. oatmeal
1/2 cucumber, diced
6 oz. sour cream
Grated rind and juice of 1
   orange
Orange segments

Juice of 1 lemon
1/8 tsp. red pepper
1/8 tsp. white pepper
1/8 tsp. basil
2 tsp. salt
2 eggs, beaten well
1 stick margarine
2 oz. wine vinegar

Peel and dice cucumbers. Place in a bowl with 1 teaspoon salt. Add wine vinegar and allow to marinate while preparing fish. Clean fish and allow head to remain. Slit belly from head to tail; place the belly face down on a board and press the backbone flat, then remove the backbone. In a small bowl, combine basil, 1 teaspoon salt, peppers, and mustard. Rub briskly on the perch. In a small bowl, add beaten eggs. Dip fish in eggs, then dredge fish in oatmeal. In a saucepan, melt margarine at 400°. Fry perch until golden brown. Remove from heat and place on a serving platter.

Drain excess liquid from cucumbers. Add sour cream and mix well. Surround fish with orange segments. Add lemon juice, orange juice and grating to the cucumbers; mix well. Pour over orange segments. Serve as a delicious light lunch. Serves 6.

SQUID VERMILLION BAY

3 lb. squid
1/2 stick margarine
1 lb. fresh mushrooms
1/4 c. parsley, chopped

1 tsp. garlic powder
Juice of 1 lemon
1/4 c. white wine
1/2 tsp. Tabasco sauce

Clean squid thoroughly and cut into 1/2 inch circles. Separate the tentacles. In a saucepan, melt margarine at 300°. Add squid and saute for 2 minutes. Warning: Do not overcook or the squid will become rubbery. Remove squid; allow drippings to remain. Set aside. Cut mushrooms in halves and saute in drippings until light brown. Add seasonings, blending well. Add remaining ingredients except wine. Saute for 2 minutes. Note: Squid will lose its transparency while set aside. Add the wine; saute for 3 to 4 minutes. Add squid and saute for an additional 2 minutes. Serve over bed of steaming rice. Serves 6.

BARBECUE SNAPPER TERREBONE BAY

5 lb. (1 inch thick) snapper fillets
    or like fish with same
    consistency
2 Tbsp. green pepper, chopped
    fine
3 Tbsp. parsley, chopped fine
Juice of 2 lemons
3 Tbsp. Worcestershire sauce

1 Tbsp. hot sauce
1/2 tsp. red pepper
1/2 tsp. white pepper
1/4 tsp. basil
1/4 tsp. thyme
1/4 c. onions, chopped fine
1 stick margarine

In a saucepan, melt 1 stick margarine at 300°. When moisture is removed, add seasonings and vegetables except parsley. Mix well. Saute snapper for 1 minute on each side. Remove from heat. Place snapper on heavy foil; fold edges up to form a boat. Place on the barbecue grill. Pour remaining drippings over the fish. Turn the fish every 10 minutes and add lemon juice. Barbecue until fillets soften.

Barbecue Sauce:

2 large cloves garlic
Juice of 1 lemon
1 tsp. smoke sauce
1 tsp. brown sugar

6 oz. ketchup
3 oz. hickory smoked mustard
6 oz. Worcestershire sauce
1/4 stick margarine

In a saucepan, melt 1/4 stick margarine at 200°. Blend in all sauce ingredients and bring to simmer. Pour over fish fillets. Turn fish every 3 to 4 minutes for another 15 minutes or until snapper is tender and coated well. Garnish with parsley and serve over a bed of steaming brown rice. Serves 8.

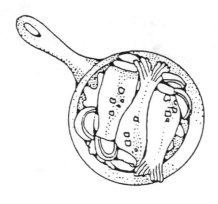

FISH IN PECAN BUTTER SAUCE BAY BOUDREAU

2 large trout fillets
1/2 c. milk
1 egg, beaten
1 tsp. salt
1 tsp. onion powder
1 tsp. paprika
1/4 tsp. red pepper
1/4 tsp. white pepper
1/2 tsp. garlic powder
1/2 tsp. black pepper
1/4 tsp. dried mustard
1/4 tsp. oregano
1/4 tsp. thyme
1 c. all-purpose flour
Corn oil (enough to fry fish)

In a bowl, thoroughly combine seasonings. Add 1 teaspoon seasoning mix and combine with flour. In a separate bowl, add milk, eggs and remaining seasoning; blend thoroughly. Spread flour on a flat plate. Dredge each fillet in seasoned flour. Lightly shake off excess. Dip fillets in egg mixture, then dredge again in flour. Heat corn oil in a large skillet at 400°. Fry fillets until golden brown. Remove from pan and place on a paper towel to drain off excess oil.

Pecan Sauce:

1/2 c. dry roasted pecans, chopped
1/4 stick margarine, softened at room temperature
2 Tbsp. onions, chopped fine
1 tsp. lemon juice
1/4 tsp. Tabasco sauce
1/4 tsp. garlic powder

In a saucepan, melt margarine at a low temperature. Combine all ingredients with margarine. Blend well and remove from heat. Place in a food processor and puree for 10 minutes. Pour over fish and serve. Serves 6.

SAUTEED CATFISH BARATARIA BAY

1 lb. catfish, cut in 1 inch fingers
2 sticks margarine
2 cloves fresh garlic, minced
1/2 c. green onions, chopped fine
1 c. oyster soup
2 c. cooked rice
1/2 tsp. white pepper
1/2 tsp. salt
1/4 tsp. red pepper
1/2 tsp. black pepper
1/2 tsp. basil
1/4 tsp. dried mustard
1/2 tsp. Tabasco

In a small bowl, combine seasonings and set aside. In a saucepan, melt 1/2 stick margarine at 350°. Add onions and garlic; saute for 1 minute. Remove from pan; save drippings. Add remaining margarine and melt at 350°. Add catfish, Tabasco sauce and seasoning mix; saute for 2 minutes, stirring well. Slowly add oyster soup, stirring well. Cook over a high heat, shaking pan constantly, for 4 minutes. Cook for an additional 2 minutes. Serve over a heaping mound of rice. Serves 4.

CATFISH STICKS BRETON SOUND

3 lb. catfish fillets, cut in 1 inch
    sticks
4 eggs
½ c. sour cream
1 c. corn meal

½ tsp. red pepper
½ tsp. white pepper
½ tsp. oregano
1 tsp. salt

In a small bowl, blend together seasonings. In a large bowl, mix eggs, sour cream and ½ seasonings together. Beat well. In a separate bowl, combine corn meal and remaining seasonings. Dip fish into egg mix, then dredge through corn meal. Shake off excess and fry until golden brown. Serves 6.

This works well with any easy frying fish.

FISH IN CHEESE MUSHROOM SAUCE BIENVILLE

3 lb. fish fillets
¼ c. onion, chopped fine
2 Tbsp. parsley, chopped fine
1 tsp. thyme
1 c. dry white wine
½ c. Parmesan cheese

3 c. white roux
1 pack fresh mushrooms
4 egg yolks, beaten
½ stick margarine
½ tsp. white pepper
¼ tsp. red pepper

In a saucepan, melt margarine at 400° until very hot. Remove all moisture. Saute fish on both sides for 2 minutes. Remove from heat and set fish aside. Place the fillets in a lightly oiled baking dish. Return pan to the heat. Add vegetables and saute until soft at 200°. Add the 3 cups of white roux slowly. Blend in seasonings for 2 minutes and reduce heat to 150°. Add white wine, stirring briskly. Add Parmesan cheese. When melted, remove from heat and blend in egg yolks. Mix well. Pour sauce over fish. Bake at 325° for 15 minutes or until tender. Serves 8.

SPECKLED TROUT IN RUM GRAND ISLE

3 lb. trout fillets
1 c. buttered rum
Juice of 1 lemon
½ stick margarine

¼ tsp. red pepper
¼ tsp. white pepper
¼ tsp. oregano

In a saucepan, melt margarine at 400°. Stir in seasonings. Fry fish until tender. Reduce heat to 200°. Pour in rum and lemon juice; saute for 5 minutes. Serve. Serves 8.

Note: For a different texture, serve with wild rice. Slowly add rum, lemon juice and ½ cup of dark brown roux. Control thickness with additional hot rum.

FLAMING FISH LEBEAU

6 fish fillets (preferably in the
    trout family)
½ stick margarine
Juice of 1 lemon

1 tsp. coarse black pepper
¼ tsp. red pepper
½ c. whiskey
3 Tbsp. flour

In a saucepan, melt margarine at 400°. Add fish and saute on both sides until light brown. Remove fish from pan and place on heated platter; allow drippings to remain. Sprinkle fish with seasonings and lemon juice. Bring temperature to 200°. Add flour and blend until it gels. Add ¼ cup whiskey to flour mixture. Blend thoroughly and remove from heat. Add fish carefully. Heat remaining bourbon in a ladle. Light the bourbon and pour slowly over fish. Continue to lightly shake the dish as you are pouring the bourbon. Allow bourbon to thoroughly burn itself out. Serve with heaping mounds of mashed potatoes. Serves 6.

FISH STEAKS WITH WINE AND MUSTARD SAUCE OPELOUSAS

8 large fish steaks (this should
    be a heavy type of fish,
    such as grouper, cobia, etc.)
1 stick margarine
1 c. sweet white wine

¼ c. Creole mustard
½ c. sour cream
¼ tsp. white pepper
¼ tsp. red pepper
2 tsp. Worcestershire sauce

In a saucepan, melt margarine at 400°; allow to arrive at a light smoke. Dash in Worcestershire sauce. Add fish steaks and saute for 3 minutes on each side. Remove from heat; set aside. Allow drippings to remain. Reduce heat to 200°. Stir in sour cream. If sour cream begins to simmer, reduce the heat. Blend in mustard. Add peppers and bring to a slow simmer. Whisk in wine. Return to a slow simmer. Carefully add fish steaks. Simmer on both sides for 5 minutes. Serve on a bed of steaming rice. Serves 6.

STUFFED FISH WITH RICE AND PECANS VILLE PLATTE

1 whole fish (6 to 8 lb.)
½ stick margarine
Juice of 1 lemon
2 c. cooked rice
½ c. dry roasted pecans, finely
    chopped

½ tsp. white pepper
¼ tsp. red pepper
¼ tsp. Louisiana hot sauce
½ c. thick brown roux

Clean fish and allow head to remain. In a saucepan, melt ½ margarine on a low heat. Add white pepper, red pepper and Louisiana hot sauce. Blend in roux thoroughly. Dredge fish in roux mixture and place in a lightly oiled baking dish. Add rice and pecans to remaining roux mixture. This should become a wet stuffing consistency. Stuff fish cavity. Pin together with toothpicks. Bake fish at 350°. Baste with juice frequently. Bake until tender. Remove from heat and add lemon juice. Serves 6.

FRIED TROUT WITH CORN FLAKE CRUST GRAMERCY

6 trout fillets
3 egg yolks, beaten
2 Tbsp. margarine, melted
2 c. crushed corn flakes
¼ tsp. white pepper

¼ tsp. red pepper
¼ tsp. dried mustard
¼ tsp. basil
1 c. corn oil

In a bowl, combine seasonings and 1 tablespoon melted margarine. Rub fillets with this mixture. Combine remaining seasoning with egg yolks. Dip fillets in beaten egg yolks. Roll fish into corn flakes. Fry at a low temperature for 20 minutes or until fish are tender. Serves 6.

Note: Corn flakes have a tendency to burn. This dish must be attended carefully. Serve with French fries.

GAR FISH SAUCE PIQUANT KAPLAN

4 lb. gar fish chunks
1 c. all-purpose flour
Corn oil (enough for frying fish)
2 c. onions, chopped
2 c. celery, chopped
2 c. green peppers, chopped
2 c. tomatoes, peeled and
    chopped
3 Tbsp. jalapeno peppers,
    chopped fine
2 Tbsp. garlic, minced

2 c. canned tomato sauce
3 tsp. Tabasco sauce
4 c. fish or oyster soup
2 c. cooked rice
3 tsp. salt
1 tsp. black pepper
2 tsp. onion powder
2 tsp. garlic powder
1 tsp. red pepper
½ tsp. white pepper
1 tsp. thyme
¼ stick margarine

In a small bowl, combine seasoning ingredients and mix well. In a brown paper bag, add flour and 1 teaspoon seasoning mix. Shake well. Dredge gar fish chunks in seasoned flour and coat well. In a large saucepan, heat oil to 400°. Fry gar fish until brown and crispy. Do not crowd together; allow time to fry separately. If oil begins to turn brown, lower temperature immediately. Remove fish and place on a paper towel. Carefully drain off oil from saucepan, allowing sediment to remain.

Add ¼ stick margarine; melt at 350°. Using a wooden spoon, blend particles into margarine. Add onions, celery and green peppers. Saute until vegetables are a light brown, stirring constantly. Add tomatoes, jalapeno peppers and garlic. Continue to stir for 2 minutes. Reduce heat to 300°. Add tomato sauce and blend for 3 minutes. Stir in Tabasco sauce and remove from heat. Place fish chunks in a large saucepan and bring temperature to 250°. Stir in half of the tomato mixture. Add fish or oyster soup. Cover and simmer for 10 minutes, stirring occasionally. Cooked rice may be folded directly into the dish. Remove from heat and serve. Serves 8.

RED SNAPPER STUFFED WITH ANDOUILLE SMOKED SAUSAGE

1 large red snapper, cleaned
(allow head to remain)
2 sticks margarine
1 c. onions, chopped fine
½ c. celery, chopped fine
1 lb. andouille sausage or any
good smoked sausage

3 c. all-purpose flour
3 c. fish or oyster soup
1 tsp. red pepper
1 tsp. thyme
1 c. cooked rice

In a saucepan, melt margarine at 300°. Add onions and celery; saute until soft. Add sausage and brown for 5 minutes, stirring frequently. Reduce heat to 200°. Blend in flour. Do not allow to stick. Stir in enough fish soup to make a thick creamy mixture. Add red pepper and thyme. Continue to saute slowly until mixture becomes syrup thick. Remove from heat and cool in refrigerator. Add 1 cup cooked rice. Lightly oil a large baking pan. Arrange fish and stuff. Pin cavity of fish with toothpicks. Pour any excess stuffing around fish. Bake slowly at 250° for 40 minutes or until fish is tender. Serves 8.

Notes

"Your crabby ways has caused
us to star in an etouffee!"

Oysters, Crabs and Crawfish

A WORD FROM CLOVICE:

Dere is all kinds of crabby situations. Now, I don't mean the kind I got in'to wit my tax advisor dis morning. Dat boy done told me the quickest and only way out of my tax problum is suicide. Other den the shell of a crab which can also be eaten when soft, dis quick-legged lil' scamper is totally edible. The fat nestled inside of a busted shell can be made into a sauce to be eaten wit de same. Find out which crab is in season, either male or female. That way you can pick out the best fat ones for yourself at any crab boil.

Neighbor, never overcook a crab. There ain't nothing that can make my wife mo crabby than someone serving her an overcooked crab.

A little honey added to the butter in which you saute onions will make a really out-of-the-ordinary dish. Don't put the onions in until the butter and honey start to sizzle.

To make rice lighter and fluffier, add 1 teaspoon of lemon juice to the cooking water.

If you have room, store potatoes in the refrigerator to inhibit the growth if "eyes". Be sure to keep them dry.

Pasta doubles in volume when it's cooked.

5-6 lb. hens make the best stewing chickens. Always remove the excess fat from the chicken before stewing.

Season poultry for stews and soups a day before cooking. The dish will be much more flavorful. Important: Be sure to remove the bird from the refrigerator before cooking so it will attain room temperature for even doneness.

Tarragon is a "must" seasoning for chicken.

If you add tomatoes to a dressed salad, do it just before serving, otherwise the juices may dilute the dressing or make the salad soggy.

OYSTERS, CRABS AND CRAWFISH

OYSTERS JAMBALAYA CROWLEY

4 doz. oysters (retain liquid)
1/4 stick margarine
1 1/2 c. onions, chopped fine
1 c. green pepper, chopped
1/4 c. ground pork
1/2 lb. ground meat
1/3 c. celery, chopped
2 cloves garlic, chopped

1/4 tsp. black pepper
1/8 tsp. red pepper
1/4 c. parsley, chopped
1/4 tsp. thyme
1/4 tsp. bay leaf
2 c. brown roux
2 c. cooked rice
Salt to taste

In a saucepan, melt margarine at 200°. Add pork and saute for 2 minutes. Add ground meat and saute until light brown. Add onions, celery, garlic, and green pepper; saute until soft. Add seasonings; continue to stir well. Slowly add roux; mix well. Take care at this point that you do not overbrown the roux. Add oyster liquid; stir in well, then add the oysters. Cook all ingredients at a slow simmer for 15 minutes. Control the liquid at this time; it may be necessary to add additional hot water. Blend in rice. Lower heat to a slow simmer. Add parsley. Stir frequently for 1/2 hour. Serve. Serves 8.

FRIED OYSTERS JEANERETTE

3 doz. oysters
1 c. bread crumbs
1 c. flour
2 eggs, beaten
1/4 tsp. white pepper
1/4 tsp. red pepper

1/4 tsp. black pepper
4 Tbsp. milk
1/4 tsp. thyme
1/4 tsp. oregano
Salt to taste
2 c. corn oil

In a small bowl, combine seasonings. In a separate bowl, combine milk, eggs and 1/2 seasonings; mix thoroughly. On a large plate, mix the bread crumbs, flour and remaining seasonings. Roll the oysters in the crumb mixture, dip into the eggs and pat again into crumb mixture. Repeat the process until the oysters are thoroughly covered. In a large saucepan, heat 2 cups of corn oil to 400°. Drop oysters in oil separately and deep-fry until golden brown. Remove from oil and place on a paper towel to drain off excess oil. Serve with French fries. Serves 4.

FRIED OYSTERS ABBEVILLE IN WINE SAUCE

3 doz. oysters
4 eggs, beaten
1/4 tsp. sweet basil
1/4 tsp. oregano
1 c. flour

1 c. corn meal
1/2 c. milk
1/8 tsp. red pepper
1/8 tsp. white pepper
Salt to taste

Drain oysters thoroughly. In a small bowl, combine seasonings. Combine eggs, milk and 1/2 seasonings. Separately combine flour, corn meal and remaining seasonings. Pat oysters into flour mixture, dip into the egg mixture and again into the flour mixture. In a deep saucepan, heat oil to 400°. Drop oysters in, one at a time, and fry until golden brown. Remove from pan and place on a paper towel, allowing to drain.

Wine Sauce:

3 Tbsp. flour
3 Tbsp. margarine

3 Tbsp. Creole mustard
1/2 c. dry white wine

In a separate saucepan, melt 3 tablespoons margarine at 200°. Stir in flour and allow to gel. Slowly add 1/4 cup white wine and bring to a simmer. Add mustard; stir well. Add remaining wine. At this point, you may decide to add the fried oysters and saute for 2 minutes, or use this delicious Wine Sauce as a dip. Serves 4.

OYSTERS IN CHEESE ST. MARTINVILLE

3 doz. large oysters
1 c. bread crumbs
1 c. grated Italian cheese
1/2 c. white wine
1 tsp. margarine
1 Tbsp. parsley leaves
1/2 tsp. thyme

1/4 tsp. bay leaf
1/4 tsp. white pepper
1/8 tsp. red pepper
2 Tbsp. Worcestershire sauce
1/4 tsp. coarse ground black
  pepper
Salt to taste

Lightly oil a casserole dish with margarine. In a small bowl, combine bread crumbs with grated cheese; mix well. Sprinkle casserole dish evenly with 1/4 cup of cheese and bread crumb mixture. Drain oysters and retain liquid. Arrange 1 1/2 dozen oysters on top of bread crumb mix. Apply another layer of 1/4 cup bread crumb mixture. Arrange remaining oysters on top of bread crumbs. Combine seasonings and sprinkle over oyster layer. Cover with 1/4 cup bread crumb mix. Cover top with white wine and Worcestershire sauce. Sprinkle with remaining bread crumbs and parsley leaves. Bake for 15 minutes at 350° or until light brown. Serves 4.

OYSTERS ARTICHOKE ESPLANADE PIE

2 doz. oysters (retain liquid)
8 oz. artichoke hearts
¼ stick margarine
3 Tbsp. flour
1 tsp. salt
¼ tsp. red pepper
½ tsp. white pepper
¼ tsp. Louisiana hot sauce

2 tsp. paprika
½ tsp. thyme
1 Tbsp. pimento, chopped
1 tsp. garlic flakes
1 c. cracker crumbs
2 oz. sherry
Bisquick

In a saucepan, melt margarine at 300°. Stir in flour until it gels. Combine seasonings, except paprika, with oyster water and blend into flour. Chop artichoke hearts and set aside. Add oysters to saucepan and saute until edges curl. Reduce heat to 200° and add artichokes and pimento. Stir thoroughly. Blend in sherry; remove from heat. Roll out enough Bisquick to cover the bottom of a 9x12 inch lightly oiled casserole dish. Place in oven and lightly brown the crust. Remove from oven. Add oyster mix; cover top with cracker crumbs. Sprinkle with paprika. Bake at 450° for 10 minutes or until crumbs brown. Serves 6.

EGGPLANT OYSTER CASSEROLE AMITE

1 doz. oysters
1 eggplant (medium)
½ c. seasoned bread crumbs
1 c. sour cream
¼ tsp. oregano
⅛ tsp. white pepper
½ tsp. black pepper

½ stick margarine
¼ c. onion, chopped
1 Tbsp. parsley, chopped
¼ tsp. garlic powder
⅛ tsp. thyme
Salt to taste

Peel eggplant and cut into 1 inch chunks. Put in a saucepan, cover with water and cook ¾ done. Drain well. In a saucepan, melt margarine at 200°. Add onion and oysters and saute until lightly curled. Add seasonings; mix well. Remove from heat and add eggplant; mix thoroughly. Try to avoid smashing the eggplant chunks. Blend in cream and ½ cup bread crumbs; stir well. Place in oiled casserole dish. Cover with remaining bread crumbs. Bake at 350° until lightly browned. Garnish with parsley. Serves 6.

This dish is excellent served cold.

EGGPLANT FILLED WITH SHRIMP AND OYSTER SAUCE FRANKLINTON

First Seasoning Mix:

2 bay leaves
1 tsp. salt
½ tsp. red pepper
½ tsp. white pepper
½ tsp. black pepper
½ tsp. thyme
3 large eggplants
2 sticks margarine
1¼ c. onions, chopped
¾ c. celery, chopped
½ c. green pepper, chopped
1 lb. shrimp, peeled and deveined
1½ c. oyster soup or oyster water
½ c. onions, chopped fine

½ tsp. salt
½ tsp. white pepper
¼ tsp. red pepper
½ tsp. sweet basil
¼ tsp. nutmeg
Juice of 1 lemon
1 tsp. garlic flakes
1½ c. flour
1 c. sour cream
3 doz. large oysters (retain liquid)
1 c. green onions, chopped fine
1½ c. bread crumbs
1 c. milk
2 eggs

Drain oysters and set aside. In a small bowl, combine First Seasoning mix; set aside. Cut eggplants in halves lengthwise, then cut a 1 inch slice from the cut end of each eggplant half. Peel each slice. Carve out centers of eggplant, forming a boat. Chop pulp into small squares; set aside. Place eggplant pulp in a saucepan with 1 stick margarine, 1 cup onions, celery, and green pepper. Saute at 350° for 5 minutes, stirring occasionally. Add First Seasoning Mix. Blend well and cook for an additional 5 minutes. Add shrimp and cook until pink, stirring frequently. Add ½ cup oyster soup or oyster water. Simmer for 3 minutes. Remove shrimp stuffing from pan and set aside.

In a saucepan, melt 1 stick margarine at 200°. Add ½ cup finely chopped onions, 1 teaspoon salt, red pepper, white pepper, basil, lemon juice, and garlic. Saute until soft. Stir in 1 cup flour and blend well until it gels. Stir in remaining cup of stock. Bring temperature to 300° and simmer. Whisk frequently and continue simmering until gravy thickens. Add sour cream; reduce heat to 200° and cook for 5 minutes. Add oysters and any remaining water. Add green onions and simmer for an additional 5 minutes. Place remaining ½ cup flour, bread crumbs and milk in 3 separate pans. Blend eggs into milk.

Second Seasoning Mix:

1 tsp. salt
1 tsp. white pepper
1 tsp. dry mustard
½ tsp. red pepper

1 tsp. paprika
1 tsp. onion powder
1 tsp. garlic powder
Corn oil (enough for frying)

In a small bowl, thoroughly combine Second Seasoning Mix. Mix half with bread crumbs and sprinkle remaining seasoning and vegetables over the eggplant. Fill a deep saucepan with 1 inch corn oil and heat at 350°. Dredge eggplant boats well in seasoned flour. Shake off excess; coat with milk mixture. Dredge in bread crumbs and fry until golden brown. Place eggplant boats in a saucepan and fill with shrimp and oyster mixture. Serve hot. Serves 6.

OYSTERS WITH CURRY RICE

3 doz. oysters (retain liquid)
1 c. white roux
1 Tbsp. margarine
2 Tbsp. parsley, chopped
1/4 tsp. thyme
1/4 tsp. bay leaf

1/2 tsp. Tabasco sauce
1 c. cooked rice
1/2 tsp. curry powder
Salt to taste
1/2 c. hot milk

In a saucepan, melt margarine at 200°. Slowly add white roux and blend well. Add hot milk; mix well. Add seasonings and bring mixture to a brisk simmer. Add oysters and simmer until ends curl. Add cooked rice and oyster water and simmer for 10 minutes or until the majority of moisture is removed. Continue to stir, as this dish will stick easy. If you wish, don't add rice. Place rice in mounds, cover with mixture and serve. Garnish with parsley. Serves 6.

OYSTERS IN PASTA CREAM BIG MAMOU

2 doz. oysters (retain liquid)
2 c. white roux
2 c. cooked noodles
3 Tbsp. green pepper, chopped
1/4 c. green onions, chopped
1/4 tsp. oregano

1/4 tsp. basil
1/8 tsp. red pepper
1/8 tsp. white pepper
3/4 c. bread crumbs
2 Tbsp. margarine
Salt to taste

Drain oysters, retain liquid and set aside. In a saucepan, melt margarine at 200°. Add green pepper and onions; saute until soft. Slowly blend in roux. Add oyster water at room temperature. Bring to simmer and remove from heat. Lightly oil a casserole dish. Place a layer of cooked noodles on bottom of casserole dish. Sprinkle with bread crumbs; pour in 1/4 cup of roux. In a small bowl, combine seasonings and sprinkle over top. Place a layer of oysters; add a layer of roux mixture. Repeat this process until ingredients are used. Bake for 40 minutes at 300° or until browning begins. Serves 6.

OYSTERS WITH PARMESAN STUFFING NEW IBERIA

2 doz. oysters (retain liquid)
1/2 c. Parmesan cheese
1 c. seasoned bread crumbs
1/4 stick margarine
1/4 c. onions, chopped
3 Tbsp. parsley, chopped

1/2 c. celery, chopped
1/8 tsp. red pepper
1/8 tsp. white pepper
1/8 tsp. thyme
Salt to taste

In a saucepan, saute oysters in own water for 5 minutes at 200°. Remove from heat. In a separate saucepan, melt margarine at 200°. Add vegetables and seasonings. Saute until soft. Add oysters; do not bring above simmer. In a separate bowl, combine bread crumbs with Parmesan cheese. Blend in with oyster mixture. Serve in mounds; top with creamy wine sauce or use as an excellent stuffing for poultry, pork or fish. Serves 4.

OYSTERS BIENVILLE KAPLAN

4 doz. oysters
2 lb. shrimp, peeled and
   deveined
2 packs fresh mushrooms, diced
2 Tbsp. garlic, chopped fine
1 large onion, chopped fine
1 1/2 c. milk
2 chicken bouillon cubes
1 1/2 c. hot water
1 1/2 sticks margarine

4 Tbsp. flour
1 lb. sharp American cheese,
   grated
1/2 c. white wine
1/2 c. sour cream
1/4 tsp. white pepper
1/4 tsp. red pepper
1/8 tsp. thyme
1/8 tsp. basil
Aluminum shells
Sprinkling of paprika

In a saucepan, melt 1/4 stick margarine at 300°. Add shrimp and saute until pink. Remove from heat; dice shrimp. Dissolve chicken bouillon cubes in 1 1/2 cups hot water. Reduce heat to 200°. Return shrimp. Combine with seasonings, bouillon, garlic, onion, and diced mushrooms. Saute for 2 minutes and remove from heat. In a separate saucepan, melt 1/4 stick margarine at 200°. Stir in flour until it gels. Add milk, sour cream and wine. Melt in 1 stick margarine. This should be whisked together well. Add shrimp mixture and simmer together slowly for 15 minutes. Arrange oysters on aluminum shells and place in a large flat casserole dish. Pour sauce generously over each oyster and broil for 2 minutes. Cover with cheese, bread crumbs and paprika. Return to broiler and brown (10 minutes maximum). Serves 4.

OYSTER CAJUN PIE

3 doz. oysters
¼ stick margarine
1 can dairy case biscuits
½ c. grated cheese (your choice)
Juice of 1 lemon
1 medium onion, chopped
1 tsp. paprika

½ c. sour cream
⅛ tsp. red pepper
⅛ tsp. white pepper
½ c. white roux
1 Tbsp. parsley, chopped
¼ tsp. basil
¼ tsp. oregano
Salt to taste

In a saucepan, melt margarine at 200°. Add onion and saute until soft. Reduce heat to 175°. Blend in sour cream, lemon juice and grated cheese until cheese is melted and blended well. Slowly add roux; mix well. Mixture should be at thick syrup consistency; if necessary, simmer additional minutes to reach this state. Pour ½ mixture into a lightly oiled baking dish. Arrange oysters over top of mixture. In a small bowl, combine seasonings, except paprika, and sprinkle on top. Cover with remaining mixture. Separate biscuits and roll into round patties. Cover dish in a leafy manner. Paint exposed surface of biscuits lightly with margarine. Sprinkle with paprika. Bake at 350° until brown. Serves 8.

This creates a lovely party dish. Garnish with parsley.

OYSTER TURNED CHICKEN GRAND ISLE

2 doz. oysters
1 lb. boneless chicken
2 c. seasoned bread crumbs
¼ stick margarine
½ tsp. paprika
¼ tsp. oregano
¼ tsp. thyme

¼ tsp. tarragon
1 can cream of chicken soup
⅛ tsp. white pepper
⅛ tsp. red pepper
Salt to taste
½ c. hot water

Drain oysters and save the liquid. Cut chicken into chunks. In a saucepan, melt margarine at 300°. Add chicken and saute until light brown. Remove from pan and set aside; retain drippings. Add oysters and saute until the ends curl, about 3 minutes. Remove from pan and arrange ½ oysters in a lightly oiled casserole dish. Spread 1 cup of bread crumbs, forming a bed, then arrange with chicken chunks.

In a bowl, combine the seasonings, except paprika, and sprinkle half over the chicken. In a bowl, blend the cream of chicken soup into the casserole dish. Cover with ¼ cup of bread crumbs, forming another bed. Arrange remaining oysters over the bed; sprinkle with remaining seasoning. Pour remaining cream of chicken over the oysters. Cover with remaining bread crumbs. Pour the oyster water over the bread crumbs. Sprinkle lightly with paprika. Bake at 450° for 20 minutes or until brown. Serves 8.

OYSTERS ON ARTICHOKE BED PLAQUEMINE

2 doz. oysters
1 c. bread crumbs
½ c. grated cheese (your
    choice - I use Feta)
1 can cream of mushroom soup
1 doz. artichoke hearts
⅛ tsp. white pepper

⅛ tsp. black pepper
½ tsp. curry powder
¼ tsp. tarragon
½ tsp. garlic powder
½ tsp. onion powder
¼ stick margarine
Salt to taste

In a small bowl, combine seasonings. In a separate bowl, combine ¾ cup bread crumbs, cheese and ½ seasoning mix. Spread ½ mixture on a lightly oiled casserole dish. Slice artichokes in halves and arrange on bed. Pour ½ of the remaining cheese/bread crumb mixture over the artichokes. In a saucepan, melt margarine at 200°. Add oysters and saute until the ends curl. Add remaining seasoning mix to the oysters; mix well. Increase temperature to 300°. Saute for 1 minute and remove from heat. Arrange on the casserole bed.

In a separate saucepan, blend ¼ cup water to mushroom soup and bring to a simmer. Pour into casserole dish. Cover with remaining bread crumbs. Bake at 450° for 15 minutes. Serves 6.

HAM FRIED OYSTERS BURAS

2 c. diced ham
2 doz. oysters
¼ stick margarine
3 Tbsp. flour
1 pack dairy case biscuits
⅔ c. white wine

⅔ c. hot milk
¼ tsp. white pepper
¼ tsp. curry powder
¼ tsp. red pepper
⅛ tsp. tarragon
Salt to taste

In a saucepan, melt margarine at 350°. Add ham and saute until edges are light brown. Remove from pan; allow drippings to remain. Add oysters and seasonings; saute until edges curl, about 2 minutes. Remove from pan; allow drippings to remain. Stir in flour carefully, stirring continuously to avoid lumping. When flour becomes light brown, slowly add hot milk. Stir frequently. When liquid comes to a simmer, slowly add white wine. Continue stirring until mixture thickens. Add oysters and ham. Stir and simmer for 5 minutes. Remove from heat and pour in a lightly oiled casserole dish. Divide biscuits in halves, making thin wafers. Arrange over top of dish. Bake until biscuits are brown. Serve. Serves 6.

OYSTERS MUSHROOM DELUXE VENICE

3 doz. oysters
1 can cream of mushroom soup
1 pack fresh mushrooms
¼ c. celery, chopped
1 c. sour cream
½ c. onions, chopped
4 Tbsp. parsley leaves
2 Tbsp. Worcestershire sauce

½ tsp. white pepper
¼ tsp. red pepper
⅛ tsp. oregano
¼ tsp. Tabasco sauce
Juice of 1 lemon
½ stick margarine
1 c. hot water
Salt to taste

In a saucepan, melt margarine at 250°. Add vegetables, except mushrooms, and saute until soft. Wash mushrooms and twist off stems from the caps. Chop stems fine and allow caps to remain intact. Add to vegetables and saute until caps begin to brown. Reduce heat to 200° and blend in sour cream. Stir well and add soup and 1 cup hot water. Continue to blend and add seasonings, Worcestershire sauce, lemon juice, and Tabasco, then oysters. Cook for 15 minutes at 200°, stirring frequently. Serve over pasta and sprinkle with Italian cheese. Serves 8.

OYSTERS IN ASPARAGUS CREAM BRETON SOUND

3 doz. oysters
1 can chopped asparagus
¼ c. onions, chopped fine
2 cloves garlic, chopped fine
¼ stick margarine
1 egg, beaten
¼ c. sour cream

½ c. bread crumbs
½ c. grated Italian cheese
¼ tsp. black pepper
¼ tsp. red pepper
¼ tsp. oregano
¼ tsp. basil
Salt to taste

In a saucepan, melt margarine at 250°. Add oysters and saute until curled. Remove from pan. Add onions and garlic; saute until soft. Return oysters. In a separate bowl, blend together asparagus and sour cream; mix well. Slowly add to oyster mixture. Combine and add seasonings; blend in well. Simmer for 5 minutes. Remove from heat. Blend in beaten egg; slowly fold in bread crumbs. Return to heat at 175°. Be careful, this dish will stick. Blend in ⅔ cup cheese and remove from heat. Pour into individual serving bowls or a lightly oiled casserole dish. Sprinkle remaining cheese on top instead of blending in mixture. Bake at 350° for 5 minutes. Serves 6.

OYSTERS CURRY CRABMEAT PEARL RIVER

1 c. crabmeat
2 doz. oysters (retain liquid)
2 c. white roux
1/4 stick margarine
1 tsp. curry powder
1/8 tsp. white pepper
1/8 tsp. red pepper
2 cloves garlic, chopped
1/4 c. onions, chopped fine
1 lb. cooked pasta
1/2 c. hot water
Salt to taste

In a saucepan, melt margarine at 200°. Add onions and garlic; saute until soft. Add crabmeat; saute for 3 minutes. Add oysters; saute until ends curl. Remove from heat. In another saucepan, add 1/2 cup hot water and bring to simmer. Blend in white roux. In a small bowl, combine seasonings. Blend well into roux. Keep a close watch on stirring as mixture thickens. Add oyster water to control thickness. Combine the two mixtures; bring to simmer. Serve over pasta and lightly sprinkle with Italian cheese. Serves 6.

In Houma, the pasta and cheese are blended directly into mixture and served with fried trout.

OYSTER BIENVILLE NEW ORLEANS

3 doz. oysters (retain water)
1/2 stick margarine
3 Tbsp. flour
1 clove garlic, chopped fine
2 Tbsp. onions, chopped fine
1 Tbsp. celery seed
1 small can mushrooms
1 can cream of mushroom soup
1 Tbsp. Worcestershire sauce
1 doz. shrimp
2 oz. sherry
1/2 c. Parmesan cheese
1 tsp. paprika
1/2 tsp. coarse black pepper
1/2 tsp. white pepper
Salt to taste

In a saucepan, melt 1/4 stick margarine at 200°. Blend in flour until it gels; do not allow it to brown. Add onions and garlic. Add Worcestershire sauce and seasoning except paprika and celery seeds. Reduce heat and blend in oyster water. Add mushrooms, shrimp, soup, and sherry. In a separate saucepan, melt remaining margarine at 300°. Add oysters and saute for 2 minutes. Remove from heat and add Parmesan cheese. Arrange oysters in a casserole dish. Cover with sauce; sprinkle with paprika. Broil for 8 minutes or until mixture begins to bubble. Serves 6.

CREOLE DEVILED OYSTERS OBERLIN

3 doz. oysters (retain liquid)
1 c. celery, chopped fine
1 c. onions, chopped fine
1 c. green pepper, chopped fine
½ c. parsley, chopped fine
¾ stick margarine
2 eggs, beaten well

2 c. cracker crumbs
2 Tbsp. Worcestershire sauce
½ tsp. red pepper
½ tsp. white pepper
Juice of ½ lemon
½ tsp. garlic flakes or powder
Salt to taste

In a saucepan, melt ¼ stick margarine at 300°. Add oysters and saute until ends curl. Remove from heat and chop fine. Melt an additional ¼ stick margarine. Add onions, celery, green pepper, and parsley. Saute until soft and remove from heat. Blend in seasonings. Remove from heat. Blend in eggs with oysters. In a separate bowl, soak cracker crumbs in oyster water. Allow to absorb as much liquid as possible; drain off excess liquid. Combine mixtures and cook at 200°, stirring frequently, for 5 minutes. Add remaining ingredients except margarine. Remove from heat and place mixture in aluminum oyster shells or ramekins. Dot with remaining margarine and brown in a hot oven. Serves 6.

OYSTER SHRIMP BROCHETTE YSCLOSKEY

3 doz. oysters
3 doz. shrimp, peeled and
    deveined
1 stick margarine
1 large onion, cut into 1 inch
    squares
1 large green pepper, cut into 1
    inch squares
Bacon slices

1 c. bread crumbs
½ tsp. red pepper
½ tsp. thyme
½ tsp. basil
1 tsp. salt
½ tsp. white pepper
½ tsp. black pepper
½ tsp. oregano

Melt ¼ stick margarine at 400°. Add seasonings, stirring briskly. Reduce heat to 300°. Add shrimp and saute until light pink. Remove from heat; set shrimp aside. Retain drippings. Wrap oysters in bacon and skewer one oyster, then an onion square, then a shrimp, then a green pepper on a skewer. Repeat process until all materials are skewered. Return saucepan with seasoning to the heat and melt remaining margarine. Place on side of barbecue grill. Do not allow to simmer. Dip skewer into bread crumbs, then into melted margarine.

Barbecue until bacon is crisp over hot coals. You may prefer using a broiler. Serve with tartar sauce. Serves 6.

CREOLE OYSTER SALAD GRAND CHENIER

2 doz. oysters
1 small jar chopped pimentos
Juice of 1 lemon
1 Tbsp. onions, chopped
1/2 tsp. red pepper
1/2 tsp. thyme
1/2 tsp. basil
1/2 tsp. salt
1/4 tsp. white pepper

1/4 tsp. oregano
1 tsp. brown sugar
1/2 tsp. celery salt
4 hard-boiled eggs, diced
1 c. celery, chopped large
1 c. lettuce, shredded
1 head lettuce
2 Tbsp. margarine
1/4 c. parsley leaves, chopped

Drain oysters; discard water. In a saucepan, melt margarine at 200°. Add oysters until ends curl. In a small bowl, combine seasonings, including brown sugar. Sprinkle oysters with seasoning; blend well. Remove from heat. Peel head of lettuce and use the leaves to form a cup in a large salad bowl. Shred center of lettuce and line the leaves. Arrange vegetables. Arrange oysters; decorate edges with eggs. Top with mayonnaise. Sprinkle generously with parsley leaves. Add lemon juice and garnish with pimentos. Chill and serve. Serves 6.

OYSTERS ROCKEFELLER LAKE PONTCHARTRAIN

4 doz. oysters
1 pack frozen spinach
2 bunches green onions
1 stalk celery
1/2 bunch parsley
4 sticks margarine
2 1/2 c. bread crumbs

1 Tbsp. anchovy paste
3 oz. absinthe
1 c. grated Parmesan cheese
1 tsp. Worcestershire sauce
1/4 tsp. white pepper
1/4 tsp. red pepper

Place spinach, onions, parsley, and celery in a food processor. Grind fine, forming a sauce. In a saucepan, melt margarine at a low temperature and blend in 1 1/2 cups bread crumbs. Add Worcestershire sauce, anchovy paste and seasonings. Place oysters in the shells on a bed of rock salt. Blend in absinthe before covering oysters with sauce. Cover each oyster with sauce. Cover with cheese and bread crumb mixture. Bake at 450° until brown. Serve hot. Serves 6.

CREOLE OYSTER SOUFFLE BURGUNDY

2 doz. oysters
1 c. white roux
1 tsp. salt
½ tsp. white pepper
½ tsp. dry mustard
½ tsp. red pepper

½ tsp. paprika
½ tsp. onion powder
¾ tsp. garlic powder
⅛ tsp. nutmeg
4 egg whites
4 egg yolks

In a saucepan, bring ½ cup water to simmer. Blend in roux. Add oysters and seasonings. Reduce heat and add well beaten egg yolks. Mix well. Remove from heat. In a separate bowl, beat egg whites until stiff. Fold stiff egg whites into mixture. Place into an oiled casserole dish. Bake at 350° until brown. Serves 6.

OYSTERS IN A FRENCH BED BOAT REEVES

1 loaf French bread (Italian or
   Greek)
2 doz. oysters (retain liquid)
1 c. sour cream
1 stick margarine
½ c. seasoned bread crumbs
2 eggs, beaten

Juice of 1 lemon
¼ tsp. garlic powder
¼ tsp. red pepper
¼ tsp. basil
¼ tsp. thyme
½ tsp. Tabasco sauce
Salt to taste

Slice off top of French bread; scoop out the interior to form a boat. In a saucepan, melt ½ stick margarine at 200°. Blend in garlic powder and Tabasco sauce. Paint inside of boat with this mixture. Place boat in a broiler and toast until light brown. Place aside and keep warm. Melt remaining margarine at 200°. Add oysters and saute until ends curl. Reduce heat to a simmer. Add sour cream and beaten eggs. In a separate bowl, combine bread crumbs and enough oyster water to make bread crumbs damp, but not wet. Combine all ingredients, including seasonings; fold in slowly. Fill boat with this mixture. Bake in oven for 10 minutes at 300°. Serves 8.

It is necessary to control this dish; make sure bread does not get too hard in oven.

CAJUN CREAM OF OYSTER AND SCALLOP STEW

3 doz. oysters
1 pt. scallops
1 qt. milk
1/2 c. green onions, chopped
1/4 c. celery, chopped
2 Tbsp. parsley leaves, chopped
2 Tbsp. flour
1/4 tsp. red pepper
1/4 tsp. white pepper

1/4 tsp. thyme
1/4 tsp. basil
1/4 tsp. oregano
1/4 tsp. black pepper
1 tsp. salt
1 Tbsp. Worcestershire sauce
1 c. croutons
1/2 stick margarine
1 c. hot water

In a saucepan, melt 1/4 stick margarine at 300°. Add vegetables and saute until light brown. Remove from heat. In a separate saucepan, heat the milk. Do not boil; reduce the heat to 150°. Slowly add the flour to the milk, blending well. Add seasonings and Worcestershire sauce. Drain water from the oysters. Return vegetable mixture to the heat and simmer at 200°. Add the water to the vegetable mixture. Add oysters to the milk and simmer until they are plump or curled. Blend two mixtures together; keep at simmer for 5 minutes or until stew thickens.

In a separate saucepan, melt remaining margarine at 300°. Add scallops and saute for 5 minutes at 200°. Add to stew and simmer for 5 additional minutes. Remove from heat; blend in croutons. Sprinkle with parsley and serve. Serves 8.

CAJUN OYSTERS POULETTE

3 doz. oysters
2 c. white roux
1 c. ham, diced
1/2 stick margarine
1/4 c. green onions, chopped
1/4 c. parsley, chopped
1 pack fresh mushrooms
1/4 c. sherry

3 egg yolks, beaten
1/4 tsp. thyme
1/4 tsp. basil
1 tsp. salt
1/2 tsp. white pepper
1/2 tsp. red pepper
1/4 tsp. oregano

In a saucepan, melt margarine at 300°. Add ham and saute until light brown. Remove from pan; set aside. Retain drippings. Add oysters and saute until lightly curled. Remove and set aside; retain drippings. Add vegetables and saute until light brown. Reduce heat to 200°. Slowly add white roux. If roux is thick, add 1/2 cup hot water. Add ham and slowly blend in egg yolks. Add oysters and remaining ingredients. Blend well and bring to simmer for 5 minutes; control thickness with hot water. The dish should have the consistency of a thick syrup. Serves 8.

This is an excellent dish to serve over thick sliced ham placed on a platter of Holland rusk. Cooked rice may be blended into this dish and served cold.

CAJUN OYSTER FRITTERS

2 doz. oysters (retain liquid)
1 c. all-purpose flour
¼ tsp. red pepper
¼ tsp. white pepper
⅛ tsp. oregano
⅛ tsp. basil

3 eggs, beaten
½ c. milk
2 Tbsp. baking powder
Salt to taste
¼ stick margarine
Corn oil for frying

In a saucepan, melt margarine at 300°. Add oysters and saute for 2 minutes. Remove from pan. Chop oysters in fourths. In a separate bowl, combine all ingredients, including oyster liquid. Control the thickness of the fritters by the amount of oyster water added. Take tablespoon size quantities, drop into deep fat and fry until brown. Serve with Spicy St. Charles Tartar Sauce. Serves 4.

OYSTER BOURBON STREET

2 doz. oysters
2 doz. party shells
2 c. white roux
2 eggs, beaten
½ c. green peppers, chopped
½ c. celery, chopped
¼ stick margarine
1 Tbsp. pimentos

¼ tsp. basil
¼ tsp. oregano
⅛ tsp. white pepper
⅛ tsp. red pepper
¼ tsp. thyme
Salt to taste
½ c. bread crumbs
½ c. grated Italian cheese

In a saucepan, melt margarine at 200°. Add oysters and saute until ends curl. Remove from heat and set aside. Add vegetables and saute until soft. Reduce the heat to 200°. Slowly add the white roux. Blend well. If this becomes too thick, add oyster water at room temperature. In a small bowl, combine seasonings and add, blending thoroughly. Add remaining ingredients, including oysters. Simmer until mixture has a heavy consistency. Pour into a casserole dish or party shells. Blend together bread crumbs and Italian cheese. Top and bake for 5 minutes at 300°. Serve. Serves 6.

Makes a wonderful appetizer in ramekins.

CREOLE OYSTER SOUP

3 doz. oysters
1 qt. milk
½ stick margarine
½ tsp. white pepper
1 tsp. coarse ground black
    pepper
¼ tsp. oregano

⅛ tsp. basil
1 Tbsp. Worcestershire sauce
3 Tbsp. parsley leaves
¼ c. celery, chopped
¼ c. green onions, chopped
¼ c. Italian cheese
Salt to taste

Melt margarine in saucepan. Add oysters and simmer until ends curl. Remove from heat. In a separate pan, bring milk to simmer. Add remaining ingredients; blend well. Simmer for 10 minutes. Do not let milk boil. Serve in a bowl; sprinkle lightly with Italian cheese. Serves 6.

OYSTER STUFFING CAJUN STYLE

2 doz. oysters (retain liquid)
1 c. seasoned bread crumbs
1 c. onions, chopped
¼ stick margarine
2 Tbsp. parsley, chopped
¼ tsp. basil
⅛ tsp. oregano

1 chicken bouillon cube
⅛ tsp. red pepper
⅛ tsp. black pepper
⅛ tsp. thyme
⅛ tsp. bay leaf
1 c. hot water
Salt to taste

In a saucepan, melt margarine at 300°. Add vegetables and saute until soft. In a separate bowl, combine seasonings; set aside. Add oysters to vegetable mix, including water. Simmer until oysters firm. Reduce heat to 150°. Add bread crumbs and mix well. Add seasonings, making sure it is well blended. Dissolve 1 bouillon cube in 1 cup of hot water. It may be necessary to add this additional liquid. Serves 6.

This is an excellent stuffing for any type of poultry or rabbit.

FRENCH QUARTER OYSTER PIE

½ can dairy case crescent rolls
2 doz. oysters
1 c. sour cream
¼ stick margarine
2 Tbsp. flour
6 hard-boiled eggs, chopped

½ tsp. Tabasco sauce
1 Tbsp. Worcestershire sauce
6 strips bacon, cooked crisp
⅛ tsp. oregano
⅛ tsp. basil
Salt to taste

Unroll ½ of crescent dough and line bottom of a lightly oiled pie pan. Place in oven and bake until light brown. Remove and set aside. In a saucepan, melt margarine at 300°. Add oysters and saute until ends curls. Reduce heat to 200°. Slowly blend in sour cream. Arrange oysters in bottom of pie plate. Sprinkle with layer of chopped hard-boiled eggs, then layer with bacon strips. In a bowl, combine remaining ingredients; pour into pie shell. Take care that dish does not become runny. If necessary, add a minimum amount of bread crumbs for control. Cover with remaining crescent dough. Bake until brown. Serve. Serves 6.

OYSTERS ON SPINACH BED LAKE ST. FRANCISVILLE

2 doz. oysters
2 packs frozen spinach, thawed
    and liquid removed
½ c. onions, chopped
½ stick margarine
2 Tbsp. flour
¼ tsp. oregano

⅛ tsp. white pepper
⅛ tsp. black pepper
¼ tsp. nutmeg
¼ tsp. cayenne pepper
2 eggs, beaten
¼ c. grated Italian cheese
1 c. sour cream
Salt to taste

In a saucepan, melt ¼ stick margarine at 300°. Add onions and saute until soft. Add spinach and saute for 3 minutes. Reduce heat to 200°. Blend in flour slowly and allow to gel. In a separate bowl, combine sour cream, cheese, seasonings, and eggs. Beat well and blend with spinach mixture. Add oyster water at room temperature. In a separate saucepan, melt remaining margarine at 300°. Add oysters and saute for 2 minutes. Combine with spinach mixture. Place in a lightly oiled casserole dish. Bake at 400° for 30 minutes. Remove from heat.

Sauce:

1 c. light brown roux
1 tsp. salt
¼ tsp. white pepper
¼ tsp. dry mustard
¼ tsp. red pepper

¼ tsp. paprika
¼ tsp. onion powder
¼ tsp. garlic powder
½ c. white wine
¼ c. hot water

In a small saucepan, add ¼ cup water; bring to a simmer. Blend in roux and seasonings. Pour ½ sauce over casserole and bake for an additional 15 minutes. Add ½ cup wine to remaining sauce and simmer for 15 minutes. Serve with rice. Serves 6.

DILL

CHICKEN IN OYSTER BED VILLE PLATTE

1 lb. boneless chicken, sliced
   into rings
2 doz. oysters
1 c. cream of chicken soup
6 strips thick, crisp bacon
¼ stick margarine
1 Tbsp. parsley leaves, chopped

½ tsp. onion powder
¼ tsp. garlic powder
¼ tsp. black pepper
1 egg, beaten
1 c. seasoned bread crumbs
Salt to taste

In a saucepan, melt margarine at 300°. Add chicken and saute until light brown. Remove from pan and set aside. Add oysters and saute until ends curl. Remove from heat. In a separate bowl, combine ½ cup bread crumbs and seasonings. Cover bottom of slightly oiled casserole dish with ½ bread crumb mixture. In a separate bowl, combine egg, parsley and soup; mix well. Arrange oysters in a casserole dish. Pour a layer of soup mixture over oysters. Arrange a layer of chicken over oysters. Add additional soup mixture. Break bacon into bits and sprinkle over soup mix. Pour in remaining soup mixture; add remaining bread crumbs. Bake for 20 minutes at 350° or until brown. Serves 6.

10/10/94

CRABMEAT JAMBALAYA VINTON

2 lb. crabmeat
1 c. onions, chopped
1 c. celery, chopped
½ c. green pepper, chopped
1¼ lb. can tomatoes
1 c. chopped bacon or diced
   ham
¼ stick margarine

2 Tbsp. Worcestershire sauce
1 tsp. Tabasco sauce
¼ tsp. thyme
¼ tsp. bay leaf
1 c. uncooked rice
¼ tsp. white pepper
¼ tsp. red pepper
Salt to taste

In a large saucepan, melt margarine at 350°. Add bacon or ham and saute until light brown. Add vegetables; saute until tender. Reduce heat to 200° and add tomatoes, including water. Add seasonings, Worcestershire sauce and Tabasco sauce. Add rice and blend well. At this point, it may be necessary to add additional hot water to cook rice. Simmer until tender. This dish will require frequent stirring. When the rice is nearly cooked, add crabmeat. Stir carefully until mixture is entirely blended and rice has absorbed the moisture, about 5 minutes. Serves 6.

STUFFED CRAB CREOLE MUSTARD SAUCE HOUMA

1½ lb. crabmeat
8 crab shells
6 strips bacon
½ c. onions, chopped
¼ c. celery, chopped
2 c. bread crumbs
1 c. milk
¼ c. green onion tops, chopped

2 cloves garlic, chopped
3 eggs, beaten
½ tsp. red pepper
¼ tsp. black pepper
¼ tsp. white pepper
¼ tsp. basil leaves
¼ c. parsley sprigs
Salt to taste

Chop bacon into bits. Place in a large saucepan and saute at 350° until light brown. Add onions and celery and saute until light brown. Remove from heat and set aside. In separate bowl, soak bread crumbs in milk until moistened. Return celery, onion and bacon mixture to the heat. Add crabmeat and seasonings; simmer at 200° for 3 minutes. Add remaining ingredients. After mixture is thoroughly blended, about 2 minutes, remove from heat and fill crab shells. Bake at 350° until golden brown. Serves 8.

Sauce:

¼ c. Creole mustard
¼ c. sour cream

¼ c. white wine

Sauce: Combine mustard, wine and sour cream. Pour over crab shells or use as a dip.

CAJUN CRAB SOUFFLE BAY ST. LOUIS

1½ lb. crabmeat
¼ stick margarine
¼ c. flour
1 c. milk
3 egg yolks, beaten
3 egg whites, beaten
Juice of ½ lemon

1½ c. grated cheese
½ Tbsp. parsley flakes
½ tsp. onion powder
¼ tsp. garlic powder
½ tsp. dry mustard
1 c. cooked rice, cooled
Salt to taste

In a large saucepan, melt margarine at 250°. Blend in flour until it gels. Add the necessary quantity of milk to create a thick and smooth consistency. Reduce heat to 175°. Add salt and cheese. Remove from the heat and add rice. Add egg yolks, stirring continuously. Add crabmeat and seasonings. Fold in egg whites. Add lemon juice. In a lightly oiled casserole dish, pour in mixture. Bake at 350° for 35 minutes. Serves 6.

In Jennings, they lay trout fillets on the bottom of the casserole dish before baking. Garnish with parsley.

CRABMEAT SALAD LAKE MAUREPAS

2 lb. chunky crabmeat
1 c. mayonnaise
Juice of 1 lemon
1 tsp. paprika
¼ tsp. red pepper
¼ tsp. white pepper
2 Tbsp. celery, chopped fine

¼ tsp. Creole mustard
2 Tbsp. parsley leaves, chopped
1 Tbsp. capers, chopped
1 head lettuce
¼ stick margarine
Salt to taste

In a saucepan, melt ¼ stick margarine at 250°. Add crabmeat and saute for 5 minutes. Shake the pan continuously. Do not stir or this will cause crabmeat to lose its chunkiness. Remove from heat and allow to cool. In a large bowl, combine all ingredients, except paprika, and blend together well. Do not beat. Fold in crabmeat. Arrange the bottom of a salad dish or individual bowls with lettuce leaves. Serve in a mound, taking care not to break up the crabmeat. Sprinkle top with paprika and serve. Serves 4.

FRIED SOFT SHELLED CRABS
LA PECAN SAUCE BAYOU SEGNETTE

8 soft shelled crabs, halved
1 c. milk
1½ c. flour
2 eggs, beaten
¼ tsp. red pepper
¼ tsp. white pepper

¼ tsp. coarse ground black
  pepper
⅛ tsp. oregano
⅛ tsp. thyme
Salt to taste

In a bowl, combine seasonings; set aside. After preparing the soft shelled crabs, dry and put in a large bowl. In bowl, mix eggs, milk and ½ seasoning mix thoroughly. Pour over soft shelled crabs and let stand for ½ hour. In a separate bowl, combine flour and remaining seasoning mix. Remove crabs from mixture and dredge in flour. Dip again into egg mix and dredge again in flour; shake off excess. In a large saucepan, heat 2 cups corn oil at 400°. Fry crabs until reddish brown. Remove from heat.

Sauce:

¼ stick margarine
½ c. dry roasted pecans,
  chopped

2 tsp. onions, chopped fine
¼ tsp. red pepper
¼ tsp. white pepper

Place ingredients in a food processor, except margarine, and blend until smooth. In a saucepan, melt ¼ stick margarine at 200°. Add crabs. Cover with sauce and bring to simmer. Remove from heat and serve. Serves 8.

CRAB GUMBO ST. MARTINVILLE WITH SMOKED SAUSAGE

6 large blue crabs, quartered
2 lb. shrimp, peeled
1 doz. oysters
1 lb. smoked sausage, diced
1 can whole tomatoes
1 stick margarine
1 c. celery, chopped
1/2 c. green peppers, chopped
4 cloves garlic, chopped
2 Tbsp. Worcestershire sauce

1/2 c. green onions, chopped
1/4 c. parsley, chopped
1/2 tsp. black pepper
1/2 tsp. white pepper
1/2 tsp. red pepper
1/4 tsp. thyme
1/4 tsp. oregano
1 c. onions, chopped
2 c. brown roux
Fresh okra (optional)

In a large saucepan, melt 1/2 stick of margarine at 350°. Add vegetables and saute until soft. If you intend to use okra, saute in a separate saucepan for 5 minutes in 1/4 stick of margarine at 200°; add to vegetable mixture. Remove from heat and set aside. In a separate saucepan, melt remaining margarine at 200°. Blend in roux. Bring to a simmer. Add remaining seasonings, including Worcestershire sauce. Combine above ingredients and simmer briskly for 30 minutes. Control thickness by adding hot water.

While this is cooking, clean crabs. Remove the claws and split the bodies into quarters. In a separate saucepan, add smoked sausage and saute at 350° until light brown. Add crab parts, shrimp and oysters. Cook for an additional 5 minutes at 450°, stirring continuously. According to the size crabs and pan used, additional cooking time may be necessary. Combine all ingredients and cook 25 minutes. Serve over a bed of rice. Serves 8.

CRABMEAT PARMESAN ST. FRANCISVILLE

1 1/2 lb. crabmeat
3 c. spaghetti
1/4 c. Parmesan cheese
1 c. canned tomatoes
8 oz. tomato sauce
1/2 c. onions, chopped
3 cloves garlic, chopped

3 Tbsp. parsley, chopped
1/4 stick margarine
1/4 tsp. oregano
1/8 tsp. white pepper
1/8 tsp. black pepper
3 Tbsp. olive oil
Salt to taste

In a large saucepan, melt margarine at 300°. Add vegetables and saute until soft. Add tomatoes, tomato sauce and seasonings; blend well. Bring to a simmer for 15 minutes. Add crabmeat; bring to simmer. Cook spaghetti at the same time. After spaghetti is drained, do not rinse in cold water. Place in a bowl and add olive oil. Blend well and add Parmesan cheese, blending well into spaghetti. Blend crabmeat with spaghetti or serve crabmeat over a mound of spaghetti. Serves 6.

STUFFED ZUCCHINI WITH CREAMED CRABMEAT AMITE

8 large zucchini
1 lb. crabmeat, well drained
½ lb. shrimp or crawfish tails,
    peeled and deveined
1 c. minced celery
1 c. minced onions
¾ c. minced green peppers
¾ tsp. sweet paprika
½ tsp. coarse ground black
    pepper
¼ tsp. white pepper
¼ tsp. onion flakes
¼ tsp. garlic flakes
¼ tsp. dry mustard

¼ tsp. thyme
¼ tsp. sweet basil
2 sticks margarine
1 Tbsp. garlic, chopped fine
1 bay leaf
3 cans oyster soup
1¼ c. bread crumbs
½ c. green onions, chopped fine
3 Tbsp. flour
1 c. sour cream
Corn oil for frying
¼ tsp. file powder (optional)

Cut 6 zucchini in halves lengthwise. Allow stem to remain. With a melon baller, scoop out pulp and retain. With a sharp teaspoon, carefully clean out remaining pulp. Coarsely grate the pulp. It will be necessary to grate the other 2 zucchini to compile enough pulp. In a separate bowl, combine celery, minced onion and green pepper; set aside. In a small bowl, combine seasoning mix; blend well. Set aside. In a large ovenproof skillet, melt ½ stick margarine at 200°. Add half the vegetable mix and saute for 3 minutes. Add garlic, bay leaves and 1 stick margarine. Add 1 tablespoon seasoning mix; blend well. Saute until mixture browns, stirring frequently. Add ¾ of remaining vegetables and 5 cups grated zucchini. Stir in well. Cook at a brisk simmer for 3 minutes. Place skillet in the oven and bake at 450° until surface is brown. This should take 15 to 20 minutes.

Remove from oven and stir in 1 cup soup; return to oven for 10 minutes. Sprinkle 1 cup bread crumbs on the surface and stir in well. Continue baking for 15 minutes. Stir in remaining bread crumbs well. Bake for an additional 10 minutes; remove from oven. Blend in green onions, peppers, ½ the shrimp or crawfish, and ½ crabmeat. Spoon this mixture into the zucchini halves. Place the zucchini halves in a lightly oiled casserole dish, making sure that the shells fit snugly. Bake at 450° for 12 minutes.

In a saucepan, combine remaining 2 cans soup, 1 cup grated zucchini and chopped onions. Bring to a boil at 350° for about 15 minutes. Remove from heat and set aside. In a small bowl, blend together ½ stick softened margarine and flour. Return soup mixture to heat at 350°; whisk in flour briskly. Add sour cream, remaining seasoning mix and remaining shrimp or crawfish. Reduce the heat to 175°; whisk continuously for 1 minute. Stir in remaining crabmeat. Cook for 2 additional minutes while whisking. Remove from heat and set aside. Pour over cooked zucchini and serve. Serves 8.

FRIED CRAB CLAWS LAKE VERRET

2 doz. crab claws
2 eggs, beaten
1/8 tsp. red pepper
1/8 tsp. white pepper
1/8 tsp. oregano
1/8 tsp. basil
1/8 tsp. thyme
1 tsp. salt
1 c. all-purpose flour
2 c. corn oil

In a bowl, combine seasonings. Blend together well; this is important. Crack the crab claws with a nut cracker, taking care to slide the shell free without damaging the meat. Remove the flexible side of the claw. In a separate bowl, combine the beaten eggs and 1/2 seasoning mix together thoroughly. In a separate bowl, combine the flour and remaining seasoning mix. Dip crab claws into the egg mixture, then into flour. Repeat this action continuously until forming a thick coat. Heat 2 cups corn oil in a deep saucepan at 350°. Fry crab claws until golden brown. Serve with French fries and remoulade sauce. Serves 6.

CRABMEAT APPETIZER COVINGTON

1 lb. crabmeat, drained
36 round Melba toast slices
Equal number thinly sliced onion
    rounds
Equal number thinly sliced
    tomato rounds
1/4 c. Parmesan cheese
1 c. mayonnaise
1/8 tsp. white pepper
1/8 tsp. red pepper

Thoroughly mix crabmeat, mayonnaise, cheese, and seasonings. Place a thin layer on each Melba round. Cover with onion and tomato ring and cover with crab mixture. Serves 8.

SOFT SHELL CRABS AT THEIR BEST

6 soft shell crabs, properly
    prepared and cleaned
1½ c. pecans, chopped
1 c. brandy
1 c. sour cream
2 doz. green tomato slices
1¼ sticks margarine
6 eggs, beaten
12 slices French bread, cut in
    sections and toasted

¼ tsp. red pepper
¼ tsp. white pepper
¼ tsp. basil
¼ tsp. oregano
¼ tsp. thyme
½ tsp. onion powder
1 Tbsp. parsley, chopped fine
1 tsp. salt
¼ tsp. black pepper
1 c. all-purpose flour

Cut soft shell crabs in halves. In a bowl, combine seasonings; mix well. In a large bowl, combine ½ seasoning mix with the flour. Pour mixture in a flat soup plate. In a separate bowl, combine well beaten eggs with remaining seasoning mix. Dredge crabs into the seasoned flour, then into eggs. Repeat this procedure twice; shake off excess. Retain egg mixture. In a large sauce-pan, melt 1 stick margarine at 350° until moisture is removed. Arrange crabs carefully. Saute crabs on each side until light brown. Remove from pan and place on a hot plate to keep warm; retain drippings. Add onion powder, parsley and brandy; simmer for 10 minutes.

While this is in process, combine egg mixture and sour cream to-gether. Reduce the heat to 200°. Combine this with the brandy mixture. Blend well. Do not allow to boil. Add pecans; mix well. Add crabs; bring to simmer. In a separate saucepan, melt ¼ stick margarine at 250°. Add green tomatoes and saute for 3 minutes. Place tomatoes on the grilled toasted bread. Arrange crab mixture over bread and tomato rounds. Serve. Serves 12.

MUSHROOMS WITH CRABMEAT STUFFING ROYAL STREET

2 doz. large mushrooms
1 lb. crabmeat
½ tsp. dry mustard
½ stick margarine
¼ c. celery, chopped
1 Tbsp. pimentos, chopped
1 c. sour cream
½ c. mayonnaise
¼ c. white roux

1 c. hot milk
Juice of 1 lemon
½ c. Italian cheese or like
½ tsp. onion powder
¼ tsp. garlic powder
⅛ tsp. red pepper
⅛ tsp. white pepper
1 tsp. Creole mustard

Separate mushroom caps from the stems. Chop the stems fine. Place mushroom caps in a slightly oiled casserole dish. In a saucepan, melt ¼ stick margarine at 250°. Add vegetables, including mushroom stems, and saute until soft. Remove from heat. In a separate saucepan, melt remaining margarine at 250°. Add seasonings and crabmeat. Saute for 3 minutes. Remove from heat and set aside. In a large bowl, blend together mayonnaise, sour cream, Italian cheese, and lemon. Mix well; blend in crabmeat. Blend in remaining ingredients. Fill each mushroom cap. In a saucepan, add milk and heat at 175°. Blend in roux and remaining mixture. Pour generously over mushrooms. Bake at 300° for 15 minutes. Serves 6.

CRAB, SHRIMP AND SMOKED HAM JAMBALAYA

½ lb. smoked ham, chopped
1 lb. crabmeat
½ lb. shrimp, peeled and
   deveined
1 c. onions, chopped
1 c. celery, chopped
¾ c. green peppers, chopped
1 tsp. garlic flakes
½ c. tomato sauce
1 c. green tomatoes, peeled and
   chopped

2 c. cream of mushroom soup
1½ c. uncooked rice
2 bay leaves
¼ stick margarine
¼ tsp. sage
¼ tsp. black pepper
1 tsp. thyme leaves
1 tsp. white pepper
1 tsp. salt
1 tsp. red pepper

In a small bowl, combine seasonings and blend well. Set aside. In a saucepan, melt margarine at 400°. Add ham and saute until light brown. Add shrimp; continue to saute until pink. Reduce the heat to 200°. Add crabmeat and saute for an additional 3 minutes. Stir in seasoning mix. Add ½ cup celery, onions, green peppers, and garlic. Continue to saute until vegetables are soft. Stir mixture frequently; do not allow to stick. Raise the temperature to 300°. Stir in tomato sauce and remaining onions, celery, green peppers, and tomatoes. Remove from heat. Blend in cream of mushroom soup and uncooked rice. In a lightly oiled casserole dish, pour in mixture. Bake at 300° until rice is tender. Serves 6.

CREOLE CRAB SPREAD CONTI

8 oz. crabmeat
4 slivers mashed anchovies
3 hard-boiled eggs, chopped
    fine
1 c. mayonnaise
2 Tbsp. parsley leaves, chopped

½ tsp. hot sauce
¼ tsp. dry mustard
¼ stick margarine
4 slices Italian or Greek bread
Salt to taste

In a saucepan, melt margarine at 250°. Add crabmeat and saute for 5 minutes. Remove from heat. In a bowl, blend together all ingredients thoroughly. Toast 4 slices of Greek or Italian bread; arrange in shallow baking pan. Cover with spread. Warm and serve. Do not melt. Serves 6.

CREOLE CREAM OF CRAB STEW CAMP STREET

2 lb. crabmeat
2 chicken bouillon cubes
1½ c. hot water
½ c. onion, chopped
¼ c. celery, chopped
2 c. light brown roux
1 pt. milk
3 Tbsp. parsley, chopped

¼ tsp. garlic powder
¼ tsp. onion powder
⅛ tsp. oregano
⅛ tsp. white pepper
⅛ tsp. black pepper
½ stick margarine
1 c. cooked rice

Dissolve 2 bouillon cubes in 1½ cups hot water. Set aside. In a saucepan, melt ¼ stick margarine at 250°. Add vegetables and saute until soft. Remove from heat and set aside. In a separate saucepan, melt remaining margarine at 300°. Add crabmeat and saute for 3 minutes. Remove from heat. Return vegetable mixture to the heat and raise temperature to 200°. Add bouillon. Blend in roux slowly. Add seasonings. Raise temperature to 300°. Keep this mixture moving at a fast simmer. Add milk and allow dish to simmer until reaching a desired thickness of a heavy cream. Add 1 cup cooked rice; blend well. Remove from heat and serve. Serves 6.

Another way to serve this dish: Lightly oil a casserole dish. Cover bottom with a layer of bread or cracker crumbs. Pour in mixture. Sprinkle top with a mixture of bread crumbs and Italian cheese. Bake at 300° until light brown.

CRABMEAT OYSTER BIENVILLE LOAF

½ lb. crabmeat
1 doz. oysters (retain liquid)
1 can clam or oyster chowder
½ c. uncooked bacon, chopped
½ c. smoked sausage, chopped
    fine
1 c. onions, chopped
1 c. celery, chopped
2 c. fresh mushrooms, sliced
½ c. green peppers, chopped

1 tsp. garlic, minced
½ c. all-purpose flour
¼ stick margarine
¼ c. sour cream
½ c. green onions, chopped fine
Bread crumbs
¼ tsp. white pepper
¼ tsp. red pepper
⅛ tsp. basil
⅛ tsp. oregano

In a small bowl, combine seasonings. In a large saucepan, fry bacon at 350° until crisp. Add sausage and saute at 300° for 3 minutes. Remove from heat and drain any excess oil. Return to the heat at 200°. Add onions, celery and green peppers. Saute for 5 minutes. Add mushrooms. Stir briskly at this point for 3 minutes. Add crabmeat and oysters, including liquid, and simmer for 3 minutes. Stir in chowder. Blend in garlic and seasonings. Bring to a brisk simmer for 5 minutes. Remove from heat. Blend together ¼ stick margarine at room temperature with flour. Blend into mixture. Return to heat at 200°. Simmer slowly for an additional 5 minutes. Remove from heat and stir in sour cream. Blend in green onions. If too much moisture remains, add bread crumbs to form into loaves. In a slightly oiled casserole dish, add mixture, forming 4 individual loaves. Bake at 300° until light brown.

Sauce:

1 c. cream

3 Tbsp. green onions

Heat 1 cup of mixture at 200°. Stir in 1 cup cream and 3 tablespoons green onions, whisking constantly until sauce is smooth. This should take no more than 5 minutes. Top with sauce and serve. Serves 6.

CRABMEAT AND MUSHROOMS IN WINE SAUCE RAMPART

1 lb. crabmeat
1 pack fresh mushrooms
½ stick margarine
3 Tbsp. flour
1 c. hot milk
½ c. white wine

½ tsp. dry mustard
¼ tsp. tarragon
¼ tsp. white pepper
½ tsp. red pepper
¼ tsp. oregano
1 c. bread crumbs

In a saucepan, melt ¼ stick margarine at 250°. Add crabmeat and saute for 3 minutes. Set aside. In a separate saucepan, melt remaining margarine. Add mushrooms and saute until light brown. Remove from heat and add to crabmeat. Allow drippings to remain. Return drippings to the heat at 250°. Stir in flour; allow to gel. Reduce heat to 200°. Add milk, wine, mustard, and seasonings. Blend well and simmer for 3 minutes. Blend in crabmeat and mushrooms. Simmer an additional 3 minutes. In a lightly oiled casserole dish, sprinkle bottom with ½ cup bread crumbs. Pour in mixture. Cover top with remaining bread crumbs. Bake, uncovered, at 350° for 30 minutes. Serves 6.

CRABMEAT EGGPLANT CASSEROLE

2 eggplants, peeled and
    chopped
1 lb. crabmeat
½ lb. small shrimp, peeled
1 c. bread crumbs
¼ c. sherry
1 pimento, minced
2 Tbsp. parsley, minced
2 Tbsp. green onions, minced
¼ c. onions, minced

¼ c. celery, chopped
¼ tsp. black pepper
⅛ tsp. thyme
¾ stick margarine
3 Tbsp. flour
2 c. hot milk
¼ tsp. red pepper
½ tsp. coarse ground black
    pepper

In a saucepan, melt ¼ stick margarine at 350°. Add eggplants and saute until they begin to soften. Add remaining vegetables and saute until soft; set aside. In a separate saucepan, melt ¼ stick margarine at 250°. Add seasonings; blend well for 1 minute. Add shrimp and crabmeat. Saute until shrimp are pink, about 3 minutes. Blend in vegetable mixture; mix well. Reduce heat to 175°. Fold in bread crumbs. In a separate saucepan, melt remaining margarine at 200°. Blend in flour until it gels. Add hot milk and sherry. Combine all ingredients. Pour into a lightly oiled casserole dish. Bake at 300° until surface is light brown. Serves 6.

CRAB AND SHRIMP CUTLETS ST. LOUIS

1 lb. cooked crabmeat
1 lb. small shrimp, peeled and
   deveined
1/2 c. green onions, chopped
1/4 c. celery, chopped
1/4 tsp. dry mustard
1 c. bread crumbs
3 eggs, beaten
1/4 stick margarine

3 Tbsp. parsley, chopped fine
1/4 tsp. white pepper
1/4 tsp. red pepper
1/4 tsp. coarse ground black
   pepper
1 tsp. salt
Milk to control moisture
1 c. corn oil

In a saucepan, melt 1/4 stick margarine at 200°. Add shrimp and crabmeat; saute for 2 minutes. Remove from pan and set aside, allowing to cool; retain drippings. Return to pan to heat. Add vegetables and saute for 2 minutes at 350°. Remove from heat and allow to cool. In a small bowl, combine seasonings. In a separate bowl, combine shrimp, crabmeat, vegetables, bread crumbs, and 1/2 seasoning mix. In a small bowl, combine beaten eggs and remaining seasoning mix. Form crabmeat shrimp mixture into patties. Add milk, if needed, to control thickness. Dip into egg mixture and fry in corn oil at 300° until light brown on both sides. Serve with rice. Serves 6.

CRABMEAT CANAL STREET

1 lb. crabmeat (optional: Alaskan
   King crabmeat)
3/4 c. cracker crumbs
1/2 c. green peppers, chopped
1 c. onions, chopped
1 c. celery, chopped
1 pack fresh mushrooms
3 cloves garlic, chopped fine
4 strips bacon
2 chicken bouillon cubes

2 c. hot water
1 tsp. coarse ground black
   pepper
1/2 tsp. celery salt
1/2 tsp. oregano
1/4 tsp. red pepper
3/4 c. parsley, chopped
1 Tbsp. Worcestershire sauce
1/4 stick margarine

In a saucepan, fry bacon until crisp at 350°. Remove from pan and crush into bits; allow drippings to remain. Add margarine, onions, green peppers, celery, mushrooms, and garlic. Saute for 3 minutes at 300°. Add seasonings, including Worcestershire sauce, and saute for 1 additional minute. Dissolve 2 chicken bouillon cubes in 2 cups hot water. Blend into vegetable mixture. Add crabmeat; blend in thoroughly. Add 1/2 cup cracker crumbs. In a lightly oiled casserole dish, pour in mixture. Sprinkle with remaining cracker crumbs. Bake at 350° for 25 minutes. Serves 6.

CRABMEAT COGNAC WITH MUSHROOMS DAUPHINE

1 lb. chunky crabmeat
½ lb. small shrimp, peeled and
   deveined
6 large mushrooms, sliced
1½ c. sour cream
3 green onions, chopped
1 Tbsp. celery, chopped
¼ tsp. dry tarragon
⅛ tsp. red pepper

⅛ tsp. white pepper
⅛ tsp. garlic powder
1 oz. cognac
½ stick margarine
1 c. milk
3 egg yolks, beaten
1 Tbsp. tomato sauce
⅛ c. white roux

In a saucepan, melt ¼ stick margarine at 250°. Add mushrooms and saute until edges begin to brown. Add green onions, celery and tomato paste. Continue to saute for 5 minutes. Reduce heat to 200°. Add sour cream; blend well. Bring to a low simmer for 3 minutes; remove from heat. In a separate saucepan, melt remaining margarine at 300°. Add seasonings; blend well for 1 minute. Reduce heat to 200°. Add crabmeat and shrimp; saute for 3 minutes. Combine the two mixtures and saute for an additional 5 minutes. In a separate saucepan, bring milk to a low simmer. Add white roux, beaten egg yolks and cognac; blend well. Immediately remove from heat. Pour crabmeat mixture over a mound of rice. Top with cognac sauce and serve. Serves 6.

CRABMEAT THERMIDOR CREOLE STYLE

2 lb. crabmeat
½ c. mushrooms, chopped
¼ stick margarine
¼ c. green onion, chopped
1 pimento, chopped
½ c. green peppers, chopped
2 large tomatoes, peeled and
   chopped

1 c. sour cream
2 Tbsp. parsley, chopped
8 crab shells or ramekins
¼ c. cheese of your choice
⅛ tsp. white pepper
⅛ tsp. red pepper
1 tsp. salt
Bread crumbs

In a saucepan, melt margarine at 250°. Add onion, tomatoes, green peppers, and crabmeat; saute for 5 minutes. Add mushrooms and saute for an additional 5 minutes. Reduce heat to 200°. Add sour cream and simmer for an additional 5 minutes. Add peppers, salt, parsley, pimento, and cheese. When cheese is melted, remove from heat. It may be necessary to add bread crumbs to stiffen this mixture. Fill crab shells or ramekins. Bake at 350° for 30 minutes or until brown. Serves 6.

CRABMEAT STUFFED TOMATOES IN CREOLE BUTTER SAUCE

1 lb. crabmeat
6 large firm tomatoes
1/4 stick margarine
1/4 c. parsley, chopped
Juice of 1 lemon
1/3 c. grated cheese

1/4 c. seasoned bread crumbs
1/8 tsp. white pepper
1/8 tsp. red pepper
1/8 tsp. basil
1 tsp. salt

Hollow tomatoes to form a bowl; set aside. Chop tomato pulp coarsely. In a saucepan, melt margarine at 250°. Add parsley, tomato pulp and crabmeat; saute for 3 minutes. Remove from heat and set aside. In a separate bowl, combine cheese, lemon juice, seasonings, and bread crumbs. Blend into crabmeat mixture. Arrange tomatoes in a slightly oiled casserole dish. Stuff and bake at 375° for 20 minutes.

Sauce:

1/2 stick margarine
Juice of 1 lemon
3 Tbsp. flour
1/8 tsp. white pepper

1/8 tsp. red pepper
1/8 tsp. basil
1/8 tsp. dry mustard
1 c. hot milk

In a saucepan, melt margarine at 200°. Blend in flour until it gels. Add lemon juice; blend in 1 cup hot milk. Simmer for 5 minutes. Sprinkle in seasonings. Remove from heat, whisking thoroughly. Allow to cool and pour over tomatoes. Serves 6.

CRABMEAT ARTICHOKE CASSEROLE FRERET

10/9/94

1 lb. artichoke hearts
1 lb. crabmeat
1 c. Parmesan cheese
1/4 stick margarine
3 Tbsp. flour
1 1/2 c. hot milk

not too much roux
Add onions

1/2 tsp. white pepper
1/8 tsp. dry mustard
1 tsp. Worcestershire sauce
4 hard cooked eggs, chopped
   fine

In a saucepan, melt margarine at 250°. Slowly add flour until it gels. Raise temperature to 400° and toast flour to a light brown. Remove from heat and allow to cool. Return to the heat at 200°. Add hot milk; blend well. Bring sauce to a low simmer. Add seasonings and Worcestershire sauce, blending well. Add eggs, artichoke hearts, 1/2 cup Parmesan cheese, and crabmeat. Mix well. In a lightly oiled casserole dish; pour in mixture. Sprinkle top with remaining Parmesan cheese. Bake at 350° for 30 minutes. Serve. Serves 6.

CRAWFISH ETOUFFE'S LaPLACE

2 lb. crawfish, peeled and deveined
1/4 c. green pepper, finely chopped
1/2 c. onions, finely chopped
1/2 c. celery, finely chopped
1 c. green onions, finely chopped
1 clove garlic, finely chopped
1 tsp. Worcestershire sauce
1 1/2 sticks margarine
3/4 c. all-purpose flour
4 c. cooked rice
1/2 c. shrimp, finely chopped
2 tsp. salt
Hot water
1 tsp. red ground pepper
1/2 tsp. white pepper
1/2 tsp. coarse ground black pepper
1 tsp. sweet basil
1/2 tsp. thyme

In a small bowl, thoroughly combine seasonings; set aside. In a separate bowl, combine onions, celery, garlic, Worcestershire sauce, and green pepper. In a large saucepan, melt 1/2 stick margarine at 450°. Do not allow to burn. Add flour slowly; stir until smooth and roux becomes dark red brown. Remove from heat and stir in vegetables except green onions and 1 teaspoon of seasoning mix. Continue to stir until mixture cools.

In a separate saucepan, heat 1/2 cup water to 300°. Add shrimp and saute for 3 minutes. Slowly add roux and stir continuously for 3 minutes. Remove from heat and set aside. In a large saucepan, melt 1 stick margarine at 300°. Add green onions and crawfish; saute until pink. Add remaining seasoning. Saute for 5 to 7 minutes. Remove from pan. Set aside and allow to cool. Return crawfish to the heat at 250°. Add water barely enough to cover. Add remaining ingredients; blend well. Simmer for 30 to 40 minutes, until dish is thick. At this point, you can either blend in your rice Cajun style of serve over rice. Serves 5.

CRAWFISH MIRLITON PIE

2 lb. crawfish, peeled
2 sticks margarine
2 c. all-purpose flour
3 mirlitons or squash

½ green peppers, chopped fine
½ c. onions, chopped fine
¼ c. celery, chopped fine

Seasonings:

½ tsp. bay leaf
¼ tsp. thyme
¼ tsp. basil
1 tsp. salt
2 tsp. paprika
½ tsp. white pepper
½ tsp. red ground pepper
½ tsp. onion powder
½ tsp. dry mustard
½ tsp. garlic flakes
½ gumbo file powder (optional)

¾ c. green onions, chopped fine
1 tsp. garlic salt
1 c. bread crumbs
½ c. hot milk
1 egg
2 c. corn oil
2 c. Bisquick
¼ c. sugar

In a saucepan, boil the mirlitons until tender. Cool, peel and cut into chunks. In a large saucepan, melt 1 stick margarine at 400° until light smoke occurs. Add 1 cup flour slowly, stirring continuously, until flour becomes dark red brown. Remove from heat and add green peppers, celery and onions. Continue stirring until mixture cools; set aside. In a separate saucepan, heat cream at 300° until it arrives at a quick simmer. Add roux mixture slowly, whisking constantly. Remove from heat and set aside.

In a small bowl, combine seasonings and set aside. In a large skillet, melt 1 stick margarine at 400°. Add green onions and garlic. Add crawfish and 1 teaspoon seasoning mix; saute for 4 minutes. Reduce heat to 200° and add cream mixture; simmer slowly. In a separate bowl, add ½ cup flour. Blend in bread crumbs and 1 teaspoon seasoning mix. In a separate bowl, combine milk and eggs; blend well. In a large saucepan, heat 2 cups corn oil at 400°. Dip mirlitons into egg mix, then into the flour mixture. Repeat this action twice and shake off excess. Fry until golden brown. In a separate bowl, mix 2 cups Bisquick and sugar. Roll into a crust. Spread half the dough on the bottom of baking dish; cut the remaining dough into strips. Arrange mirlitons, cover with sauce and top with strips of dough. Bake at 300° until crust is brown. Serves 6.

CRAWFISH PIE LA CROSS

2 lb. crawfish, peeled
2 cans cream of mushroom soup
1 tsp. sweet paprika
½ tsp. white pepper
¼ tsp. onion powder
¼ tsp. garlic powder
¼ tsp. dry mustard
¼ tsp. ground red pepper
¼ tsp. ground black pepper

⅛ tsp. dry thyme
⅛ tsp. sweet basil
½ stick margarine
½ c. onions, chopped
¼ c. green pepper, chopped
3 cloves garlic, chopped
¼ c. parsley, chopped
1 can dairy case biscuits
½ c. dry white wine

In a bowl, combine seasoning; set aside. In a saucepan, melt margarine at 350°. Add crawfish and saute until pink, about 3 minutes. Remove crawfish from the pan; set aside. Allow drippings to remain. Add vegetables and ½ seasoning mix; saute until soft, about 2 minutes. Reduce the heat to 200°. Return crawfish. Add soup and simmer for 15 minutes. Add wine; blend well. Simmer for 3 minutes. Pour mixture into 2 pie pans. Separate the biscuit dough into wafers. Sprinkle the top of crawfish mix with ¼ seasoning mix. Arrange biscuit wafers in overlapping layers. Sprinkle top with remaining seasoning mix. Bake at 325° until golden brown. Serves 6.

CRAWFISH STUFFED TOMATOES LaPLACE

2 lb. crawfish, peeled and
  deveined
6 large Creole tomatoes
¼ stick margarine
3 hard-boiled eggs, chopped
1½ c. yogurt
Juice of 1 lemon

¼ c. celery, finely chopped
3 Tbsp. onion, finely chopped
¼ c. salad olives, finely chopped
¼ tsp. ground red pepper
¼ tsp. white pepper
¼ tsp. dry sweet basil

Hollow tomatoes and chop pulp fine; set aside. In a bowl, combine seasonings and set aside. In a saucepan, melt margarine at 300°. Add crawfish and saute for 3 minutes. Add ½ seasoning mix and vegetables, including tomato pulp. Saute for an additional minute. Remove from heat. Pour into a large bowl and allow to cool. Blend in remaining ingredients except remaining seasoning; mix well. Stuff tomatoes; sprinkle on remaining seasoning mix. Chill and serve. Serves 6.

LIGHT STEWED CRAWFISH

2 lb. crawfish, peeled
½ stick margarine
¼ c. onions, chopped
3 cloves garlic, chopped
¼ c. green pepper, chopped
1 Tbsp. green onion, chopped
2 Tbsp. Worcestershire sauce

1 Tbsp. paprika
¼ tsp. white pepper
¼ tsp. ground red pepper
¼ tsp. thyme
¼ tsp. oregano
¼ tsp. sweet basil
3 Tbsp. all-purpose flour

In a saucepan, melt ¼ stick of margarine at 400°. Add crawfish and saute until deep pink. Remove crawfish from pan and set aside. Allow drippings to remain. In a bowl, combine seasonings and set aside. In a separate saucepan, add remaining margarine and melt at 400°. Add seasoning mix, Worcestershire sauce and vegetables; saute for 5 minutes or until vegetables are light brown. Blend in flour; saute until brown. Add crawfish drippings. Shake the pan continuously. Return crawfish and add 3 cups water. Bring to a simmer for 45 minutes. Serve over rice. Serves 4.

This dish can be used as a sauce for baking fish.

CRAWFISH SAUCE PIQUANT

2 lb. large crawfish or Florida
   crawfish (retain heads for
   stock)
4 c. cooked rice
½ stick margarine
2 c. onions, chopped
1½ bell peppers, chopped
1 c. celery, chopped
3 c. plump ripe tomatoes,
   peeled
1 c. tomato sauce

2 bay leaves
3 Tbsp. jalapeno peppers,
   chopped
2 tsp. ground red pepper
1 tsp. white pepper
1 tsp. black pepper
1 Tbsp. garlic, chopped fine
2 Tbsp. sugar
2½ c. seafood stock
1 tsp. salt
2 Tbsp. crab boil

In a large saucepan, add 3 cups hot water, crawfish heads and 2 tablespoons crab boil. Bring to a rapid boil for 4 minutes. Remove from heat; strain and discard heads. Retain liquid for stock. In a large saucepan, melt margarine at 400°. Add onions, bell peppers and celery. Saute for 2 minutes, stirring frequently. Add tomatoes, tomato sauce, jalapenos, bay leaves, peppers, and garlic; stir well. Continue to saute for 4 minutes. Reduce heat to 300°. Add stock; bring to a rapid simmer. Add sugar and salt and continue to simmer for 15 minutes. Add crawfish and cook for an additional 5 minutes. Stir well and remove from heat. Cover and set aside for 10 minutes. At this point, you may choose to blend the rice directly into the sauce or serve over mounds of rice. Serves 8.

CRAWFISH CASSEROLE IN A BISCUIT CRUST

2 lb. crawfish, peeled and
   deveined
1 pack dairy case biscuits
½ c. seasoned bread crumbs
1 c. celery, chopped
¼ c. bell peppers, chopped
1 c. onions, chopped
3 cloves garlic, chopped
¼ c. green onions, chopped
½ stick margarine

1 can cream of mushroom soup
½ tsp. ground red pepper
½ tsp. coarse ground black
   pepper
1 tsp. salt
¼ tsp. thyme
¼ tsp. dry rosemary leaves
¼ tsp. oregano

In a bowl, mix together seasonings; set aside. In a large saucepan, melt margarine at 400°. Add crawfish and saute for 3 minutes. Remove crawfish from pan and set aside; allow drippings to remain. Return pan to the heat at 300° and add vegetables and ½ seasoning mix. Saute until soft. Reduce heat to 250°. Return crawfish to the pan. Add soup, blending well. Remove from heat. Add bread crumbs and stir well. In a lightly oiled casserole dish, pour in mixture. Divide biscuits into wafers and arrange over the sauce. Sprinkle the remaining seasoning mix over the top. Bake at 350° for 30 minutes or until golden brown. Serves 6.

CRAWFISH COURTBOUILLON

2 lb. crawfish, peeled and deveined	2 c. hot water
½ c. dry white wine	½ tsp. thyme
1 large onion, chopped	2 bay leaves
¼ c. mushrooms, chopped	½ tsp. salt
	2 egg yolks

In a large saucepan, add 2 cups water and bring to a boil. Add crawfish, onion, wine, and seasonings except paprika. Simmer for 5 minutes. Remove from heat. Drain and separate courtbouillon from crawfish. In a saucepan, melt 2 tablespoons margarine at 300°. Add mushrooms and saute for 4 minutes. Remove from heat and set aside.

Sauce:

½ stick margarine	1 can dairy case biscuits
2 Tbsp. all-purpose flour	¼ tsp. white pepper
Juice from ½ lemon	¼ tsp. red pepper
3 Tbsp. bread crumbs	2 Tbsp. parsley, chopped
Ramekins	1 tsp. paprika

Return the pan used for the courtbouillon to the heat at 300°. Add ¼ cup courtbouillon. Stir in flour and cook until it gels. Whisk in the remaining bouillon. Simmer until sauce is reduced to 1 cup. Remove from heat and allow to cool. Blend in eggs. Return sauce to heat at 200°. Do not allow to boil or eggs will curdle. Whisk in remaining margarine, lemon juice and mushrooms. Add crawfish and onions; saute for 2 minutes. Add parsley and bread crumbs. Spoon mixture into ramekins. Cover with biscuit wafers. Sprinkle top with paprika and bake for 5 minutes at 350° or until biscuits brown. Serves 6.

CREOLE CRAWFISH CAKES

2 lb. crawfish, peeled, deveined and chopped	¼ tsp. ground red pepper
	¼ tsp. white pepper
¼ c. green onions, finely chopped	⅛ tsp. thyme
	⅛ tsp. ground bay leaf powder
¼ stick margarine	¼ tsp. Louisiana hot sauce
½ c. onions, finely chopped	5 potatoes, boiled
¼ c. parsley, finely chopped	1 c. all-purpose flour

Wash potatoes well; allow skin to remain and dice. Place in a large pan and boil until ¾ done. Remove from heat. Drain and set aside. In a bowl, combine seasonings. In a saucepan, melt margarine at 400°. Add crawfish and ½ seasoning mix; blend well. Saute for 3 minutes. Add remaining ingredients except the seasoning mix and flour. Mix thoroughly and saute for 2 minutes. Remove from heat. Set aside and allow to cool. Add potatoes and mash into the mixture. Blend well and shape into patties. In a separate bowl, combine flour and remaining seasoning mix. Dredge patties into the flour mixture and fry until golden brown. Serves 6.

STUFFED CRAWFISH MARKSVILLE

2 lb. crawfish, peeled and deveined (reserve heads)	1 can cream of mushroom soup
½ c. onions, finely chopped	1 c. seasoned bread crumbs
½ stick margarine	¼ tsp. ground red pepper
¼ c. bell pepper, finely chopped	¼ tsp. black pepper
¼ c. celery, finely chopped	½ tsp. dry thyme
3 cloves garlic, finely chopped	¼ tsp. rosemary
1 Tbsp. paprika	⅛ tsp. oregano
3 eggs, beaten	1 Tbsp. crawfish boil
	4 c. hot water

In a saucepan, add 4 cups hot water and 1 tablespoon crawfish boil. Boil crawfish heads for 5 minutes at 400°. Strain and reserve stock. Allow to cool and clean heads, thoroughly discarding core. In a small bowl, combine seasonings thoroughly except paprika. Set aside. In a saucepan, melt margarine at 350°. Add crawfish and ½ seasoning mix except paprika. Saute for 4 minutes. Remove the crawfish from the heat, allowing drippings to remain. Return pan to the heat. Add vegetables and saute until light brown. Reduce heat to 200°. Add eggs and soup; fold in bread crumbs. If necessary to control dryness, add crawfish stock. Remove from heat.

If crawfish heads are available, stuff with ¾ of the mixture. Add crawfish stock to remaining ¼ mix, blending well. Arrange heads in a lightly oiled casserole dish. Cover with stock mixture and bake at 300° for 20 minutes. Otherwise, pour mixture into a lightly oiled casserole dish. Sprinkle with remaining seasoning mix. Cover with Italian cheese or bread crumbs. Sprinkle top with paprika. Bake at 350° until light brown. Serves 6.

This stuffing can be used with just about any large fish.

CRAWFISH SUPREME NAPOLEON

2 lb. crawfish, peeled and
   deveined
2 packs frozen spinach, cooked
½ stick margarine
¼ c. flour
4 egg yolks, beaten
½ c. onions, finely chopped
1 can mushrooms
3 Tbsp. parsley, chopped

½ c. Parmesan cheese
¼ tsp. white pepper
¼ tsp. ground red pepper
¼ tsp. Louisiana hot sauce
¼ tsp. oregano
¼ tsp. thyme
¼ tsp. bay leaf
1 c. sour cream
1 c. hot water

In a large saucepan, melt ¼ stick margarine at 400°. Add crawfish and saute for 5 minutes. Remove crawfish from pan and set aside. Return saucepan to the heat and melt remaining margarine at 300°. Add vegetables, except spinach, and saute until soft. Add flour slowly until it gels with the vegetables. Add 1 cup hot water and bring to a simmer. Add seasonings and hot sauce, blending well. Reduce heat to 200°. Add sour cream; blend well for 1 minute. Remove from heat and slowly blend in egg yolks. Return sauce to the heat at 200° and simmer until sauce thickens. Add Parmesan cheese and crawfish and blend well for 1 minute. In a lightly oiled casserole dish, pour in ¼ mixture. Cover with ½ of well drained spinach. Cover with ½ of remaining mixture. Add rest of spinach. Cover with remaining mixture. Bake at 350° for 20 minutes. Serves 6.

CRAWFISH COCKTAIL DUPRE

1 lb. large crawfish, peeled and
   deveined
¼ stick margarine
Juice of 1 lemon
¼ tsp. white pepper

¼ tsp. ground red pepper
¼ tsp. oregano
¼ tsp. thyme
¼ tsp. sweet basil

In a saucepan, melt margarine at 400°. Add seasonings and lemon juice. Blend well for 2 minutes. Add crawfish and saute for 4 minutes. Remove from heat and drain off excess liquid. Chill.

Sauce:

¾ c. chili sauce
¼ c. finely chopped celery
1 Tbsp. lemon juice

1 Tbsp. horseradish
½ tsp. salt
¼ tsp. Louisiana hot sauce

In a bowl, combine sauce ingredients and whisk together well. Chill. Arrange crawfish in a pinwheel shape over a bed of shredded lettuce. Top with the sauce and squeeze on the lemon juice. Serves 4.

CRAWFISH JAMBALAYA GRAND ISLE

2 lb. crawfish, peeled and
   deveined
1 c. smoked ham, chopped
1 c. smoked sausage, chopped
1½ c. celery, chopped
1½ c. onions, chopped
1½ c. bell peppers, chopped
4 cloves garlic, chopped
½ stick margarine

½ tsp. thyme
½ tsp. ground cumin
½ tsp. white pepper
½ tsp. red pepper
1 tsp. dry mustard
½ tsp. bay leaf
¼ tsp. oregano
4 beef bouillon cubes
2 c. uncooked rice
4 c. hot water

In a bowl, combine seasonings and mix well. Set aside. In a large saucepan, melt ¼ stick margarine at 400°. Add ham and sausage; saute for 3 minutes. Add ½ seasoning mix and saute for 2 minutes. Add crawfish and saute for 2 minutes. Remove ham, sausage and crawfish from the pan and set aside. Return drippings to 300° heat. Add remaining margarine. Add vegetables and saute until light brown.

While this is in progress, in a separate saucepan, dissolve 4 bouillon cubes in 4 cups hot water and bring to a boil. Stir in rice and allow to cook for 7 minutes, stirring frequently. Combine all ingredients together and bring to a brisk simmer for 5 minutes, stirring frequently. Reduce the heat to 250°; continue at a low simmer until rice is cooked and most of the moisture has been absorbed. Serves 8.

DEVILED CRAB HOUMA

2 lb. crabmeat
¼ c. chopped onion
¼ stick margarine
3 Tbsp. flour
1 c. hot milk
Juice of 1 lemon
1½ tsp. dry mustard

1 Tbsp. Worcestershire sauce
1 tsp. salt
½ tsp. coarse ground pepper
¼ tsp. ground red pepper
2 beaten eggs
1 Tbsp. parsley
½ c. bread crumbs

In a saucepan, melt margarine at 400°. Add onion and saute until soft. Add flour; blend well until it gels. Reduce the heat to 250° and slowly add milk, blending well. Add seasonings and lemon juice; stir until sauce thickens. In a separate bowl, combine hot sauce and egg; blend well. Add to sauce, stirring constantly. Add crabmeat and saute for 5 minutes. Place in a slightly oiled baking dish. Top with bread crumbs and garnish with parsley. Bake at 350° for 15 minutes. Serves 6.

CREOLE CRAB CASSEROLE BUNKIE

2 lb. crabmeat
1½ c. milk
¼ c. grated cheese
1 c. mayonnaise
¼ stick margarine
½ tsp. ground red pepper

¼ tsp. white pepper
1 tsp. salt
1½ c. bread crumbs
¼ tsp. oregano
¼ tsp. basil

In a saucepan, melt margarine at 400°. Add crabmeat and saute for 3 minutes. Remove from heat and allow to cool. In a large bowl, add crabmeat, mayonnaise, milk, and seasonings. Blend thoroughly. Place in a slightly oiled casserole dish; add ½ crab mixture, then ¼ bread crumbs. Top with cheese. Add remaining crab mixture and cover with remaining bread crumbs. Bake for 35 minutes at 300°.

CRAB CAKES ROSELAND IN CREAM SAUCE

2 lb. crabmeat
1 stick margarine
½ c. bell peppers, chopped fine
½ c. onions, chopped fine
3 eggs, beaten

1½ tsp. prepared mustard
½ tsp. ground red pepper
1 tsp. coarse ground black
   pepper
2 Tbsp. mayonnaise
1½ c. crackers, crushed fine

In a saucepan, melt margarine at 400°. Add onions and bell peppers; saute until soft. Add crabmeat and seasonings; saute for 3 minutes. Remove from heat and allow to cool. Combine all ingredients and form into cakes. Place in a slightly oiled casserole dish and bake for 10 minutes. Remove from heat and set aside.

Sauce:

4 Tbsp. margarine
2 Tbsp. all-purpose flour
2 eggs, beaten

1 c. cream
1 tsp. salt
1 tsp. white pepper

In a saucepan, melt margarine at 300°. Add flour; blend well until it gels. In a separate bowl, combine milk, seasonings and eggs. Slowly add to the flour mixture and saute until sauce thickens. Pour over crab cakes and bake for an additional 10 minutes at 250°. Serves 6.

NEW ORLEANS CRAWFISH CHOWDER OR LOBSTER QUARTERS

1½ lb. crawfish, peeled and
   deveined
1 c. onions, chopped
½ c. celery, chopped
½ c. bell pepper, chopped
2 large Idaho potatoes, diced
½ lb. bacon, chopped
3 c. hot milk

2 Tbsp. all-purpose flour
½ tsp. red ground pepper
½ tsp. coarse ground pepper
¼ tsp. oregano
¼ tsp. basil
1 bay leaf
1 tsp. crab boil
1 c. hot water

In a saucepan, add 1 cup hot water, crawfish and 1 tablespoon crab boil. Boil for 5 minutes. Remove from heat and drain. Place the water and crawfish in separate bowls; set aside. In a separate saucepan, fry the bacon at 400° until light brown. Add celery and onions and saute until golden brown. Add bell pepper, potatoes, seasonings, and crawfish water. Bring to a boil for 10 minutes. Remove from heat and set aside. In a separate bowl, combine ½ cup milk and 2 tablespoons flour; stir until smooth. Blend into chowder and return to the heat at 250°. Add the remaining milk and crawfish. Simmer for 10 minutes or until done. Serves 6.

LOBSTER IN SWEET WHITE WINE ABBEVILLE

1 lb. lobster claw meat
1 c. sour cream
1 c. sweet white wine
½ c. white onions, chopped fine
¼ stick margarine

1 pack whole small mushrooms
2 Tbsp. all-purpose flour
½ tsp. salt
½ tsp. red ground pepper
2 c. cooked rice

In a saucepan, melt margarine at 400°. Add onions and lobster meat; saute until lobster is pink. Add mushrooms and saute for 5 minutes. Add the flour, pepper and salt; blend well. Reduce heat to 200°. Stir in sour cream slowly and simmer for 10 minutes. Add the wine and simmer for 3 minutes. Make an oblong boat with the rice in a serving dish. Fill with lobster mixture. Serve. Serves 6.

CRAWFISH BORDELAISE ROYAL STREET

1½ lb. crawfish, peeled and
   deveined
3 Tbsp. olive oil
2 Tbsp. green onions, chopped
   fine
7 peppercorns
¼ stick margarine
¼ c. leeks
¼ c. carrots
¼ c. onions
½ c. celery

2½ Tbsp. tomato sauce
2 Tbsp. potato starch
2 c. red burgundy wine
½ tsp. garlic powder
1 bay leaf
2 chicken bouillon cubes
1 c. hot water
3 tsp. red currant jelly
2 Tbsp. crawfish fat
1 truffle, chopped fine

Dissolve 1 chicken bouillon cube in 1 cup hot water; set aside. In a saucepan, heat olive oil at 250°. Add green onions and saute until soft. Add wine, garlic, peppercorns, and bay leaf; simmer for 15 minutes. Set aside. In a separate saucepan, melt the margarine at 350°. Add the vegetables and saute until golden brown. Slowly blend in the red currant jelly, tomato paste and potato starch. Add bouillon, crawfish fat and wine mixture. Simmer until it becomes a thick brown sauce. Remove from the heat. Strain the sauce. Add the truffles and crawfish. Continue to simmer for 10 minutes. Serve with mounds of steaming rice. Serves 6.

CRAWFISH OR SHRIMP MARINATE LaPLACE

5 lb. crawfish, peeled and
   deveined
1 box Creole crab boil
1 large onion, chopped
2 c. Gardineira

2 c. wine vinegar
½ stick margarine
1 qt. water
1 lemon, cut into quarters

In a large pot, bring 2 quarts of water to a boil. Add crab boil and boil for 20 minutes. Add crawfish and lemon; boil until crawfish are a deep pink. Remove from heat and drain at once. In a large bowl, add the crawfish and remaining ingredients. Blend well and refrigerate overnight. Drain and serve on a bed of shredded lettuce. Serves 6.

LOBSTER OR CRAWFISH IN IRISH CHANNEL POTATO SALAD

2 cans Irish potatoes (retain
    water)
1/2 lb. crawfish, peeled and
    deveined
1/2 tsp. sugar
1/2 head lettuce, shredded
1/4 tsp. dry mustard

1/2 tsp. white pepper
1 1/2 c. hot water
1/2 tsp. salt
2 Tbsp. salad oil
1 Tbsp. Creole crab boil
Juice from 1 lemon

In a saucepan, bring 1 cup water and crab boil to a brisk boil. Add crawfish and boil for 5 minutes. Drain at once and set aside. In a saucepan, bring 1/2 cup of water to a simmer. Add potatoes, including water, and simmer for 5 minutes. Drain and place the potatoes, salt, pepper, mustard, salad oil, and sugar in a large bowl. Mix well. Add all but 6 crawfish. Mix well. In a salad bowl, make a bed with the shredded lettuce. Using an ice cream scoop, form mounds with the potato crawfish salad. Top with remaining crawfish, sprinkle with lemon juice and serve. Serves 6.

OYSTERS BIENVILLE CHARTER HOUSE

3 doz. small oysters (retain
    water)
1 stick margarine
3 c. hot cream
4 Tbsp. all-purpose flour
1/2 c. chopped parsley
1/2 c. onions, chopped fine
1/3 c. dry white wine
1 c. mushrooms
1/2 c. shrimp, cooked and
    chopped

6 egg yolks
1/2 tsp. thyme
1/2 c. grated Parmesan cheese
1/2 tsp. white pepper
1/2 tsp. ground red pepper
1/4 tsp. oregano
1/4 tsp. basil
8 pastry shells

In a large saucepan, melt the margarine at 450°. Add flour; stir until it gels. Reduce the heat to 250° and stir in the cream until it thickens. Add all the remaining ingredients except oysters and egg yolks. Stir until cheese is blended well. Remove from the heat and stir in eggs slowly until well blended. In a separate saucepan, bring the oyster water to a simmer. Add oysters and simmer until the edges curl. Remove from heat and separate the oysters from the water and reserve. Add the oysters and seasonings to the mixture. Cook for 5 minutes at 300°. If the sauce is too thick, add oyster water. Place 4 oysters in each pastry shell. Place the shells in a shallow baking pan. Fill the shells with sauce; bake at 400° until piping hot. Serve. Serves 8.

Notes

"The Cajuns are coming!
The Cajuns are coming!"

Chicken on the Run

A WORD FROM THE AUTHOR:

Chicken On The Run is that dish I prepare when my darling little wife phones me at the last minute and says, "We are rendezvousing with friends this evening. I'm going to be terribly on the run, so please prepare one of your delicious chicken dishes."

Chicken, as we all know in its boneless fillet stage possesses an unlimited variety of faces. Heck Cajun cousin, it can even be fried.

You always want to fix too much chicken because tomorrow night you might just be on the run again. I guarantee you this, chicken is a leftover masterpiece.

I don't know which one of you is subject to steal a nice piece of fried chicken from the fridge or a ladle full of chicken gumbo on a cool comfortable night but if you don't, I sure will.

Chicken to me always seems to be running towards delicious.

3/4 pound of cooked crabmeat equal 1 1/2 cups. The cooked meat of 4 blue crabs equals 1 cup.

Never overcook or dry out crabmeat. When you buy fresh-packed crabmeat, pick over it again; it usually contains small pieces of shells.

You can tell a ripe avocado by squeezing it lightly. It will feel soft under its leathery skin. If only unripened ones are available, place them in a brown paper bag in a warm place for 2 or 3 days.

Always have eggs at room temperature before boiling. Cold eggs crack when put into boiling water. If you must add eggs to hot water, prick the rounded end with a pin. This will stop them from cracking.

Cook eggs for potato salad for six minutes; this will allow them to remain tender.

When you buy cabbage, avoid those which show separate leaves growing from the main stem below the head - such cabbages usually have a strong flavor and coarse texture.

Fresh asparagus continues to age and toughen after it has been cut, so the sooner you cook it after buying, the better.

CHICKEN ON THE RUN

CAJUN CHICKEN WITH RICE

8 large pieces boneless chicken,
    cut into chunks
2 c. uncooked rice
1/4 c. onions, chopped
1 (8 oz.) can tomatoes
1 1/2 qt. water
1/4 tsp. powdered bay leaf
1/4 tsp. white pepper

1/4 tsp. coarse ground black
    pepper
1/4 c. bell pepper, chopped
1 can mushrooms
1 small jar pimentos
1/4 tsp. saffron
1 c. corn oil
1/2 tsp. black pepper

In a large saucepan, heat the corn oil to 400° and fry chicken until light brown. Remove from heat and place the chicken on a paper towel. Drain off as much oil as possible from the saucepan. Do not scrape off the particles from the bottom of the pan. Return the saucepan to the heat at 250°. Add vegetables and saute for 2 minutes. Add tomatoes, including water, and blend well. Add remaining ingredients except rice and water. Cook briskly for 20 minutes. Add water and rice; continue to cook for 20 minutes or until rice is tender. Serves 8.

CHICKEN ETOUFFE'S ST. CHARLES

3 lb. boneless chicken
1 tsp. garlic powder
1 stick margarine
1/2 c. celery, chopped
1/2 c. onions, chopped
1/2 c. bell peppers, chopped
1 tsp. black pepper
1/2 c. green onion, finely
    chopped
3 c. rice, cooked 3/4
1/2 tsp. dry mustard

1/2 tsp. sweet paprika
1 tsp. garlic powder
1 tsp. coarse ground black
    pepper
1/4 tsp. white pepper
1/4 tsp. onion powder
1/4 tsp. ground red pepper
1/4 tsp. thyme
4 chicken bouillon cubes
4 c. water
2 c. brown roux

Cut chicken into generous chunks. In a saucepan, melt 1/4 stick margarine at room temperature. Rub chicken thoroughly with the margarine. In a bowl, combine seasonings and rub chicken thoroughly with 1/2 seasoning mix. In a separate saucepan, melt remaining margarine at 350°. Add chicken and saute on both sides until light brown. Remove chicken and set aside on a paper towel. Add vegetables and saute until soft. In a separate saucepan, dissolve bouillon in 4 cups hot water; bring to a simmer. Add the remaining seasoning, blending well. Add roux slowly, whisking continuously. Return chicken to mixture. Add rice; cook until moisture is absorbed and rice is tender. This should take about 25 minutes. Serve. Serves 8.

CHICKEN SEAFOOD JAMBALAYA BAYOU BOUDREAU

1 lb. shrimp, peeled and deveined
2 lb. chicken fryer parts
1 doz. oysters
¾ c. smoked ham, diced
¼ c. Italian or Polish sausage
1 large can tomatoes
¾ c. tomato sauce
2 c. uncooked rice
½ tsp. garlic powder
1 c. onions, chopped
1 c. celery, chopped
½ c. green onions, chopped
¾ c. bell peppers, chopped
1 tsp. salt
¼ tsp. white pepper
¼ tsp. red pepper
1 tsp. coarse ground black pepper
1 stick margarine
¼ tsp. thyme
2 bay leaves
1½ tsp. garlic, minced
2 chicken bouillon cubes
2 c. hot water

Dissolve chicken bouillon in 2 cups hot water; set aside. In a bowl, combine seasonings; set aside. In a saucepan, melt ¾ stick margarine. Add sausage and saute at 400° for 4 minutes; stir frequently. Reduce heat to 300°. Add onions, celery and bell peppers. Saute for an additional 4 minutes. Stir well. Add chicken and saute for 2 minutes. Reduce heat to 250° and add ½ seasoning mix. Add garlic and cook for an additional 3 minutes. Stir constantly; do not allow dish to stick. Add tomatoes and simmer for 5 minutes. Add tomato sauce and simmer for an additional 5 minutes. If dish becomes too thick, remove from heat.

In a separate saucepan, add ¼ stick margarine. Melt at 400°. Add shrimp and oysters and saute for 2 minutes. Remove from heat and allow to cool. Return to heat at 200° and blend in bouillon. Combine all ingredients, including rice and cook for 5 minutes. Remove from heat. Cover and set aside for 10 minutes or until rice is tender. Serve. Serves 8.

CHICKEN CREOLE CASSEROLE

3 lb. chicken parts
1 c. celery, chopped
½ c. onions, chopped
2 c. light brown roux
½ tsp. white pepper
½ tsp. black pepper
2 eggs, beaten
1 can cream of mushroom soup

1 c. bread crumbs
2 bay leaves
1 tsp. salt
1 stick margarine
2 chicken bouillon cubes
2 c. hot water

In a bowl, combine seasonings; set aside. In a saucepan, melt margarine at 350°. Rub chicken with ½ seasoning mix and saute until light brown. Remove chicken; set aside. Return drippings to the heat at 250°. Add vegetables and saute until soft. Slowly add roux and bring to a simmer for 1 minute. Dissolve 2 cubes bouillon in 2 cups hot water. Add bouillon and blend well. Add soup and continue to simmer for 3 minutes. Add remaining ingredients except eggs and remaining seasoning mix. Blend well and continue to simmer for an additional 3 minutes. Remove from heat, allow to cool and carefully blend in eggs. Fold in half the bread crumbs. In a lightly oiled casserole dish, arrange chicken pieces and cover with mixture. In a small bowl, combine the remaining seasoning mix with remaining bread crumbs. Sprinkle over dish. Bake at 350° until chicken is tender. Serve with mashed potatoes. Serves 8.

CHICKEN PIE VIEUX CARRE

3 lb. boneless chicken
2 c. brown roux
1 c. peas
1 c. small carrots
1 pack dairy case biscuits
¼ c. onions, chopped
¼ c. celery, chopped
¼ tsp. black pepper
¼ tsp. white pepper

¼ tsp. ground red pepper
½ tsp. oregano
½ tsp. thyme
¼ tsp. dry sweet basil
¼ tsp. margarine
1 heaping tsp. powdered chicken
  bouillon
2 c. hot water

Cut chicken into bite-size pieces. In a small bowl, combine seasonings; set aside. In a saucepan, melt margarine at 400°. Add ½ seasoning mix and saute for 1 minute. Add chicken and saute until light brown. Remove chicken and set aside. Reduce the heat to 300°. Add onions and celery and saute until soft. In a separate saucepan, add 2 cups hot water. Bring to a simmer and add bouillon. Add peas and carrots, simmering for 5 minutes. Add remaining seasoning mix and continue to simmer for 5 minutes. Add roux, blending well. Simmer for 15 minutes until sauce thickens. Add chicken and simmer for 10 minutes. In a lightly oiled casserole dish, pour in chicken mixture. Unroll biscuits and roll into a pie crust. Place on top of the mixture. Bake at 350° until biscuits are golden brown. Serves 8.

CHICKEN SPAGHETTI CASSEROLE ST. LOUIS

3 lb. boneless chicken
1 lb. Italian or Polish smoked
   sausage
1 stick margarine
2 cloves garlic, chopped
2 c. canned tomatoes
1 lb. spaghetti, ¾ cooked (retain
   liquid)
½ c. grated cheese
¼ c. bell pepper, chopped

¼ c. celery, chopped
¼ c. onions, chopped
¼ tsp. oregano
¼ tsp. coarse ground black
   pepper
¼ tsp. thyme
2 bay leaves
¼ tsp. white pepper
⅛ tsp. red pepper
3 chicken bouillon cubes

In a small bowl, combine seasonings; set aside. In a saucepan, melt ½ stick margarine at 400°. Add ½ seasoning mix and sausage and saute for 3 minutes. Add chicken and saute until light brown. Remove from pan; set aside. Allow drippings to remain. Add remaining margarine and reduce heat to 350°. Add vegetables and saute until soft. Add tomatoes and remaining seasonings; bring to a simmer. Add chicken bouillon and 2 cups of spaghetti liquid; simmer until dissolved. Add chicken and sausage; bring to a brisk simmer, about 350°. Continue at a brisk simmer for 20 minutes or until mixture thickens. Add spaghetti and blend well. Cook for 5 minutes. Remove from heat. Blend in grated cheese. Place mixture in a lightly oiled casserole dish. Cover and bake for 30 minutes at 350°. Serves 8.

CHICKEN IN CREAM OF GARLIC SAUCE

2 lb. chicken fryer
1½ tsp. garlic powder
½ tsp. onion powder
2 c. dark brown roux
¼ tsp. red pepper
¼ tsp. white pepper
½ tsp. oregano

4 Tbsp. parsley, chopped
Juice of 1 lemon
1 stick margarine
2 cubes chicken bouillon
2 c. hot water
½ c. dry white wine

In a small bowl, combine seasonings; set aside. In a saucepan, melt ¾ stick margarine at 350°. Add ½ seasoning mix and chicken; saute until light brown. Remove chicken from the pan and set aside. Dissolve chicken bouillon in 2 cups hot water. In a separate saucepan, melt remaining margarine at 450° until light smoke occurs. Add roux, whisking continuously until roux thickens. Remove from heat. Blend in parsley, lemon juice and remaining seasoning mix. Immediately blend in chicken bouillon or roux will continue to darken. Add chicken and wine. Simmer for 30 minutes until most of the moisture has evaporated. It should form a thick consistency. The recipe requires attention, because it will stick easily. Serves 6.

CHICKEN IN WINE SAUCE PLAQUEMINE

8 chicken breasts
1 stick margarine
1 can mushrooms
1 (6 oz.) can small onions
2 cubes chicken bouillon
2 c. hot water
1 c. white roux
1 c. white wine

1 oz. brandy
¼ tsp. white pepper
¼ tsp. black pepper
¼ tsp. red pepper
¼ tsp. oregano
¼ tsp. thyme
1 can cream of mushroom soup

In a small bowl, combine seasonings. Sprinkle ½ seasonings over breasts. In a saucepan, melt margarine at 350°. Add chicken breasts and saute until light brown. Raise the heat to 450°. Pour brandy over chicken. Light brandy and allow the alcohol to burn off. Remove chicken from the pan; set aside and allow drippings to remain. Add onions and mushrooms; saute at 300° until soft. Remove from heat and set aside.

In a separate saucepan, add 2 cups hot water and bring to a simmer at 300°. Add bouillon, stirring until it dissolves. Slowly whisk in roux. Add wine and cream of mushroom soup. Reduce heat to 250° and combine all ingredients, blending well. Cover and simmer for 30 minutes or until chicken is tender. Serve with mounds of steaming rice. Serves 8.

CHICKEN LIVERS IN MUSHROOMS DAUPHINE

1½ lb. drained chicken livers
¼ lb. uncooked bacon, chopped
    into bits
1 stick margarine
1 c. flour
¼ tsp. white pepper
¼ tsp. red pepper
¼ tsp. thyme

¼ tsp. oregano
¼ tsp. sweet basil
1 large can mushrooms
1 can cream of chicken soup
1 c. sour cream
2 Tbsp. parsley, chopped
¼ c. onions, chopped

In a bowl, combine seasonings; set aside. In a saucepan, add bacon bits and saute until brown. Remove from heat; drain well and crush. In a large bowl, combine ½ seasoning mix and bacon bits with flour. Dredge the livers in the flour mixture and coat livers thoroughly. Let excess flour remain on livers. In a saucepan, melt margarine at 350°. Add livers and saute until brown. Allow flour residue to remain in pan. Remove livers and set aside. Add onions, parsley and mushrooms; stir in thoroughly into flour residue. Saute until flour and vegetables are light brown. Reduce heat to 250°. Add chicken soup and bring to a simmer for 3 minutes. Add sour cream, livers and remaining seasoning. Continue to simmer for 10 minutes. Control thickness with hot water. Remove from heat and cover for 5 minutes. Serve over a bed of rice. Serves 6.

TURKEY ROUCHAMBEAU

8 slices toast
8 slices turkey (¼ inch thick)
8 slices ham
8 slices aged Swiss cheese
¼ stick margarine
2 Tbsp. flour
2 egg yolks, beaten
Juice of 1 lemon
1 Tbsp. parsley leaves, chopped

1 (6 oz.) can drained mushrooms
3 cubes chicken bouillon
1 c. hot water
¼ tsp. white pepper
⅛ tsp. red pepper
¼ tsp. sweet basil

Dissolve bouillon cubes in 1 cup hot water; set aside. In the bottom of an oiled casserole dish, arrange toast. On each slice of toast, place 1 slice each of ham, turkey and cheese. In a saucepan, melt margarine at 350°. Stir in flour until it gels. Do not allow to brown. Add chicken bouillon and bring to simmer. Add remaining ingredients, except eggs, and simmer for 30 minutes. Remove from heat and allow to cool. Blend in beaten egg yolks. Pour this mixture over top of casserole dish. Bake at 350° for 20 minutes. Serves 8.

BAKED CHICKEN STUFFED WITH
OYSTER AND RICE DRESSING

1 large baking hen
1 c. hot water
2 sticks margarine
½ c. green onions, chopped
½ c. celery, chopped
½ c. bell pepper, chopped
1 qt. oysters
Giblets from chicken
¼ c. parsley, chopped
3 c. cooked rice

⅛ tsp. red pepper
¼ tsp. black pepper
½ tsp. garlic powder
½ tsp. white pepper
½ tsp. onion powder
¼ tsp. ground cumin
¼ tsp. sweet paprika
1 piece cheesecloth
1 c. hot water
1 chicken bouillon cube

In a saucepan, add 1 cup hot water; bring to a simmer. Add giblets and simmer for 5 minutes. Remove from the heat; drain and chop. Set aside. In a bowl, combine seasonings; set aside. In a separate saucepan, melt 1 stick margarine at 200°. Add ½ seasoning mix and remove from heat. Allow to cool and rub chicken thoroughly with margarine mixture inside and out. Set extra margarine aside for later basting. Cover chicken with cheesecloth and allow cavity in back to be exposed. Place chicken in an oiled baking pan.

In a deep saucepan, melt 1 stick margarine at 300°. Add onions, parsley, celery, and bell peppers and saute until soft. Add giblets and oysters, continuing to saute. Add remaining seasonings. Add rice and blend well. Remove from heat and stuff the chicken. Sew the chicken cavity and bake at 300° until done. Place excess stuffing in a casserole dish. Dissolve 1 cube of chicken bouillon in 1 cup of hot water. Pour over casserole dish. Bake until moisture is absorbed. Serve with baked chicken. Serves 8.

CHICKEN IN SPANISH RICE DELACROIX

2 lb. boneless chicken
4 strips bacon
1½ c. uncooked rice
¼ lb. smoked sausage
¼ lb. smoked ham
4 chicken bouillon cubes
1 qt. hot water
1 c. uncooked rice

¼ tsp. red pepper
¼ tsp. white pepper
¼ tsp. dry mustard
¼ tsp. black pepper
¼ tsp. thyme
½ c. onions, chopped
2 cloves garlic, chopped
1 can peas and onions

In a saucepan, fry bacon until crisp. Remove and crush; set aside. Allow drippings to remain. Add pork and smoked ham. Saute in drippings until light brown. Remove and set aside. Allow drippings to remain. Add chicken, seasonings, onions, and garlic; saute until light brown. In a separate saucepan, add 1 quart hot water and bring to a boil. Add bouillon cubes and rice; cook until rice is ¾ done. Remove from heat. Pour a layer of rice into a lightly oiled casserole dish. Add a layer of chicken, a layer of pork and sausage. Add a layer of peas and onions; sprinkle with seasoning. Continue this process until all ingredients are used. Bake at 350° for 20 minutes or until chicken is tender. Serves 6.

CHICKEN LOAF IN CREAM SAUCE GROSSE TETE

4 lb. chicken, diced
1 can cream of chicken soup
1½ c. cooked rice
½ c. seasoned bread crumbs
1 c. sour cream
4 eggs, beaten well

¼ tsp. white pepper
¼ tsp. garlic powder
¼ tsp. black pepper
¼ tsp. thyme
¼ tsp. oregano
½ stick margarine

In a saucepan, melt margarine at 450° until a light smoke occurs. Stir in seasonings and quickly add chicken. Braise on each side for 2 minutes. Remove chicken and set aside. Allow residue and drippings to remain. Return pan to the heat at 200°. Blend in soup and sour cream. Remove from heat and blend in eggs. Add the chicken. Fold in bread crumbs and rice to form a loaf. Set aside.

Sauce:

3 Tbsp. all-purpose flour
3 Tbsp. margarine
½ c. sour cream
¼ c. pimentos, chopped
1 can mushrooms, drained

¼ c. parsley, chopped
¼ c. green onions, chopped
¼ tsp. white pepper
⅛ tsp. red pepper
1 Tbsp. Worcestershire sauce

In a saucepan, melt margarine at 200°. Combine all ingredients and saute until sauce is very thick, about 15 minutes. Form the chicken into loaves and arrange in a lightly oiled casserole dish. Cover with sauce and bake in a moderate oven until chicken is tender. Serves 12.

CAJUN CHICKEN IN PARSLEY SAUCE

3 lb. chicken fryer
½ c. onions, chopped
½ stick margarine
¼ c. celery, chopped
1 Tbsp. green onions, chopped
1 tsp. salt

½ tsp. coarse ground black
   pepper
½ tsp. garlic powder
¼ tsp. ground red pepper
¼ tsp. white pepper
¼ tsp. thyme

In a bowl, combine seasonings; set aside. Thoroughly rub the seasoning on the chicken. In a saucepan, melt margarine at 450°. Add chicken and saute on both sides until light brown. Remove from pan; set aside. Allow drippings to remain. Reduce heat to 350°. Add vegetables and saute until soft. Remove from pan and set aside.

Sauce:

1 c. white roux
1 c. sour cream
1 can cream of chicken soup
½ c. parsley, chopped

¼ tsp. white pepper
2 egg yolks, beaten
1 Tbsp. lemon juice

In a saucepan, bring roux to a low simmer at 200°. Add parsley and remaining seasonings. Blend well. Add chicken soup and continue to stir. Reduce heat to 150°; add egg yolks. Whisk constantly. Remove from heat. Add sauteed vegetables; stir in thoroughly. Add sour cream and blend well. In a lightly oiled casserole dish, arrange chicken and cover with sauce. Bake at 350° until chicken is tender. Garnish with sprigs of parsley. Serve with mounds of steaming rice. Serves 8.

BAKED CHICKEN IN MUSHROOMS CLAIBORNE

3 lb. chicken fryer
½ stick margarine
1 tsp. salt
¼ tsp. black pepper
¼ tsp. white pepper
½ tsp. garlic powder

2 packs fresh mushrooms
1½ c. sherry wine
¼ tsp. thyme
1 chicken bouillon cube
1 c. hot water
1 c. dark brown roux

Dissolve bouillon cube in 1 cup hot water; set aside. In a bowl, combine seasonings; set aside. Thoroughly rub and coat chicken with ½ seasoning mixture. In a saucepan, melt margarine at 450° until a light smoke occurs. Add chicken and fry on both sides until light brown. Remove from heat and set aside. Allow drippings to remain. Reduce heat to 300°. Add mushrooms and saute until light brown. Add remaining seasoning. Blend in roux, whisking continuously. Add bouillon and wine; bring to simmer for 3 minutes. In a lightly oiled casserole dish, arrange chicken. Pour mixture over chicken. Bake at 350° until chicken is tender. Serves 8.

CHICKEN IN CHERRY SAUCE VENICE

3 lb. chicken fryer
1 large can black cherries
1/2 c. red wine
1 c. white roux
1/4 tsp. white pepper
1/4 tsp. ginger

1 stick margarine
1 cube chicken bouillon
1 c. hot water
1/4 tsp. red pepper
1/4 tsp. white pepper

Dissolve bouillon in 1 cup hot water; set aside. In a saucepan, melt margarine at 450° until a light smoke occurs. Add chicken and saute until golden brown. Remove from heat and set aside. Reduce heat to 250°. Slowly add roux, bringing to simmer. Add bouillon liquid and blend well. Add wine; continue to simmer and stir. Carefully add cherries, including liquid and seasonings; blend well. Return chicken to mixture. Cook for 25 minutes at a low simmer. Stir frequently and control the moisture. Serve on bed of rice. Serves 8.

CHICKEN CACCIATORE NAPOLEONVILLE

4 lb. chicken parts
1/2 stick margarine
3 cloves garlic, chopped
1/4 c. celery, chopped
1/2 c. onions, chopped
1 can Italian tomatoes
1 can tomato sauce
1/4 c. bell pepper, chopped

1 tsp. salt
1/4 tsp. black pepper
1/8 tsp. red pepper
1/2 tsp. oregano
1/4 tsp. bay leaf
1/4 tsp. thyme
1 c. red wine

In a bowl, combine seasonings. Thoroughly rub 1/2 seasoning mix on chicken parts. In a saucepan, melt margarine at 450°. Add chicken and saute until light brown. Remove from pan and set aside. Reduce heat to 350°. Add vegetables and remaining seasoning; saute until light brown. Add tomatoes and tomato sauce. Bring to a simmer. Return chicken. Add wine, blending well. Cook for 45 minutes. Serve with noodles and sprinkle with Parmesan cheese. Serves 8.

CHICKEN DIVAN AMITE

6 boneless chicken breasts, flattened
2 packs fresh broccoli
1 c. grated American cheese
¼ tsp. white pepper
⅛ tsp. red pepper
½ tsp. garlic powder
2 cans cream of chicken soup
1 c. sour cream
1 c. toasted croutons
¼ c. sherry
1 chicken bouillon cube
½ stick margarine

In a saucepan, add broccoli and enough water to cover it. Bring to a boil and add the bouillon cube. Cook until tender. Drain and set aside. In a saucepan, melt margarine at 450°. Add chicken and seasonings; saute until light brown. Remove from heat and set aside on a paper towel. In a slightly oiled casserole dish, arrange broccoli. Add chicken and a layer of grated cheese. In a bowl, combine soup, sour cream and sherry. Pour into casserole dish. Sprinkle with additional cheese; cover with a layer of croutons. Add remaining cheese and bake at 375° for 45 minutes. Serves 6.

CHICKEN CURRY JEAN LaFITTE

4 lb. chicken parts
½ c. celery, chopped
½ c. onions, chopped
¼ c. green onions, chopped
4 chicken bouillon cubes
2 c. hot water
1 c. tomato juice
1½ tsp. curry powder
¼ tsp. white pepper
½ tsp. red pepper
½ stick margarine
1 c. light brown roux

Dissolve bouillon cubes in 2 cups hot water; set aside. In a saucepan, melt margarine at 450°. Add chicken and saute until light brown. Remove from pan, set aside and allow drippings to remain. Reduce heat to 350°. Add vegetables and saute until soft. Add curry and seasonings; blend well. Add tomato juice. Add bouillon; mix well. Blend in roux. Return chicken to pan and bring to a simmer. Continue to simmer until chicken is tender. It may be necessary to control thickness with additional hot water.

Serve over rice and with an excellent condiment, apple chutney. Serves 8.

CHICKEN IN ARTICHOKES AND WINE PITKIN

3 lb. chicken parts	2 chicken bouillon cubes
1 c. white wine	1 c. hot water
½ c. onions, chopped	2 packs artichoke hearts
1 stick margarine	¼ tsp. white pepper
2 cans tomato sauce	¼ tsp. red pepper

In a saucepan, melt margarine at 450°. Add chicken and saute until light brown. Remove from pan, set aside and allow drippings to remain. Add onions and seasonings; saute until soft at 300°. Add tomato sauce and wine; blend well. Simmer for 10 minutes; set aside. In a separate saucepan, bring 1 cup hot water to a simmer. Dissolve bouillon cubes. Add artichokes and simmer for 5 minutes. Remove from heat and drain. In a lightly oiled casserole dish, arrange artichokes. Cover with the chicken and pour over sauce mixture. Bake at 350° for 30 minutes. Serves 8.

CHICKEN ANDOUILLE SMOKED SAUSAGE BURAS

3 lb. hen parts
1 c. all-purpose flour
2 c. onions, chopped
2 c. bell peppers, chopped
1½ c. celery, chopped
4 cubes chicken bouillon cubes

16 c. water
1 c. corn oil
1 tsp. garlic flakes
2 bay leaves
½ lb. Polish sausage, cut into pieces
2 c. cooked rice

Seasoning:

1 tsp. salt
1 tsp. white pepper
1 tsp. garlic powder
1 tsp. onion powder

½ tsp. ground red pepper
½ tsp. black pepper
½ tsp. onion powder
½ tsp. cumin

In a small bowl, combine seasonings. Blend thoroughly and set aside. Rub 1 teaspoon seasoning mix thoroughly on chicken parts. In a separate bowl, combine 1 teaspoon seasoning mix to 1 cup flour; mix well. Dredge chicken parts in flour and set aside. In a separate bowl, combine ½ cup onions, bell peppers and celery. In a large saucepan, add 8 cups water and bring to a simmer. Blend in 2 bouillon cubes. In a skillet, heat 1 cup corn oil to 350°. Fry the chicken parts until brown on both sides. Remove from pan and set on a paper towel.

Pour all but ¼ cup oil from the skillet, allowing the sediment to remain. Return oil to the heat at 400°. Add any remaining flour to make ¼ cup. Add flour slowly to the hot oil; whisk briskly until the roux is a dark red brown. Remove from the heat and immediately stir in the remaining onions, bell peppers and celery; mix well. Add this mixture to the simmering stock, blending in thoroughly. Stir in 1 teaspoon seasoning mix; simmer for 30 minutes. Add the remaining water and 2 bouillon cubes. Boil for an additional 5 minutes. Remove from the heat and strain thoroughly. Discard the solids and return the liquid to the saucepan. Heat the liquid to 350°. Add chicken and remaining onions, bell peppers, celery, garlic, and remaining seasoning. Stir in sausage and simmer the gumbo until the chicken begins to disintegrate. Serve with heaping mounds of rice. Serves 8.

CHICKEN DIJON LaFOUCHE

8 pieces boneless chicken,
flattened
½ c. bell peppers, chopped
1 pack fresh mushrooms
1 large firm tomato, diced
½ c. green onions, chopped
1 c. Dijon mustard
1 c. Creole mustard
½ tsp. garlic powder

1 Tbsp. minced onion
½ c. white wine
½ c. milk
¼ tsp. white pepper
½ tsp. ground black pepper
½ c. sour cream
½ stick margarine
1 c. corn oil

In a saucepan, heat corn oil to 450°. Add chicken and saute on both sides until light brown. Remove from heat and place on a paper towel. Discard the oil. Add margarine to the saucepan and melt at 350°. Add bell peppers, mushrooms, tomatoes, and green onions; saute until soft. Remove from heat. In a separate saucepan, combine mustards, seasonings, onions, and wine. Saute at 200° for 2 minutes. Add milk and sour cream; bring to a simmer. Stir in sauteed vegetables. In a lightly oiled casserole dish, arrange chicken and cover with mustard sauce. Bake at 350° for 30 minutes or until chicken is tender. Serves 6.

CHICKEN IN SAUCE PIQUANT VACHERIE

3 lb. boneless chicken
½ stick margarine
1 c. bell pepper, chopped
1 c. onions, chopped
1 c. celery, chopped
3 c. tomatoes
1 can tomato sauce
1 jalapeno pepper, peeled and
chopped
⅓ tsp. bay leaf

½ tsp. garlic powder
1 tsp. white pepper
1 tsp. red pepper
2 Tbsp. dark brown sugar
½ tsp. thyme
¼ tsp. oregano
1 tsp. black pepper
3 chicken bouillon cubes
3 c. hot water

In a bowl, combine seasonings; set aside. In a saucepan, bring 3 cups hot water to a simmer. Add bouillon cubes and dissolve; set aside. In a separate saucepan, melt margarine at 450°. Add chicken and saute until light brown. Remove from pan and set aside. Return the drippings to the heat at 350°. Add vegetables and saute until soft. Add jalapeno pepper, tomatoes and tomato sauce; blend well. Add ½ seasoning mix; blend well. Add bouillon liquid and bring to a boil for 10 minutes. Return chicken to the pan and cook for 15 minutes. Control moisture if necessary. Remove from heat. Blend in remaining seasoning. Cover and set aside for 10 minutes.

You may add 1 pound cooked rice to this mixture or serve over rice. Serves 8.

CHICKEN CREOLE

4 lb. chicken parts with skin
3 chicken bouillon cubes
3 c. hot water
2 c. celery, chopped
1 c. bell pepper, chopped
2 c. onions, chopped
4 cloves garlic, chopped
½ tsp. bay leaf
½ tsp. red pepper

½ tsp. black pepper
½ tsp. white pepper
1 tsp. thyme
1 can tomatoes
2 c. tomato sauce
1 Tbsp. brown sugar
½ tsp. Tabasco sauce
1 tsp. sweet basil
½ tsp. oregano

In a bowl, combine seasonings; set aside. Dissolve bouillon cubes in 3 cups hot water; set aside. Strip the skin, including fat, from chicken and cut into strips. Heat a saucepan to 450°. Add chicken skin, fats and 1 teaspoon seasoning mix. Fry until skin is crispy. Remove skin from pan, allowing drippings to remain. Return pan to the heat. Add chicken parts and saute until light brown. Remove from pan and set aside. Reduce heat to 350°. Add vegetables and saute in chicken juices until light brown. Add remaining seasonings, including Tabasco sauce; blend well. Add tomatoes and tomato sauce; stir constantly for 10 minutes. Add bouillon liquid and sugar; simmer for an additional 10 minutes. Return chicken to the pan, stirring well. Add crispy chicken skins and saute for an additional 5 minutes or until chicken is tender. Serve over a bed of rice. Serves 8.

CHICKEN FRIED DIRTY RICE

2 lb. boneless chicken with skin
¼ c. onions, chopped
¼ c. celery, chopped
¼ c. parsley, chopped
2 c. cooked rice

½ tsp. black pepper
¼ tsp. oregano
¼ tsp. thyme
1 tsp. salt
2 Tbsp. Worcestershire sauce

Remove skins from chicken, including fat. Chop into small pieces. Heat a saucepan to 450°. Fry skins and fat until crispy. Remove skin from the heat and allow drippings to remain. Cut chicken into small pieces and saute in drippings until golden brown. Add vegetables, stirring frequently, and saute until light brown. Add Worcestershire sauce; blend in well. Add crispy chicken skins and seasonings. Reduce heat to 200°. Add rice and blend in well for 3 minutes. Do not allow to stick. Serves 6.

ORANGE CHICKEN WITH RAISIN RICE TERREBONE BAY

2 lb. boneless chicken
½ stick margarine
1 Tbsp. shredded orange rind
1 c. orange juice
½ c. white raisins
1 c. rice (uncooked)

1 Tbsp. brown sugar
1 tsp. white pepper
¼ tsp. sweet basil
1 tsp. salt
2 c. hot water

Cut chicken into bite-size cubes. In a saucepan, melt margarine at 450°; saute until light brown. Remove from pan and set aside, allowing juices to remain. Reduce heat to 250° and add orange juice. Bring to a simmer. Add 1 cup water, sugar, seasonings, raisins, and orange rind. Increase heat to 350° and bring to a brisk simmer. Return chicken to pan. Add 1 cup hot water; blend well. Add rice and reduce heat to a low simmer. Cook until moisture is absorbed and rice is tender. Garnish with orange slices. Serves 6.

GRILLED CHICKEN BREASTS WITH
CREAM OF THYME SAUCE JEANERETTE

4 large boneless chicken
    breasts, flattened
Juice of 1 lemon
1 c. olive oil
⅓ c. soy sauce
4 cloves garlic, minced
1 tsp. coarse ground black
    pepper
¼ tsp. rosemary

¼ tsp. thyme
¼ tsp. oregano
2 eggplants
4 strips thick cut bacon
3 c. pearl onions, peeled and cut
    in halves
8 strips fresh thyme
2 c. sour cream

In a large bowl, combine lemon juice, olive oil, soy sauce, garlic, and black pepper; blend together well. Add herbs and mix well. Cover and let stand for 3 hours. Strain marinade thoroughly into a large baking dish. With a fork, prick chicken thoroughly and arrange in marinade, turning occasionally for 3 hours.

Trim eggplants; cut ½ inch off bottom of each to form a square. Cut each eggplant lengthwise to form 4 slices. Brush well with olive oil and saute at 350° until light brown on both sides; set aside. In the same pan, saute bacon in the olive oil until well brown. Add pearl onions and saute for 3 minutes. Remove from the heat. Remove chicken from marinade and grill for 3 minutes on each side. Add ⅔ of the remaining marinade to the bacon mixture; blend well. Add sour cream, stirring well. Reduce heat to 200°. In a lightly oiled casserole dish, arrange eggplant slices. Pour in ½ sauce; add chicken. Cover with remaining sauce. Sprinkle with fresh thyme and serve. Serves 6.

SWEET RAISIN PINEAPPLE CHICKEN EUNICE

3 lb. boneless chicken
1 stick margarine
1 small can pineapple juice
1 can chunky pineapple
½ c. white raisins
1 c. uncooked rice

3 chicken bouillon cubes
2 c. hot water
1 tsp. white pepper
½ tsp. salt
2 tsp. dark brown sugar

Dissolve bouillon cubes in 2 cups hot water. Cut chicken into bite-size chunks. In a saucepan, melt margarine at 400°. Add chicken, salt and pepper; saute until lightly browned. Reduce the heat to 350°. Add bouillon liquid, sugar and pineapple juice; blend well. Add raisins and pineapple and simmer for 15 minutes. Add rice and bring to a boil. You may have to add additional liquid. Reduce the heat to 250°. Simmer for 25 minutes or until rice is tender. Liquid should be absorbed.

Use good judgment in the amount of liquid in this dish; it should not be sloppy. Serve in mounds; sprinkle with finely chopped mixed nuts. Serves 6.

RICH CAJUN CHICKEN WITH LOUISIANA YAMS

6 lb. stewing hen, cut in parts
2 cans Louisiana yams
1½ c. all-purpose flour
3 c. chopped onions
1 c. chopped celery
4 chicken bouillon cubes
6 c. hot water
¼ tsp. sage
1 tsp. salt
1 tsp. white pepper
½ tsp. thyme
¼ tsp. basil
¼ tsp. oregano
½ stick margarine
1 tsp. onion powder
1 tsp. garlic powder
½ tsp. red ground pepper
½ tsp. coarse ground black
   pepper
1 c. corn oil

Dissolve 4 bouillon cubes in 6 cups of hot water. In a small bowl, combine seasonings and set aside. Generously rub 3 teaspoons of seasoning mix on chicken parts. Combine ⅔ of remaining seasoning with the flour; mix well. Pour into a large flat plate. Dredge chicken into the seasoned flour. Retain excess flour.

In a large skillet, heat 1 cup corn oil at 350°. Fry chicken on both sides until light brown. This should take about 15 minutes per side. Remove from heat and place on a paper towel. Pour off corn oil, allowing the sediment to remain at the bottom of the skillet. Return the skillet to the heat at 450° and add ½ stick margarine. Add ¾ cup of the reserved flour. Whisk in until roux becomes a medium brown. Immediately add onions and celery; saute until soft. Remove from heat.

In a separate saucepan, bring bouillon to a brisk simmer. Blend in roux mixture; mix well. Add chicken pieces and remaining seasoning mix. Simmer until chicken is tender. In a lightly oiled casserole dish, arrange yams in a circular pattern, including the juice. Place chicken mixture in the center and bake at 350° for 15 minutes. Serve. Serves 8.

CHICKEN PASTA

3 lb. boneless chicken
¼ c. celery, chopped
½ c. onions, chopped
1 c. dry white wine
2 Tbsp. tomato paste
1 tsp. garlic powder
1 tsp. onion powder
½ tsp. coarse ground black
  pepper

¼ tsp. oregano
¼ tsp. thyme
½ tsp. white pepper
1 lb. elbow macaroni, cooked
1 c. Parmesan cheese
3 eggs, beaten
½ c. bread crumbs
1 stick margarine

In a bowl, combine seasonings; set aside. In a saucepan, melt margarine at 400°. Add chicken and saute until light brown. Remove chicken from the pan and set aside. Return drippings to the heat at 300°. Add vegetables and ½ seasoning mix; saute until soft. Add wine and bring to simmer. Stir in tomato paste, blending well. Return chicken to the pan. Continue to simmer for 15 minutes. Place ½ the macaroni in a lightly oiled casserole dish. Sprinkle with ½ cup Parmesan cheese and remaining seasoning mix. Reduce the heat to 175°. Remove the chicken and place in the casserole dish. Slowly blend eggs into the sauce. Blend in ½ the bread crumbs. Pour ½ the sauce mixture over the chicken. Add remaining macaroni. Cover with remaining cheese. Cover with remaining sauce mixture. Cover with remaining bread crumbs.

Sauce:

2 c. milk
4 Tbsp. margarine

3 Tbsp. all-purpose flour
¼ tsp. salt

In a small saucepan, heat the milk to a slow simmer. Add margarine and salt, blending well. Add flour, blending continuously. Do not allow to boil. Pour sauce over casserole dish. Bake at 375° for 35 minutes. All moisture should be absorbed. Serve in squares. Serves 12.

CHICKEN POTATO WHITE CASTLE

8 chicken breasts
2 c. smoked ham
4 c. white potatoes, diced
1 large pack mushrooms, sliced
1 c. green onions, chopped
1 c. corn oil
¼ stick margarine
1 tsp. salt

1 tsp. sweet paprika
1 tsp. ground red pepper
1 tsp. white pepper
1 tsp. onion powder
1 tsp. garlic powder
½ tsp. sweet basil
½ tsp. black pepper
¼ tsp. thyme

In a small bowl, combine peppers. In a separate bowl, combine remaining seasonings. Combine ½ pepper mixture with seasoning mix. In a saucepan, boil potatoes until tender but firm. Drain, set aside and retain water. Thoroughly rub chicken breasts with the seasoning mix. In a skillet, heat 1 cup corn oil at 400°. Add chicken and saute until light brown on both sides. Remove chicken from the pan and set aside. Pour off oil, retaining sediment.

Return skillet to the heat at 450°. Add margarine and potatoes. Saute until potatoes turn a golden brown. Remove potatoes, set aside and retain drippings. Return skillet to the heat at 400°. Add ham and pepper mixture; saute until ham is brown. Blend well. Stir in mushrooms and saute for 1 minute. Stir in green onions and saute for 3 minutes. Arrange potatoes on a heated serving platter. Top with chicken. Cover with ham mixture.

Sauce:

4 egg yolks, beaten
1 stick margarine
Juice of ½ lemon
1 Tbsp. tarragon vinegar

¼ tsp. salt
1 tsp. parsley, chopped
1 tsp. onion juice
⅛ tsp. ground red pepper

Place egg yolks with ⅓ stick margarine at the top of a double boiler. Add remaining margarine as sauce thickens; stir constantly. Remove from the heat and add remaining ingredients. Pour over serving platter. Serve. Serves 6.

CREOLE CHICKEN IN CREAM OF PEANUT SAUCE

4 large chicken breasts
1 egg white
1 c. unsalted roasted peanuts
1 Tbsp. brown sugar
1 c. corn oil
3 slices ginger
1 Tbsp. garlic, chopped

¼ tsp. red pepper
¼ tsp. white pepper
1 Tbsp. soy sauce
¼ c. sherry
2 Tbsp. all-purpose flour
2 Tbsp. margarine
¼ tsp. salt

In a small bowl, combine salt and peppers. Rub chicken thoroughly. In a saucepan, add corn oil and heat to 400°. Add chicken and saute until golden brown. Remove from the heat and cut chicken into 1 inch chunks. Allow to cool. In a separate saucepan, melt margarine at 250°. Blend in flour until it gels. Reduce the heat to 200°. Add sherry; blend well. Add remaining ingredients, including chicken. Continue to stir well, glazing chicken thoroughly for 10 minutes. Serve over a bed of steaming rice. Serves 4.

SWEET FRUIT CHICKEN VIEUX CARRE

4 large chicken breasts
1 c. onions, chopped
1 chicken bouillon cube
½ c. hot water
¼ c. all-purpose flour
¼ stick margarine
1 can pineapple rings (retain
    juice)

1 c. seedless grapes
¼ c. dry sherry
½ tsp. chili powder
¼ tsp. white pepper
¼ tsp. red pepper
1 orange, sliced into rings

Dissolve chicken bouillon in ½ cup hot water; set aside. In a small bowl, combine seasonings with the flour, including chili powder. Coat chicken thoroughly; retain excess flour. In a saucepan, melt the margarine at 350°. Add chicken and saute until brown. Remove chicken and place on a paper towel; retain drippings. Return pan to 350°. Add onions. Slowly add remaining flour until it gels. Add pineapple juice and bouillon; bring to a simmer for about 3 minutes. Add remaining ingredients, including chicken pieces. Toss lightly until chicken is well coated, about 10 minutes. Place on a heaping bed of rice. Surround with orange slices. Serves 6.

CHICKEN BREASTS, NEW ORLEANS STYLE

2 lb. boneless chicken breasts
1 lb. Italian or Polish sausage
½ c. all-purpose flour
4 Tbsp. olive oil
2 zucchini, cut into ½ inch
   rounds
¼ stick margarine
¼ tsp. red ground pepper
½ c. dry white wine

2 garlic cloves, sliced thin
1 chicken bouillon cube
½ c. hot water
1 (6 oz.) jar roasted peppers,
   drained and chopped fine
1 Tbsp. parsley, chopped
½ tsp. coarse black ground
   pepper
1 tsp. salt

Dissolve chicken bouillon cube in ½ cup hot water; set aside. Cut chicken breasts into ½ inch slices. In a bowl, combine red pepper, salt and flour. Dredge chicken; shake off excess flour, retaining flour mixture. Set chicken aside. In a saucepan, heat olive oil at 350°. Add zucchini and saute until brown, approximately 3 minutes. Remove from the heat and set aside. In the same saucepan, add sausage and saute until brown. Drain off excess oil. Add margarine and black pepper, stirring in thoroughly. Add chicken and saute until brown. Add wine, continuing to stir briskly. Add garlic and bouillon; bring to a brisk simmer. Add remaining ingredients and simmer for 10 minutes. Serve with mounds of steaming rice. Serves 6.

Notes

"Where's the beef, Cajun?"

Meat in a Hurry

A WORD FROM CLOVICE:

Meat, neighbor, dat is what I eat. I read a whole lot of dem scienti'fic suggestions dat you are sup'pose to eat a 4 ounce serving. Dis boy follows dat rule religiously because I find it v'ery difficult to get mo' den 4 ounces of meat on my fork and in'to my mout at de same time.

I'm very particular 'bouts eatin' meat. I limit my'self to biting the hind end off a charging buffalo as he go by. And I never eat meat so rare that the butcher ain't had time to skin the critter. In other words, neighbor, if I get the first bite I done won.

Add 1 tablespoon vegetable oil to the water in which you cook pasta. This helps prevent the pasta from sticking together and also helps keep the pot from boiling over when the water rises during cooking.

To store watercress, wash it, then stand upright in a glass of cold water. Wrap the glass in a plastic bag and refrigerate. Fresh cress will keep about a week this way.

If you shape hamburgers lightly, with not too much pressure, they'll be juicier.

Mushrooms may be sliced in an egg slicer to get uniform slices for a sandwich.

When buying a cured ham, ask the butcher to remove the rind and all but a thin layer of fat. Do not remove all the fat or the ham will tend to dry out.

Sausage will be less greasy if put in a cold frying pan with no added fat and become more tender.

When making a sauce, it is imperative that you add hot liquid to the flour-fat base. Add all liquids one at a time vigorously whisking in between each ingredient. Cream sauces are easily scorched and overly browned; control of the heat is imperative.

MEAT IN A HURRY

CAJUN BEEF JAMBALAYA

3 lb. beef, cubed
½ lb. Italian or Polish sausage
3 Tbsp. all-purpose flour
1 c. onions, chopped
½ c. bell pepper, chopped
½ c. green onions, chopped
½ c. celery, chopped
¼ c. parsley, chopped
2 c. rice (uncooked)
¼ tsp. red pepper
¼ tsp. black pepper

½ tsp. thyme
½ tsp. cumin
½ tsp. dry mustard
½ tsp. white pepper
1 tsp. salt
3 bay leaves
3 cloves garlic, chopped
¼ stick margarine
2 beef bouillon cubes
4 c. hot water

Dissolve 2 beef bouillon cubes in 4 cups hot water. In a small bowl, combine seasonings; set aside. In a large skillet, melt margarine at 400°. Add sausage and saute for 5 minutes. Add onions, celery, green pepper, garlic, and seasoning mix. Saute for an additional 5 minutes. Remove from heat. Set aside and retain drippings. Return skillet to 400°. Add beef and saute until light brown. Add flour; stir in well until it gels. Blend in bouillon; stir well. Add sausage mixture and simmer for 5 minutes. Reduce heat to 300°. Add rice and parsley; simmer until rice is tender. Serves 8.

TENDERLOIN STEAK IN RED WINE VERSAILLES

3 lb. beef tenderloin, cut in ¾
    inch strips
Juice of 1 lemon
¼ tsp. oregano
1 tsp. salt
¼ tsp. white pepper
1 tsp. fennel seeds
1 tsp. coarse ground black
    pepper

1 tsp. dry mustard
½ tsp. ground red pepper
1 c. water
1 c. red wine
½ tsp. garlic powder
½ tsp. onion powder
½ stick margarine

In a bowl, combine seasonings; set aside. Rub meat thoroughly with ½ seasoning mix. In a saucepan, melt margarine at 400°. Add beef and saute until brown on both sides. Remove from the heat. Set aside and allow drippings to remain. Return saucepan to the heat at 300°. Blend together all remaining ingredients, except beef, and saute for 4 minutes. In a lightly oiled casserole dish, pour in half the mixture. Add the beef; cover with remaining mixture. Bake at 350° until beef is tender. Serve with whole boiled potatoes. Serves 8.

HASH LOCKPORT

2 lb. top round steak, cubed
¼ stick margarine
¼ c. flour
2 beef bouillon cubes
4 c. hot water
2 large onions, chopped
2 cloves garlic, crushed
½ c. celery, chopped
2 tsp. Worcestershire sauce
¼ tsp. thyme
¼ tsp. oregano

1 bay leaf
¼ c. dry red wine
1 tsp. coarse ground black pepper
1 tsp. soy sauce
½ bunch parsley, chopped
1 pack fresh mushrooms, sliced
2 Idaho potatoes, peeled and diced

Dissolve bouillon cubes in 4 cups hot water; set aside. In a small bowl, combine seasonings; set aside. In a saucepan, melt ¼ stick margarine at 400°. Add meat and ½ seasoning mix; saute until golden brown. Remove from pan and save drippings. Return pan to the heat and add onions, garlic, celery, and remaining seasonings; saute until soft. Add flour until it gels and becomes a light brown. Reduce heat to 300°. Stir in mushrooms for 1 minute. Blend in bouillon, stirring well. Combine remaining ingredients. Simmer until potatoes are soft and beef is tender. Sprinkle with parsley and serve. Serves 6.

CREOLE EGGPLANT SMOTHERED IN MEAT SAUCE

3 lb. ground beef
½ stick margarine
3 cloves garlic, chopped
¼ c. parsley, chopped
1½ c. tomato sauce
¾ c. red wine
1 c. grated Italian cheese
1 c. bread crumbs

4 large eggplants
¼ tsp. white pepper
¼ tsp. oregano
½ tsp. coarse ground black pepper
½ tsp. garlic flakes
½ tsp. dry mustard
1 tsp. salt

In a bowl, combine seasonings; set aside. Peel eggplants and dice into ½ inch cubes. In a saucepan, melt ¼ stick margarine at 350°. Add vegetables, including eggplants and ½ seasoning mix; saute until soft. Remove from heat and set aside. In a separate saucepan, melt remaining margarine at 400°. Add ground meat and remaining seasoning mix; saute for 10 minutes or until light brown. Add tomato sauce, blending well. Add wine and continue to cook for 15 minutes or until thickened. Add vegetable mixture; blend well. Reduce heat to 200°. Fold in bread crumbs and cheese. Reserve a small amount of cheese to sprinkle on top. Place in a lightly oiled casserole dish; sprinkle with cheese. Bake at 350° for 30 minutes. Serves 8.

MARINATED ROAST BEEF RACELAND

4 lb. eye of the round beef
2 tsp. beef bouillon powder
3 c. white wine
¾ c. salad oil
1 tsp. salt
1 tsp. rosemary

¼ tsp. sage
¼ tsp. thyme
1 Tbsp. black pepper
2 onions, chopped
2 Tbsp. margarine
1 tsp. celery seeds

Pierce surface of roast in many places with a fork and sprinkle with powdered bouillon; rub thoroughly. Place roast in a deep casserole dish. In a separate bowl, combine wine, salad oil, salt, rosemary, sage, thyme, pepper, and onions. Pour over meat and let stand in the refrigerator 12 hours, turning occasionally. At the end of the marinating time, remove meat but save marinade and insert spit through center. Combine 2 cups of marinade, 2 tablespoons melted margarine and celery seeds. Place roast in an electric rotisserie for about 1 hour and 20 minutes or until thermometer registers your desired doneness. Baste frequently with marinade. Serves 6 to 8.

PORK CHOPS IN CREAM OF CURRY SAUCE

3 lb. pork chops, cut ¾ inch
   thick
1 tsp. curry powder
¼ tsp. thyme
½ tsp. black pepper
½ tsp. white pepper
½ c. raisins
½ c. apples, diced

1 can cream of mushroom soup
½ c. sour cream
¼ stick margarine
½ c. onions, chopped
2 cloves garlic, chopped
1 tsp. salt

In a bowl, combine seasonings; set aside. In a saucepan, melt margarine at 450°. Add pork chops and ½ seasoning mix; saute on both sides until light brown. Remove chops from heat. Set aside and retain drippings. Return pan to 350°. Add onions and saute until soft. Add apples and raisins and saute for 5 minutes. Add remaining ingredients except pork chops. Bring to a simmer for 5 minutes. Stir continuously and remove from heat. Pour half ingredients into a lightly oiled baking dish. Add pork chops. Pour remaining mixture over top. Cook at 350° until pork chops are done. Serve with Louisiana yams. Serves 8.

CROWN BAKED HAM RUSTON

2 lb. smoked ham, diced
2 lb. ground veal shoulder
3 eggs
¾ c. milk
3 c. bread crumbs
½ c. claret
2 tsp. Worcestershire sauce
⅓ c. onions, minced

¾ tsp. coarse ground black
  pepper
1 tsp. salt
½ c. currant jelly
2 red apples, cored and sliced
3 Tbsp. margarine
3 Tbsp. brown sugar
Parsley for garnish

In a mixing bowl, beat eggs well. Add milk and blend in the bread crumbs; let stand 10 minutes. Add claret, Worcestershire sauce, onions, salt, and pepper. Stir in well; do not beat. Add ham and veal. Mix well. Pack in a greased tube pan, 10 inches in diameter. Bake at 350° for 30 minutes. Unmold in a shallow pan. Spread top and sides with jelly. Return to oven; bake at 350° for an additional 30 minutes. In a saucepan, melt margarine at 400°. Add apples and saute on both sides. Add brown sugar and toss apples well for 1 minute. Place meat on platter, garnish with parsley and surround with apples. Serves 6 to 8.

SUNDAY MEATLOAF AT ABBEVILLE

3 lb. ground meat
½ c. sour cream
1 can cream of mushroom soup
2 Tbsp. horseradish
⅔ c. tomato sauce
3 Tbsp. parsley, chopped
3 Tbsp. Worcestershire sauce
3 cloves garlic, finely chopped
⅔ c. celery, chopped
½ c. green pepper, chopped

1 c. seasoned bread crumbs
3 eggs, beaten
½ tsp. black pepper
¼ tsp. thyme
⅛ tsp. bay leaf
½ tsp. fennel seeds
¼ tsp. dry mustard
¼ tsp. ground red pepper
1 tsp. salt
2 tsp. margarine, melted at room
  temperature

In a bowl, combine seasonings; set aside. In a large bowl, combine ½ mushroom soup, horseradish, tomato sauce, and sour cream; blend well. Add bread crumbs; stir in well, but do not beat. Add well beaten eggs and ½ seasoning mix. Add vegetables; mix well, using your hands. Add ground meat; mix well, using your hands. Shape into a loaf. Combine melted margarine with remaining seasoning mix and rub outside of the meatloaf. In a bowl, combine Worcestershire sauce and remaining soup; blend well. Pour over top of meatloaf. Bake at 350° until done. Garnish with parsley. Serves 8.

CAJUN ROAST BEEF

5 lb. sirloin roast (pin bone in)
1 clove garlic, minced
1/4 c. onions, chopped fine
1/4 c. celery, chopped fine
1/4 c. bell pepper, chopped fine

1 tsp. white pepper
1/2 tsp. black pepper
1/2 tsp. dry mustard
1 1/2 tsp. salt
1/4 tsp. ground red pepper
1/2 stick margarine

In a bowl, combine seasonings; set aside. In a large saucepan, melt margarine at 450°. Add roast and brown on both sides. Remove from heat. Set aside and retain drippings. In a separate bowl, combine celery, bell pepper, onions, and 1/2 seasoning mix. Place the roast in a slightly oiled roasting pan. Take the point of a knife and puncture the roast and insert slithers of garlic. Slice the center of the roast in 2 longitudinal strokes, about 1 inch deep. Do not penetrate completely. Fill slots with the vegetable mix. Combine remaining seasoning mix with roast drippings. Pour over the roast. Cover and bake at 350° until the thermostat reads 160°. This will produce a medium rare roast. Serves 8.

SWEET DOUGH NATCHITOCHES CREOLE MEAT PIE

½ lb. ground meat
½ lb. ground pork
½ lb. Italian smoked sausage
1 stick margarine
½ c. celery, chopped
½ c. onions, chopped
¾ tsp. garlic flakes
½ tsp. thyme
½ tsp. black pepper

½ tsp. red pepper
½ tsp. white pepper
1 tsp. paprika
½ tsp. basil
2 c. red potatoes, coarsely
   grated
2 beef bouillon cubes
2 c. hot water

Dissolve bouillon in 2 cups hot water; set aside. In a large saucepan, melt margarine at 450°. Add celery and onions until soft. Reduce heat to 350°. Add pork, garlic and seasonings; saute for 5 minutes, stirring continuously. Reduce heat to 300°. Add remaining meat, blending well for 5 minutes. Add bouillon and potatoes; simmer for an additional 5 minutes. Remove from the heat, place in a strainer and allow to drain while preparing the dough.

Dough:

4 Tbsp. margarine
¼ tsp. salt
3 Tbsp. milk

1 egg
¼ c. sugar
1⅓ c. all-purpose flour

In a food processor, combine margarine, sugar and salt; blend well to form a creamy consistency. Add egg and milk; blend thoroughly. Add flour and beat just until it blends. Mold the dough into 2 separate patties. Allow to set while preparing the topping.

Topping:

12 oz. cream cheese, softened
   at room temperature
1 c. heavy cream

⅛ tsp. oregano
½ tsp. thyme

Combine ingredients in a bowl and beat together with a mixer until smooth. Roll dough large enough to cover two 9 inch pie plates. Spoon in filling. Cover with topping. Bake at 350° for 35 minutes or until crust is golden brown. Serves 6.

CABBAGE ROLLS VACHERIE

1 large head cabbage
1 lb. ground beef
1 lb. ground pork
1 Tbsp. margarine
1 Tbsp. salt

½ tsp. black pepper
2 small onions, minced
1 clove garlic, minced
1 c. cooked rice
1 (No. 2) can tomatoes

Gently pull off 8 large cabbage leaves from the head. Simmer leaves in 1 inch boiling water, covered, for 5 minutes. Drain and lay out for filling. Combine ground beef and pork. Melt margarine in a saucepan at 400°. Add meat and saute until brown. Add salt, pepper, onions, garlic, and rice. Blend well and remove from the heat. Fill each leaf with ⅛ of the mixture. Roll up each, folding ends to center. Secure the leaves with a toothpick. Place in a lightly oiled saucepan. Add tomatoes. Cover and simmer for 30 minutes, or bake in an oven at 350° for 30 minutes. Remove toothpicks. Serves 4.

MEATLOAF DELGADO

3 lb. ground meat
½ c. salad olives with pimentos,
  chopped
3 cloves garlic, chopped
½ c. celery, chopped
½ c. onions, chopped
½ c. seasoned bread crumbs
3 eggs, beaten

⅓ c. bell pepper, chopped
3 Tbsp. parsley, chopped
1 tsp. coarse ground black
  pepper
½ c. tomato sauce
¼ tsp. bay leaf
¼ tsp. thyme
¼ stick margarine

In a large saucepan, melt margarine at 350°. Add garlic, onions, bell pepper, and celery; saute until soft. Remove from heat and place in a large mixing bowl. Add seasonings, blending well. Add remaining ingredients; mix well with your hands. Shape into a meatloaf. Use tomato sauce and olive liquid to control thickness. Place meatloaf in a lightly oiled casserole dish. Bake at 350° for 30 minutes.

Sauce:

1 c. brown roux
2 c. beef consomme
1 Tbsp. soy sauce
¼ tsp. garlic powder

¼ tsp. onion powder
¼ tsp. coarse ground black
  pepper
2 Tbsp. margarine

While meatloaf is baking, combine ingredients in a bowl, mixing well. In a saucepan, melt 2 tablespoons margarine at 200°. Add mixture and simmer until it thickens. After meatloaf has cooked for 30 minutes, remove from oven and cover with gravy. Return to oven and cook until done. Garnish with parsley and serve. Serves 8.

HAM AND CHICKEN JAMBALAYA BOUTTE

3 lb. chicken, cut in chunks
1 lb. smoked ham, cut in chunks
1½ c. celery, chopped
1½ c. onion, chopped
½ stick margarine
½ tsp. bay leaf
1 tsp. garlic powder
¼ tsp. white pepper
¼ tsp. red pepper
¼ tsp. black pepper
¼ tsp. thyme
1½ c. green pepper, chopped
1 c. tomato sauce
2 c. uncooked rice
2 cans chicken soup
1 can cream of chicken soup

In a bowl, combine seasonings; set aside. In a saucepan, melt margarine at 450°. Add chicken, ham and ½ seasoning mix; saute until brown. Remove from pan and allow drippings to remain. Return pan to the heat at 250°. Add vegetables and saute until light brown. Add remaining seasonings; blend well. Keep this dish constantly moving. Add tomato sauce and bring to a simmer. Return meats to pan and saute for another 10 minutes. Add soups and any remaining ingredients except for rice. Bring to a boil. Add rice and bring to a simmer. Cook until rice is tender, but not mushy. Serve. Serves 8.

CAJUN GLAZED MEATLOAF

2 lb. ground meat
1 lb. smoked ham, chopped fine
1 c. cream of mushroom soup
3 eggs, beaten
1 c. bread crumbs
4 strips bacon
½ tsp. black pepper
1 tsp. salt
½ tsp. thyme
½ tsp. marjoram
½ c. onions, chopped
½ c. celery, chopped

In a large saucepan, fry bacon strips at 400° until crispy. Remove from the pan. Crush bacon and allow drippings to remain. Add meat and ham; saute until brown. Remove from heat. In a large bowl, combine all ingredients and shape into loaf. If meat mixture is too soft to form into a loaf, add more bread crumbs. Place loaf in a lightly oiled baking pan.

Glaze:

¾ c. dark brown sugar
2 tsp. dry mustard
¾ c. sweet white wine
¼ c. honey

In a saucepan, combine dark brown sugar, dry mustard and sweet white wine. Bring to a brisk simmer. Remove from the heat. Stir in honey. Baste meatloaf often to form a surface glaze. Bake at 350° until done. Slice and serve on a steaming bed of rice. Serves 8.

BEEF GUMBO LULING

3 lb. lean chuck, chopped into chunks
1/2 lb. thick sliced bacon, cut into 1 inch pieces
2 (1 lb.) packs okra
1 1/2 c. celery, chopped
1 1/2 c. bell pepper, chopped
2 c. onion, chopped
2 bay leaves
1 tsp. black pepper
3/4 tsp. dry mustard
1 tsp. basil

1/2 tsp. red pepper
1 tsp. garlic powder
1 tsp. thyme
1/2 tsp. white pepper
1 1/2 tsp. onion powder
1 tsp. salt
2 c. brown roux
3 bouillon beef cubes
8 c. hot water
1 tsp. paprika
2 cans tomatoes

Dissolve bouillon cubes in 8 cups of hot water; set aside. In a large saucepan, fry bacon at 400° until crisp. Remove from pan and retain drippings. Add chuck and saute until light brown. Remove from pan and retain drippings. Add vegetables and seasonings; saute until soft. Reduce heat to 300°. Slowly blend in the roux. Add bouillon, blending well. Return meat and add remaining ingredients, mixing well. Cook for 45 minutes at a fast simmer. Serve over rice. Serves 12.

VEAL FETTUCINI INDEPENDENCE

8 slices veal, passed once
   through a tenderizer
2 c. bread crumbs
1 tsp. parsley, chopped fine
½ tsp. onion powder

½ tsp. garlic powder
2 tsp. olive oil
1 tsp. white pepper
3 eggs, beaten

In a bowl, combine bread crumbs, parsley, olive oil, white pepper, garlic powder, and onion powder; mix well. Spread in a large soup plate. In a separate bowl, beat eggs well. Add 4 tablespoons Parmesan cheese. Dip the veal slices individually in the egg mixture, coating thoroughly. Dredge thoroughly in bread crumbs. Shake off excess and set aside. In a saucepan, melt margarine at 400°. Add veal and saute on both sides until golden brown. If excess bread crumbs develop in pan, discard immediately and add more margarine. Set aside.

Fettucini:

1 c. grated Parmesan cheese
2½ c. heavy cream
2 sticks margarine
1 pack fettucini, cooked and well
   drained (hot)

1 tsp. salt
¼ tsp. ground red pepper

In a large saucepan, melt margarine at 350°. Blend in heavy cream. Remove from heat immediately and add cheese and seasonings. Add fettucini, tossing together well. In a large heated serving platter, form a bed with the fettucini. Arrange veal in a leafy pattern. Garnish with parsley and serve. Serves 8.

BEEF STROGANOFF, CAJUN STYLE

2 lb. steak, cut into slithers
½ c. onions, chopped
1 c. tomato sauce
2 Tbsp. Worcestershire sauce
3 cloves garlic, chopped
1 c. brown roux
1 pack fresh mushrooms
2 c. sour cream

2 Tbsp. teriyaki sauce
1 bay leaf
¼ tsp. thyme
1½ tsp. coarse ground black
   pepper
1 tsp. salt
¼ stick margarine

In a saucepan, melt margarine at 400°. Add beef and saute until light brown. Add vegetables and saute until soft. Add tomato sauce; bring to simmer. Reduce heat to 300°. Slowly blend in roux and simmer for 5 minutes. Blend in sour cream. Add seasonings and remaining ingredients. Blend well and continue to simmer until beef is tender.

Watch the moisture content of this dish. Serve over a bed of noodles or rice. Serves 8.

VEAL IN A CREOLE MUSHROOM PASTA SAUCE

2 lb. veal, cubed
½ c. onions, chopped
¼ stick margarine
½ bell pepper, chopped
1 can cream of mushroom soup
¼ c. Parmesan cheese
1 c. yellow grated cheese (your choice)
½ can pimentos
1 c. sour cream
1 lb. noodles, cooked
¼ tsp. garlic powder
¼ tsp. white pepper
¼ tsp. thyme
½ tsp. sweet paprika

In a saucepan, melt margarine at 400°. Add veal and saute for 5 minutes. Add vegetables and saute until soft. Reduce heat to 250°. Add sour cream, blending well. Add seasonings and remaining ingredients except noodles and Parmesan cheese. Blend well. Bring to a rapid simmer for 10 minutes. Blend in cooked noodles. Remove from heat immediately. Pour the mixture into a lightly oiled casserole dish. Top with Parmesan cheese. Bake at 325° for 45 minutes. Serves 8.

CAJUN MEATBALLS IN ONION SAUCE

2 lb. lean ground beef
½ c. bread crumbs
2 eggs, beaten
½ stick margarine
1½ c. sweet onions, chopped
½ c. milk
2 Tbsp. ketchup
¼ tsp. red pepper
¼ tsp. white pepper
3 Tbsp. all-purpose flour
1 tsp. paprika
2 beef bouillon cubes
2 c. hot water
1 tsp. salt

Dissolve bouillon cubes in 2 cups hot water; set aside. In a saucepan, melt ¼ stick margarine at 350°. Add onions and saute until soft. Remove from pan and set aside. In a large bowl, combine ground beef, ketchup, bread crumbs, eggs, milk, and seasonings except paprika. Shape into fist-sized meatballs. Return pan to the heat at 400°. Melt remaining margarine. Add meatballs and saute until light brown. Remove meatballs and set aside. Blend flour and paprika in the drippings until it gels. Gradually add bouillon and cook until sauce thickens. Reduce heat to 350°. Return onions and meatballs to the pan. Cover and simmer until meatballs are done. Serve. Serves 6.

STUFFED HAM

1 (1½ inch thick) round ham
   steak
2 eggs, beaten
1 c. bread crumbs
2 tsp. celery seed
¼ c. onion, chopped

1 Tbsp. Creole mustard
½ c. brown sugar
¼ tsp. sage
½ tsp. black pepper
¼ tsp. red pepper

Cut a 4 inch hole in center of the ham steak. Remove bone and chop the 4 inch center piece small. In a bowl, combine all ingredients except for eggs and brown sugar. In a separate bowl, blend together the eggs and brown sugar. Combine all ingredients, including the chopped ham. Place ham steak in a lightly oiled casserole dish. Heap mixture in center of ham steak. Bake at 300° until ham is tender. Serves 4.

SHERRIED LAMB ROSELAND

2 lb. lamb fillets
4 Tbsp. flour
¼ c. dry sherry
¼ c. orange juice
½ tsp. garlic flakes
¼ tsp. red pepper

¼ tsp. white pepper
2 beef bouillon cubes
2 c. hot water
¼ stick margarine
1 orange, sliced into rounds

Slice lamb into cubes. In a saucepan, melt margarine at 400°. Add lamb and seasonings and saute until light brown; set aside. In a bowl, blend together flour and sherry until smooth. Slowly add orange juice, blending well. Dissolve bouillon cubes in 2 cups hot water. Stir in bouillon and whisk well. Return lamb to the heat at 300°. Add sherry mixture and orange; bring to a simmer. Cook until lamb is tender. Serves 6.

VEAL IN CREAM OF WINE SAUCE DUPRE

6 (½ inch thick) veal cutlets
½ stick margarine
1 can mushrooms
½ c. white wine
3 Tbsp. all-purpose flour
¼ tsp. garlic powder

¼ tsp. garlic salt
1 Tbsp. Worcestershire sauce
¼ tsp. white pepper
¼ tsp. red pepper
⅛ tsp. tarragon

Use a mallet to tenderize cutlets. In a saucepan, melt ¼ stick margarine at 400°. Add cutlets and saute on both sides until light brown. Add mushrooms, including water. Add seasonings and Worcestershire sauce; simmer briskly, stirring well for 5 minutes. Remove from heat and set aside. In a separate saucepan, melt remaining margarine at 300°. Blend in flour until it gels. Reduce heat to 200°. Add wine, blending well. Simmer briskly for 20 minutes or until mixture thickens. Combine the 2 mixtures. Control thickness by adding wine or water. Cover and simmer slowly for an additional 20 minutes or until veal is tender. Serve on a steaming bed of rice. Serves 6.

CALF LIVER SMOTHERED IN ONIONS OPELOUSAS

1 lb. calf liver
1 large onion, cut in half and
sliced
3 Tbsp. all-purpose flour
¼ stick margarine
3 Tbsp. margarine
2 cloves garlic, chopped

¼ tsp. white pepper
¼ tsp. black pepper
1 Tbsp. Worcestershire sauce
¼ bell pepper, chopped
1 beef bouillon cube
1 c. hot water

Dissolve bouillon cube in 1 cup hot water. In a saucepan, melt ¼ stick margarine at 400°. Add liver and saute on both sides for 2 minutes. Remove liver from the pan and set aside. Return pan to the heat at 450°. Add 3 tablespoons margarine. Add flour and whisk briskly until it browns. Add vegetables and saute until soft. Reduce heat to 300°. Blend in bouillon and bring to simmer. Return liver and any juices to mixture. Add seasonings, blending well. Continue to simmer until liver is tender. Turn over frequently. Control thickness with hot water. Serves 4.

CREOLE BEEF FANDINO WITH EGGPLANT

2 lb. ground beef
¼ stick margarine
2 eggplants
2 eggs, beaten
2 cans tomato sauce
1 tsp. oregano

¼ c. grated Parmesan cheese
1 c. grated Cheddar cheese
1 c. flour
½ tsp. black pepper
1 tsp. white pepper
1 tsp. salt

In a bowl, combine seasonings; set aside. In a separate bowl, combine beaten eggs and ½ seasoning mix; blend well. In a separate bowl, combine the flour and remaining seasoning mix. Peel eggplants and slice into ½ inch rounds. In a saucepan, melt margarine at 400°. Dip eggplant rounds into the eggs, then dredge into the flour. Fry on both sides until lightly browned. Arrange eggplant rounds on the bottom of a lightly oiled casserole dish. In a bowl, combine remaining ingredients except tomato sauce and Cheddar cheese. Form mixture into patties; arrange over eggplant. Spread Cheddar cheese over top. Carefully cover with tomato sauce. Bake at 300° for 40 minutes. Serves 8.

CREOLE STUFFED GREEN PEPPERS

2 lb. ground veal
8 large bell peppers
4 strips bacon
¼ c. celery, chopped
¼ c. onions, chopped

1½ c. bread crumbs
½ tsp. ground red pepper
½ tsp. white pepper
1 tsp. salt

In a saucepan, fry bacon at 400° until crisp; remove from drippings. Crush into pieces and set aside. Add veal and saute until white. Add vegetables and saute until soft. Remove from heat. In a bowl, blend all ingredients together. Core bell peppers and discard cores. Stuff bell peppers with mixture. In a lightly oiled casserole dish, add water ¼ inch deep. Arrange bell peppers so they will not turn over. Bake at 400° for 45 minutes. Serves 8.

BARBECUED SPARERIBS, CAJUN STYLE

Marinade:

1 beef bouillon cube
½ c. tomato sauce
4 tsp. honey
3 tsp. wine vinegar
¼ c. dry sherry

1 Tbsp. brown sugar
2 cloves garlic, chopped fine
½ tsp. cinnamon
¼ tsp. allspice

Sauce:

2 tsp. sesame oil

2 tsp. honey

Place a 3 pound sparerib slab in a shallow pan with a rack. In a bowl, combine the ingredients for the marinade; mix well. Pour over ribs. Marinate at room temperature for 3 hours, turning frequently. Remove ribs from marinade and place on a baking rack, meaty side down. In a bowl, combine honey and sesame oil. Mix well. Add marinade and blend in well. Roast the ribs for 20 minutes at 450°, basting well. Turn the roast over for another 15 minutes, basting well. After ribs are brown and well coated, remove from the baking pan and cut into individual ribs. Serve. Serves 6.

CAJUN PEPPER STEAK

2 lb. round steak, cut into 2 inch strips
1/4 stick margarine
2 c. hot water
2 beef bouillon cubes
1 bell pepper, cut into strips

1/4 c. soy sauce
2 Tbsp. flour
1/4 tsp. ground red pepper
1/2 tsp. coarse ground black pepper
1/4 tsp. tarragon

Dissolve 2 bouillon cubes in 2 cups hot water; set aside. In a bowl, combine seasonings; set aside. In a saucepan, melt margarine at 450°. Add steak strips and 1/2 seasoning mix; saute until brown. Add bell pepper; saute for 2 minutes. Add flour, stirring until light brown. Add bouillon slowly, stirring well; saute for 10 minutes. Add soy sauce and remaining seasoning mix. Simmer for an additional 10 minutes. Serve when sauce thickens. Serve over steaming bed of rice. Serves 4.

PANEED VEAL IN CAJUN SAUCE

6 slices baby veal, pounded with tenderizing hammer
1/2 stick margarine
3/4 c. all-purpose flour
1 large onion, cut into rings
1 large zucchini, cut into rings
1 large yellow squash, cut into rings
Juice of 1 lemon

1 c. sour cream
1 c. shrimp, peeled, deveined and diced
1/2 c. grated Parmesan cheese
2 tsp. salt
1 tsp. sweet paprika
1/2 tsp. onion powder
1/2 tsp. ground red pepper
1/2 tsp. garlic powder
1/4 tsp. dry mustard

In a small bowl, combine seasonings; mix well. Set aside. Dust veal steaks well with 1/2 seasoning mix. In a separate bowl, mix the flour with 1/2 of the remaining seasoning mix. Dredge the veal in the seasoned flour and shake off excess. In a large skillet, melt 1/4 stick margarine at 450°. Add the veal and fry until brown. Remove veal from the heat and set aside. Allow drippings to remain. Reduce the heat to 350°. Add zucchini, onion, and yellow squash; saute for 3 minutes, stirring frequently. Add lemon juice and remaining margarine. Stir well. Add any remaining seasoning mix and blend in sour cream. Bring to a simmer and add shrimp. Simmer for an additional 2 minutes. Reduce heat to 250°. Add veal. Add cheese and remove from heat when melted. Serve with steaming mounds of rice. Serves 6.

BEEF STUFFED MUSHROOMS IN WINE SAUCE

12 large mushrooms
1 lb. ground beef
1/4 c. green pepper, chopped fine
1/4 c. celery, chopped fine
1/4 c. onions, chopped fine
1 c. rice, cooked

1 can cream of mushroom soup
1/3 tsp. black pepper
1/4 tsp. thyme
1/4 tsp. white pepper
1/4 tsp. oregano
1/4 stick margarine

Remove stems from the mushrooms and chop fine; set aside. In a large saucepan, melt margarine at 450°. Add meat and saute until lightly browned. Add vegetables and mushroom stems (not the mushroom caps); saute until soft. Reduce heat to 250°. Blend in all ingredients, including rice. Stuff mushroom caps. Arrange mushroom caps in a lightly oiled casserole dish. Bake at 250° until mushrooms are soft.

Sauce:

1/2 c. dry white wine
1/4 stick margarine
1 c. sour cream

3 Tbsp. all-purpose flour
Juice of 1/2 lemon

In a saucepan, melt margarine at 300°. Blend in flour until it gels. Slowly add wine and lemon juice. Reduce heat to 200°. Add sour cream; blend well. Remove from heat. Pour over the mushrooms and serve over a bed of rice. Serves 6.

DELICIOUS SPAGHETTI MEAT SAUCE FRANKLIN

2 lb. ground beef
2 cans tomato paste
1/4 stick margarine
2/3 c. onions, chopped
2/3 c. celery, chopped
1/3 c. parsley, chopped
1 Tbsp. sugar
1/2 c. green pepper, chopped
1/2 tsp. thyme

1/2 tsp. bay leaf
1/4 tsp. oregano
3 garlic cloves, chopped
1/2 tsp. black pepper
1/4 tsp. white pepper
1/4 tsp. ground red pepper
4 beef bouillon cubes
4 c. hot water
1 tsp. salt

In a bowl, combine seasonings; set aside. Dissolve bouillon cubes in 4 cups hot water. In a large skillet, melt 1/8 stick margarine at 450°. Add tomato paste and 1/2 seasoning mix. Fry until dark red and paste separates. Add vegetables and saute until soft. Remove from heat and set aside. In separate saucepan, melt remaining margarine at 450°. Add ground beef and saute until light brown. Add vegetable mixture. Blend well, stirring frequently. Add remaining seasoning mix. Reduce the heat to 300°. Add sugar and blend well. Add bouillon, blending slowly, and bring to a simmer. Simmer for 45 minutes or until sauce becomes thick. Serve over spaghetti and sprinkle with Italian cheese. Serves 6.

VEAL SCALLOPINI, CAJUN STYLE

2 lb. veal cutlets
¾ c. Italian cheese, grated
¼ c. parsley, chopped
1 c. flour
1 tsp. garlic powder
1 tsp. oregano
2 c. brown roux

2 cans mushrooms
1 tsp. sugar
½ c. onions, chopped
¼ tsp. white pepper
¼ tsp. red pepper
½ stick margarine
3 eggs, beaten

Pound veal with a tenderizing hammer until flat. In a bowl, combine seasonings; set aside. In a separate bowl, combine ½ seasoning mix and beaten eggs; stir well. In a separate bowl, mix the flour and remaining seasoning mix. Dip the veal into the egg mix, then dredge thoroughly into seasoned flour. Coat well and set aside. In a saucepan, melt ¼ stick margarine at 400°. Add vegetables and saute until soft. Slowly add 2 cups brown roux, blending well. Bring to a slow simmer for 10 minutes.

In a separate saucepan, melt ¼ stick margarine at 450° and saute veal until light brown on both sides. Remove from heat and set aside. Return roux mixture to the heat at 350°. Add ¼ cup Italian cheese, controlling thickness with hot milk. Pour half of this mixture into a lightly oiled casserole dish. Sprinkle with ¼ cup Italian cheese. Arrange cutlets on top. Pour remaining mixture over top and sprinkle with remaining Italian cheese. Cover and bake at 350° for 30 minutes or until cutlets are done. Serves 8.

CREOLE BREADED VEAL CUTLETS

2 lb. veal cutlets, sliced thin and
　　pounded (breakfast steaks
　　can be substituted for veal)
½ stick margarine
2 c. seasoned bread crumbs
½ tsp. garlic powder
½ tsp. onion powder

¼ tsp. thyme
¼ tsp. white pepper
⅛ tsp. red pepper
¼ tsp. oregano
4 eggs, beaten
¼ c. heavy cream
¼ c. Italian cheese

In a small bowl, combine seasonings; set aside. In a separate bowl, combine cream with beaten eggs and seasonings. Blend well. Dip cutlets into egg mixture, then pat thoroughly into bread crumbs. It may be necessary to repeat this process to form a thick coat. In a saucepan, melt margarine at 350°. Add cutlets and saute until brown on both sides. Add ¼ cup Italian cheese to a cream of wine sauce and serve over cutlets. Serves 6.

CAJUN PORK CHOPS IN CREAM OF APPLESAUCE

8 (½ inch thick) pork chops
1 c. sherry
½ tsp. cinnamon
½ tsp. nutmeg
1 large can applesauce
½ c. dried apples

½ stick margarine
3 Tbsp. all-purpose flour
½ tsp. white pepper
¼ tsp. ground red pepper
Juice of 1 lemon
1 tsp. salt

In a saucepan, melt margarine at 450°. Add pork chops and saute until brown on both sides. Remove from the heat. Remove pork from the pan; allow drippings to remain. In a separate bowl, combine seasonings, lemon juice, wine, apples, and applesauce together, blending well. Add the mixture to the drippings and return pan to the heat at 300°. Bring mixture to a simmer for 3 minutes. In a lightly oiled casserole dish, pour in half of the mixture. Arrange cutlets on top. Cover with remaining mixture. Bake for 30 minutes at 350°. Surround the outer edge of a serving platter with mounds of rice. Fill the center with pork chops. Pour sauce over rice and serve. Serves 6.

SPICY MEAT PATTIES IN RED WINE SAUCE

2 lb. ground beef
1 stick margarine
½ c. salad olives, finely chopped
½ c. onions, finely chopped
½ c. celery, finely chopped
½ tsp. oregano

1 c. seasoned bread crumbs
1 can cream of mushroom soup
½ tsp. black pepper
½ tsp. ground red pepper
1 tsp. salt
1 c. all-purpose flour

In a large bowl, combine ingredients except flour. Form into 1 inch thick patties. In a separate bowl, add flour and pat in patties well; shake off excess. In a large saucepan, melt margarine at 400°. Add patties and fry on both sides until brown. Cover and reduce heat to 200°.

Sauce:

3 Tbsp. all-purpose flour
3 Tbsp. margarine
1 c. sweet red wine

2 Tbsp. Parmesan cheese
½ c. sour cream

In a small saucepan, melt margarine at 300°. Add flour and saute until it gels. Add wine, stirring well. Add sour cream and cheese; saute for 3 minutes. Pour over top of patties. Cover and cook for an additional 15 minutes. Serves 6.

THIBODEAUX RED WINE POT ROAST

2 lb. beef, cut into chunks
1 large onion, sliced
4 large carrots, sliced
1½ c. red wine
¼ stick margarine
4 Tbsp. all-purpose flour
1 c. hot water

2 beef bouillon cubes
1 tsp. garlic flakes
½ tsp. rosemary
½ tsp. thyme
½ tsp. coarse ground pepper
¼ tsp. ground red pepper

Dissolve bouillon cubes in 1 cup hot water; set aside. In a small bowl, add seasonings; mix well. Set aside. In a large bowl, mix onion, red wine and ½ seasoning mix. Add meat and allow to marinate for 2 hours. Remove the meat and retain the wine marinade.

In a large saucepan, melt margarine at 450°. Add meat and saute until brown on both sides. Remove meat from pan. Add flour and stir until dark brown. Add onion and wine marinade, blending well for 2 minutes. Add bouillon, stirring in well. Add meat, remaining seasoning mix and carrots. Reduce heat to 300°. Cover and cook until done. Serve with steaming rice. Serves 6.

GROUND VEAL EGGPLANT CASSEROLE BIENVILLE

2 lb. ground veal
1 eggplant
½ stick margarine
½ c. flour
2 cans tomato sauce
½ tsp. oregano
¼ c. Parmesan cheese

1 c. Cheddar cheese, grated
¼ tsp. white pepper
¼ tsp. red pepper
¼ tsp. tarragon
½ tsp. coarse ground black
    pepper
1 tsp. salt

In a bowl, combine seasonings; set aside. Combine ½ seasoning mix with ground veal and shape into elongated patties. In a saucepan, melt ¼ stick margarine at 400°. Saute patties until brown. Remove patties from pan and set aside. Slice eggplant into 1 inch thick slices; do not remove the skin. Combine remaining seasoning mix with the flour. Dip eggplant quickly into the saucepan and remove from the heat. Pat thoroughly into the seasoned flour. Add remaining margarine and return eggplant to the saucepan; saute until brown on both sides. In a slightly oiled casserole dish, arrange eggplant slices. Top with veal patties. Cover with tomato sauce and alternate layers of cheese. Bake at 300° for 30 minutes. Serves 6.

CAJUN BABY LAMB CHOPS IN PARMESAN CHEESE BATTER

12 single rib chops
3/4 c. grated Parmesan cheese
3 eggs, lightly beaten
1 c. bread crumbs
1 stick margarine
1 tsp. sweet paprika
1 tsp. garlic powder

1/2 tsp. white pepper
1/4 tsp. thyme
1/4 tsp. black pepper
1/4 tsp. ground red pepper
1 tsp. onion powder
1 tsp. salt

In a bowl, combine seasonings; set aside. Combine Parmesan cheese and bread crumbs in a large soup plate. In a separate bowl, combine lightly beaten eggs and seasoning mix. Dredge the chops into the Parmesan cheese, then into the eggs. Repeat the action and shake off excess. In a saucepan, melt margarine at 350°. Fry the chops until golden brown. Serves 10.

Note: The lamb chops should fry to a golden crust within 4 to 5 minutes. Do not overcook.

CAJUN BEEF STEW CANAL STREET

2 lb. cubed beef
1 stick margarine
4 onions, chopped in squares
1 c. celery, chopped large
1/4 c. parsley, chopped large
4 cloves garlic, halved
1/2 tsp. thyme
2 bay leaves
1/4 tsp. sweet basil
1/4 tsp. sage
2 tsp. paprika
1 tsp. red ground pepper

1 tsp. coarse ground black
   pepper
1 tsp. Creole mustard
1/4 c. all purpose flour
2 Tbsp. Worcestershire sauce
4 bouillon cubes
4 c. hot water
2 cans tomatoes
3 c. red wine
2 c. carrots, chopped large
3 large potatoes, chopped in
   chunks

Dissolve bouillon cubes in 4 cups hot water; set aside. In a bowl, combine seasonings; set aside. In a large deep skillet, melt margarine at 450°. Add meat and saute until light brown. Add flour; stir in well until flour browns and coats meat well. Add 1/2 seasoning mix, blending well. Add vegetables; this dish must be stirred continuously for 5 minutes. Flour will continue to darken. Add bouillon liquid and remaining ingredients. Bring to a brisk simmer for 40 minutes. Stir frequently. If necessary, add water to control moisture. Serves 10.

BEEF CUBES IN CAJUN HOT SAUCE

3 lb. lean beef, cut into 2 inch squares
1/2 c. bell peppers, chopped fine
1/2 c. celery, chopped fine
1/2 stick margarine
3/4 c. onions, chopped fine
1/4 c. all-purpose flour
1/2 tsp. ground red pepper
1/2 tsp. white pepper
1/2 tsp. black pepper
2 bay leaves
2 jalapeno peppers, chopped fine
2 beef bouillon cubes
3 c. hot water

In a bowl, combine onions, bell peppers and celery. Mix well and set aside. Dissolve bouillon cubes in 3 cups hot water. In a large saucepan, melt margarine at 450°. Add steak chunks and seasonings; saute until brown. Remove steak and allow drippings to remain. Add flour, blending thoroughly until light brown. Remove from the heat and immediately stir in vegetables. Return pan to the heat at 300°. Saute vegetables for 2 minutes. Add remaining ingredients except bouillon and meat. Stir well for 2 minutes. Slowly blend in bouillon. Simmer for 2 minutes, stirring briskly. Add beef and simmer at 250° for 10 minutes. Control moisture with additional hot water. Serve over mounds of rice. Serves 8.

BEEF STUFFED TOMATO BURAS

2 lb. ground meat
1 c. tomato sauce
2 Tbsp. all-purpose flour
1/2 stick margarine
1/4 c. onions, chopped
1 Tbsp. parsley, chopped
3/4 c. rice, 3/4 cooked
8 large tomatoes
1/4 tsp. ground dried bay leaf
1/4 tsp. oregano
1/4 tsp. sweet paprika
1/4 tsp. thyme
1/4 tsp. basil
1/4 tsp. white pepper
1/8 tsp. red pepper

Core tomatoes and chop cores fine; set aside. In a saucepan, melt margarine at 450°. Add meat and saute until light brown. Add flour; blend well until light brown. Add vegetables, including tomato cores, and saute until soft. Add tomato sauce. Blend well and reduce heat to 250°. Add seasonings, blending well. Add rice and simmer at 250° for 20 minutes. Remove from the heat and allow to cool. If mixture contains too much moisture, add bread crumbs. Stuff tomatoes with mixture. In a lightly oiled casserole dish, add 1/4 inch deep water. Arrange tomatoes so they will not turn over. Bake at 350° for 45 minutes. Serves 8.

VEAL IN CREOLE CAJUN SAUCE

2 lb. veal, cubed bite-size
1 c. peeled tomatoes, chopped
¾ c. celery, chopped
¾ c. bell peppers, chopped
¾ c. onions, chopped
2 Tbsp. garlic, chopped fine
1 cube chicken bouillon
1½ c. hot water
1 c. tomato sauce
1 tsp. brown sugar

2 bay leaves
½ tsp. white pepper
¼ tsp. red pepper
½ tsp. sweet paprika
½ tsp. oregano
½ tsp. black pepper
½ tsp. thyme
½ tsp. sweet basil
½ stick margarine
1 tsp. salt

Dissolve bouillon cube in 1½ cups hot water; set aside. In a large skillet, melt margarine at 450°. Add veal and saute until light brown. Reduce the heat to 300°. Add bell peppers, celery, tomatoes, onions, and garlic. Stir in well and add seasonings. Continue to saute for 5 minutes, stirring frequently. Add bouillon and tomato sauce; blend in sugar carefully. Allow mixture to reach a boil for 2 minutes. Reduce the heat and simmer for 20 minutes, stirring occasionally.

Serve with just about anything. Serves 6.

POT PORK ROAST WITH SWEET POTATOES SHREVEPORT

Trim lean pork roast and slice in between each rib to the bottom bone.

3 lb. pork roast
1 large can sweet potatoes
¼ c. onions, finely chopped
2 Tbsp. parsley, finely chopped
1 tsp. garlic powder
3 Tbsp. all-purpose flour
¼ stick margarine

¼ tsp. white pepper
¼ tsp. red pepper
1 tsp. coarse ground black
   pepper
¼ tsp. basil
¼ tsp. dry mustard
1 beef bouillon cube
2 c. hot water

Dissolve bouillon cube in 2 cups hot water; set aside. Place roast in a large Dutch oven or ovenproof skillet. Melt margarine at 450°. Brown roast on both sides. Remove roast from pan and allow drippings to remain. Add flour, blending continuously until light brown. Blend in bouillon liquid for 2 minutes. Remove pan from the heat. Stand the roast up in a skillet. Sprinkle with seasonings. Cover and cook until roast begins to tender. Remove roast from heat and set aside.

Combine together potatoes, onions and parsley. Mash together and blend well. Stuff in between cut in the ribs. Return roast to heat at 300°. Cover and continue to cook until roast is tender. Serves 8.

BARBECUE SHRIMP FERRIDAY

2 lb. large shrimp with heads
   removed (retain heads)
1/4 tsp. oregano
1/2 tsp. thyme
1/4 tsp. red pepper
1 tsp. salt
1/2 tsp. black pepper

1/2 tsp. rosemary
1 1/4 sticks margarine
1 tsp. garlic powder
1 tsp. Worcestershire sauce
1 c. beer
1 c. shrimp stock

In a small bowl, combine seasonings; set aside. In a saucepan, add 2 cups hot water, 1/2 teaspoon seasoning mix and shrimp heads; saute for 5 minutes. Remove from the heat and strain. Retain the liquid and discard the heads. In a bowl, melt 1 stick margarine at room temperature. Add Worcestershire sauce and remaining seasoning mix; blend well. Heat a large skillet to 400°. Add seasoning mixture, stirring rapidly. Add shrimp and cook for 3 minutes, shaking the pan continuously.

Add remaining margarine and 1 cup shrimp stock. Shake the pan well for 2 minutes. Add the beer and cook for an additional 2 minutes. Remove from the heat. Serve in a soup bowl over a heaping mound of steaming rice. Serves 4.

CREOLE BARBECUE STEAK IN PEANUT BUTTER WINE SAUCE

3 lb. tender steak
1 c. red wine
1 c. chunky peanut butter
3/4 stick margarine
1/2 tsp. white pepper
1/2 tsp. red pepper

1/2 tsp. coarse ground black
   pepper
1 tsp. salt
1/8 tsp. garlic powder
1/8 tsp. onion powder

In a bowl, combine seasonings; set aside. In a saucepan, melt 1/2 stick margarine at 300°. Slowly blend in peanut butter, stirring continuously. When peanut butter begins to bubble, add red wine, 2 ounces at a time. When mixture gels, remove from the heat. Stir in seasonings. In a large saucepan, melt remaining margarine at 450° until smoke occurs. Add steak and sear on both sides. Remove from the heat. Place the steak on a preheated barbecue pit covered with foil. Paint heavily with the peanut butter sauce. Turn over and paint heavily again. When cooked to your desire, serve. Serves 8.

BARBECUE RIBS IN SPICY CREOLE SAUCE

3 lb. barbecue rib slab
½ lb. thick bacon, diced
1½ c. onion, diced
2 c. hot water
2 chicken bouillon cubes
1½ c. chili sauce
1 c. honey
½ tsp. ground red pepper
½ tsp. white pepper

½ tsp. black pepper
1 tsp. garlic powder
1 tsp. onion powder
1 tsp. salt
2 Tbsp. lemon juice
1 tsp. garlic flakes
½ tsp. Tabasco sauce
¼ stick margarine

Dissolve bouillon cubes in 2 cups hot water; set aside. In a bowl, combine seasonings; set aside. In a saucepan, melt margarine and fry bacon until brown at 400°. Add onion and saute until brown, stirring frequently. Blend in seasonings. Add bouillon liquid and chili sauce; saute for 1 minute. Add lemon juice and Tabasco sauce. Reduce the heat to 200° and saute for an additional 10 minutes. Remove from the heat and blend in honey. Place the ribs in a hot barbecue pit and sear until light brown on both sides. Frequently paint sauce on both sides until a rich brown glaze appears. Slice into pieces and serve. Serves 8.

BARBECUE HAM STEAK HAMMOND

8 (1 inch thick) ham steaks
1 stick margarine
2 c. cooked rice

¾ tsp. dry mustard
½ c. dark brown sugar
1 Tbsp. paprika

Marinade:

3 tsp. powdered cloves
4 c. sherry wine
6 cloves, finely chopped
1 tsp. white pepper

¼ tsp. ground red pepper
¼ tsp. coarse ground black
  pepper
¼ tsp. basil

In a large casserole dish, combine marinade ingredients, whisking thoroughly. Add ham to marinade and allow to stand for 4 hours. Remove ham from the marinade. Melt margarine at room temperature and add to marinade with remaining ingredients. Place on side of barbecue pit to keep hot. Barbecue ham steaks on a blistering hot grill; baste frequently on both sides with sauce. Lay a ½ inch thick bed of steaming rice on a large heated serving dish. Lay in ham steak. Cover with another layer of rice. Pour over remaining barbecue sauce and serve. Serves 8.

BARBECUE PORK CHOPS WITH
ORANGE MARMALADE BASILE

8 (½ inch thick) pork chops
½ lb. thick sliced bacon,
   chopped
½ c. orange marmalade
1 whole orange
1 chicken bouillon cube
2 c. hot water
1 c. chili sauce
1 c. honey

1½ tsp. coarse ground black
   pepper
1 tsp. salt
1 tsp. onion powder
1 tsp. garlic powder
½ tsp. ground red pepper
1 lemon
1 tsp. garlic powder
½ tsp. Tabasco sauce

In a small bowl, grate the orange and lemon. Squeeze juices in a separate bowl and discard the pulp; set aside. Dissolve bouillon cube in 2 cups hot water; set aside. In a bowl, combine seasonings; set aside. In a saucepan, fry bacon at 450° until brown. Remove from pan and crush; set aside. Add pork chops and sear on both sides. Remove and set aside.

Reduce the heat to 300°. Add bouillon liquid, honey, chili sauce, orange and lemon juice, orange and lemon grated rind, and Tabasco sauce. Simmer for an additional 10 minutes, stirring frequently. Remove from the heat. Blend in marmalade. Pour ½ barbecue sauce in the bottom of a broiling pan. Arrange pork chops on top. Pour remaining sauce over chops. Barbecue at a high temperature, turning the chops frequently until forming a heavy glaze. Serve. Serves 8.

BARBECUE CAJUN CHICKEN

3 lb. chicken parts
¼ stick margarine
¼ c. onions, chopped fine
2 cloves garlic, chopped fine
3 Tbsp. A.1. Steak Sauce
¼ c. dry white wine
¼ c. tomato sauce

1 tsp. hot sauce
1 tsp. white pepper
½ tsp. ground white pepper
4 Tbsp. dark brown sugar
2 Tbsp. Worcestershire sauce
¼ tsp. chili powder

In a saucepan, melt margarine at 400°. Add chicken parts and saute until light brown on both sides. Remove from pan and allow the drippings to remain. Add remaining ingredients to the drippings. Bring to a brisk simmer for 3 minutes, whisking rapidly and allowing mixture to gel. In a lightly oiled casserole dish, arrange chicken. Pour sauce over chicken. Place under a broiler; rotate frequently. Broil until done. Serves 8.

BARBECUE ROAST BATON ROUGE

1 (6 lb.) sirloin roast

Sauce:

1 Tbsp. celery seed
1 Tbsp. chili powder
½ c. brown sugar
1 tsp. sweet paprika
1 c. tomato sauce

1 stick margarine

¼ c. wine vinegar
1 tsp. salt
½ tsp. white pepper
½ tsp. red pepper

In a bowl, combine chili powder, sugar, salt, paprika, and celery seed; set aside. In a separate bowl, combine the peppers. In a saucepan, melt margarine at 450°. Rub sirloin thoroughly with pepper seasoning mix. Braise the roast until brown on both sides. Remove from heat and set aside. Reduce the heat to 250°. Combine all remaining ingredients. Allow to saute until sauce thickens. Make ½ inch slits on both sides of the roast. Place on a barbecue pit. Coat generously with sauce and barbecue until both sides form a glaze. Serves 6.

BARBECUE PORK CHOPS HOUMA

8 large boneless pork chops
¼ c. liquid smoke
1 tsp. garlic salt
1 tsp. celery salt
1 tsp. onion salt
¼ c. Worcestershire sauce

¼ c. brown sugar
Juice of 1 lemon
½ c. catsup
¼ c. hickory smoked mustard
1 stick margarine
1 c. dry white wine

Combine the first 5 ingredients in a casserole dish, whisking well. Add pork chops and allow to marinate for 4 hours. In a saucepan, melt margarine at 400°. Braise pork chops on both sides until light brown. Reduce the heat to 300°. Remove pork chops and set aside. Stir in marinade. Add remaining ingredients, blending well. Simmer until sauce thickens. Add pork chops; turn over frequently for 5 minutes. Place pork chops on a broiling pan with a rack. Broil close to the heat, painting frequently with the sauce until a heavy glaze forms. Remove from heat and place chops on a serving platter. Stir wine into the drippings. Surround pork chops with steaming rice and cover with sauce. Serves 8.

BARBECUE STEAK DE RIDDER

3 lb. sirloin steak or other tender
    type
1 c. onions, finely chopped
½ stick margarine
½ tsp. celery powder
¼ tsp. black pepper
¼ tsp. white pepper
½ tsp. oregano
½ tsp. thyme
½ tsp. rosemary
½ tsp. garlic powder
½ c. red wine

Combine ingredients thoroughly except meat. Pour over steak; marinate for 2 hours on both sides. Barbecue on hot coals. Baste frequently; cook to your desired taste. Serves 8.

QUICK CREOLE BARBECUE TURKEY BURGERS

3 lb. ground turkey
2 beaten eggs
1 stick margarine
½ c. bread crumbs
½ bottle beef steak sauce
¼ bottle Worcestershire sauce
2 Tbsp. onion juice
1 tsp. garlic salt
1 Tbsp. brown sugar
1 Tbsp. parsley, finely chopped
¼ tsp. celery seeds
½ tsp. black pepper
½ tsp. red pepper
1 tsp. salt

In a large bowl, combine ground meat, salt, peppers, garlic, eggs, bread crumbs, and parsley. Form into elongated 1 inch thick patties. In a large saucepan, melt margarine at 400°. Add patties and saute on both sides until light brown. Remove from pan and set aside. Return pan to the heat and blend in remaining ingredients. Simmer until sauce thickens. Place sauce on the barbecue pit to keep warm. Place patties on a hot barbecue pit, turning and basting often with sauce until done. Dip French bread halves into sauce. Add patties. Cover with shredded lettuce and thin sliced tomatoes and serve. Serves 8.

CAJUN BARBECUE CHICKEN IN PECAN SAUCE

8 chicken fryer quarters
1 c. dry roasted pecans,
   chopped
1 c. sweet red wine
1 orange
1 lemon
1 Tbsp. Tabasco sauce
¼ stick margarine
2 tsp. garlic, minced
1½ c. onions, chopped fine
2 chicken bouillon cubes

2 c. hot water
1 c. honey
1½ c. chili sauce
½ tsp. ground red pepper
½ tsp. white pepper
1 tsp. garlic powder
1 tsp. onion powder
1 tsp. salt
1 tsp. coarse ground black
   pepper

Use a separate bowl for each ingredient: Grate lemon and orange peel. Separate the orange into slices and remove the skins. Grind the lemon into a pulp. In a small bowl, combine seasonings; set aside. Dissolve bouillon cubes in 2 cups hot water; set aside. In a saucepan, melt margarine at 400°. Add onions and saute until light brown. Add seasoning mix, blending well for 2 minutes. Add bouillon liquid, chili sauce, orange and lemon juice, including lemon rinds and pulp. Add garlic and Tabasco sauce. Reduce the heat to 250°. Simmer for 15 minutes, stirring frequently. Remove from the heat and blend in all remaining ingredients except red wine. Return to the heat and simmer until sauce reaches a heavy thickness.

Place chicken parts, skin down on a hot barbecue pit. Paint chicken generously with the sauce. Turn over frequently and paint generously to form a heavy dark brown glaze. Add 1 cup sweet red wine to remaining barbecue sauce. Arrange chicken on a platter; surround with a mound of cooked brown rice. Cover with barbecue sauce and serve. Serves 8.

PONTCHARTRAIN BARBECUED GRILLED FISH

4 lb. grouper, red snapper or like
1 stick margarine
1 tsp. onion salt
1 Tbsp. green pepper, finely
   chopped
½ tsp. garlic powder
1 Tbsp. parsley, finely chopped

Juice of ½ lemon
1 tsp. Louisiana hot sauce
2 Tbsp. Worcestershire sauce
¼ tsp. oregano
½ tsp. coarse ground black
   pepper

In a saucepan, melt margarine at 400°. Add seasonings and stir in well. Add Worcestershire sauce and hot sauce; blend well. Reduce the heat to 200°. Add green pepper and parsley and bring to a simmer. Lay fish steaks on foil, forming a boat that can be closed at the top. Pour a generous amount of sauce over the fish. Seal top of the foil and place on a hot grill. After 25 minutes, open seal and turn the fish over. Reseal top and continue to grill until fish is flaky and tender. If fish is developing too much moisture, you can leave top of the foil open to increase the absorption rate. Squeeze with lemon juice and serve. Serves 8.

CREAMY BARBECUE SAUCE FOR STEAKS
AND HAMBURGERS RACELAND

1 c. crunchy peanut butter
1 can sliced mushrooms
1/4 c. green onions, finely
  chopped
1/2 stick margarine
1/2 c. dry white wine

1 c. sour cream
1/2 tsp. paprika
1/4 tsp. white pepper
1/4 tsp. red pepper
1/4 tsp. oregano

In a bowl, combine seasonings; set aside. In a saucepan, melt margarine at 350°. Add mushrooms and green onions; saute for 3 minutes. Slowly blend in peanut butter and bring to a simmer. Reduce heat to 250°. Blend in sour cream, whisking rapidly. Blend in wine and simmer until sauce thickens. Serves 12.

Delicious as a barbecue coating over steaks or hamburgers.

CREOLE BARBECUED GLAZED CHICKEN

6 boneless chicken breasts,
  flattened
4 c. cooked yellow rice
1/2 c. tomato sauce
1/4 c. steak sauce
1 tsp. hot sauce
Juice of 1 lemon
3 Tbsp. onions, finely chopped
1 clove garlic, finely chopped

1/2 tsp. chili powder
1/2 tsp. paprika
1 Tbsp. dark brown sugar
1 c. cream of chicken soup
1 stick margarine
1/4 tsp. dry mustard
1 Tbsp. Worcestershire sauce
1/4 c. green peppers, finely
  chopped
1/4 c. dry red wine

In a bowl, combine seasonings; set aside. In a saucepan, melt margarine at 450° until smoke appears. Rub chicken thoroughly with 1/2 seasoning mix. Braise the chicken for 2 minutes on each side and remove from the heat. Allow the drippings to remain. Add vegetables, stirring rapidly. Add remaining seasoning mix, blending well. Add remaining ingredients, except chicken and rice, whisking rapidly until sauce thickens. Remove from the heat and set aside. Place the chicken in the bottom of a shallow baking pan. Cover with the sauce. Place under a hot grill, turning frequently. Remove from the heat after a glaze has formed. Surround with steaming yellow rice and serve directly from the pan. Serves 6.

SPICY PEACH BARBECUE SAUCE
FOR CHICKEN, CAJUN STYLE

3 fresh peaches, peeled and
    diced
2 cans firm sliced peaches
1 c. brown sugar
4 c. hot water
2 chicken bouillon cubes
½ c. bell peppers, chopped fine

½ c. celery, chopped fine
½ c. onions, chopped fine
1 bay leaf
½ tsp. white pepper
½ tsp. red pepper
Juice of 1 lemon
¼ stick margarine

Dissolve bouillon cubes in 3 cups hot water. In a saucepan, add 1 cup hot water and bring to a simmer. Blend in brown sugar. Add fresh, chopped peaches, lemon juice and the water from the canned peaches. Bring to a brisk simmer. Stir until liquid thickens, about 30 minutes.

In a separate saucepan, melt margarine at 300°. Add bell peppers, onions, celery, and seasonings. Saute until tender, stirring frequently. Add bouillon and bring to a boil. Reduce the heat to a brisk simmer for 10 minutes. Add peach mixture, blending well. When sauce thickens, remove from heat. Add canned peaches. Use a hand blender, blending the ingredients for 30 seconds. This should form a heavy puree. Use this sauce to barbecue chicken under a hot grill. Serves 8.

CAJUN STYLE SWISS STEAK

2 lb. sirloin steak
1 c. flour
¼ stick margarine
½ c. onions, diced
½ c. hot water
2 c. tomato sauce

1 c. celery, diced
¼ c. bell pepper, diced
1 tsp. salt
1 tsp. coarse ground black
    pepper

Cut meat in 1 inch strips. Season well with salt and pepper. Roll the steak into flour. In a saucepan, melt margarine at 450°. Sear the meat until golden brown on both sides. Add celery, onions, tomato sauce, pepper, and water. Bring the mixture to a simmer. Simmer until steak is tender. Form a gravy by stirring and add hot water when necessary. Serve. Serves 6.

"Now, just how do you think you're going to get me in that pot, Cajun?"

Quick Game

A WORD FROM CLOVICE:

Game is sometin' a Cajun never plays wit wen it comes to huntin'. When my wife and I go to our favorite huntin' lodge in dat for'eign land called south Texas, we have found dere is all dif'ferent kind of hunters.

Dey got dese fellas dat turn up at de lodge wit guns big enough to hunt dem elephants and consider all dat hairy food out dere as game.

Dere is de timid hunter who tries not to hurt de deer wen he shoots him.

Den dere is dat serious hunter who comes equipt wit a computer printout as to why he missed. Den dere's dat ever-present liar who tries to B.S. dis expert in dat field.

Den dere's dat unbelievably embarrassing woman like my lil' wife who I am always ashamed to have around when I go huntin'. Tink about it, hoss, she neck shoots at 400-500 yards and I'm still waitin' for her to miss. Now, if you don't tink that's embarrassin' send me some of dem lies to help me es'splain why I miss and she don't.

Den dere's dat creature dat terrifies all de game, de animals too. It's called a Cajun Creole. Cause he is ordained, certified, legitimatized, and authorized as a genu'ine pot hunter. If'n he kills it, he a gonna eat it.

Cornstarch and arrowroot will give a clear quality to a sauce when used. One tablespoon of cornstarch is equal to 2 1/2 tablespoons of flour when used as a thickener.

When flour is used as a thickener, cook it for 1-2 minutes in hot melted fat, butter, margarine or oil. This helps the flour to mix easily with the liquid. Always mix flour in a hot cup of water to add to a liquid if you don't use fats or oils.

Egg yolks make a delicate thickener and adds no starch. Don't add egg yolks to a boiling liquid or they will curdle.

Pureed vegetables blended with 1 tablespoon of flour makes an excellent thickener for soups.

If raisins seem dry, blanche them quickly in boiling water and drain or steam them over a sieve over boiling water.

Always take extreme care to control the heat when cooking with sour cream; it will curdle easy. To discourage curdling, add a small amount of flour to the cream and mix well with a whisk while cooking.

For a super taste, use dark roasted, freshly ground peanuts. Most health food stores and some groceries have grinding machines for this.

QUICK GAME

CORNISH HENS IN SPICY FIG GRAVY

6 Cornish hens, split at the back and flattened
3 chicken bouillon cubes
4 c. hot water
½ stick margarine
2 jars whole figs in heavy syrup
1 c. brown sugar
1 c. onions, chopped fine

1 c. celery, chopped fine
½ c. green peppers, chopped fine
1 tsp. ground red pepper
½ tsp. thyme
½ tsp. white pepper
1 orange
Juice of ½ lemon

Peel and separate the orange sections. Remove peeling and discard. Dissolve bouillon in 4 cups hot water; set aside. Drain and separate figs from syrup and retain. In a large saucepan, melt 1 tablespoon margarine at 400°. Add syrup and blend in sugar, mixing well. Allow to caramelize. Remove from heat and set aside.

In a separate saucepan, melt remaining margarine at 400°. Add ½ cup celery, green peppers and ¾ cup onions; saute until soft, about 4 minutes. Add vegetable mix to the caramelized sauce; blend in well. Add 2 cups bouillon liquid; whisk in thoroughly. Return saucepan to the heat at 400° and cook for 10 to 15 minutes, stirring frequently. Add orange sections; cook for an additional 5 minutes. Add remaining ingredients and simmer until dish begins to thicken. Remove sauce from the heat. Pour into a food processor and puree. Arrange Cornish hens in the bottom of a shallow baking dish. Cover with sauce and bake at 350°, turning hens over twice. Bake until done. Serves 6.

CREOLE RABBIT

1 rabbit, skinned, cleaned and quartered
1 tsp. ground red pepper
¼ tsp. black pepper
1 tsp. garlic powder
1 tsp. white pepper
2 bay leaves
1 tsp. salt

1 c. celery, chopped
¼ c. green pepper, chopped
2 c. dark brown roux
4 sweet potatoes, peeled
1 c. onions, chopped
¼ stick margarine
2 c. hot water

In a bowl, combine seasonings; set aside. Place 2 cups of boiling water in a saucepan. Add half of the seasoning mix. Place rabbit parts in pan; parboil on both sides until tender. The majority of water should be removed at this time. Remove rabbit from pan. In the same saucepan, melt margarine at 400°. Add vegetables, except potatoes, and saute until tender. Slowly blend in roux and remaining seasonings; mix well. Briskly saute for 5 minutes. In a lightly oiled casserole dish, arrange rabbit parts. Circle with sweet potatoes and cover with sauce. Bake at 350° until rabbit is extremely tender. Serves 6.

PHEASANT IN SMOKED SAUSAGE GUMBO ST. TAMMANY

3 pheasants, dressed and
    quartered
½ lb. Italian or Polish smoked
    sausage
2 c. wild rice, ¾ cooked
1½ c. all-purpose flour
2 c. onion, chopped
2 c. green pepper, chopped

2 c. celery, chopped
3 qt. hot water
4 chicken bouillon cubes
1 c. corn oil
1 tsp. garlic flakes
2 bay leaves
¼ stick margarine

Seasoning Mix:

½ tsp. cumin
½ tsp. dry mustard
½ tsp. black pepper
2 tsp. salt

½ tsp. ground red pepper
1 tsp. garlic powder
1 tsp. onion powder
2 tsp. sweet paprika

Dissolve bouillon cubes in 3 quarts hot water; set aside. In a bowl, combine Seasoning Mix; blend well and set aside. Rub pheasant parts with 1 tablespoon Seasoning Mix. In a bowl, place 1 cup flour and 1 tablespoon Seasoning Mix; blend well. Dredge pheasant parts in flour; shake off excess. Retain flour; set aside. Heat the corn oil at 400° in a separate saucepan and fry pheasant pieces until light brown on each side. Remove from the pan and place on a paper towel. Drain oil from pan, allowing the flour residue to remain.

Add ¼ stick margarine to the pan and return to 450° heat. Add remaining flour, stirring briskly until roux becomes a dark red brown. Remove from the heat and stir in vegetables. Return pan to the heat at 350°. Blend in bouillon. Slowly add all remaining ingredients, one at a time. Add pheasant parts and rice last; continue to simmer until pheasant shows a tendency to disintegrate. Serve. Serves 5.

TENDER DOVES PLAQUEMINE

1 doz. doves
½ c. green onion, chopped
1 c. sherry
¼ c. parsley, chopped
1 c. flour
¼ tsp. black pepper
¼ tsp. ground red pepper
¼ tsp. onion powder

½ tsp. garlic powder
½ tsp. white pepper
1 tsp. sweet paprika
1 tsp. salt
½ stick margarine
1 chicken bouillon cube
1 c. hot water

Dissolve bouillon cube in 1 cup hot water. In a bowl, combine seasonings with the flour. Split back of doves and spread. Thoroughly pat with seasoned flour. In a saucepan, melt margarine at 450°. Add doves and saute until light brown on both sides. Remove doves and set aside. Add vegetables and saute for 3 minutes. Add the doves, shaking the pan while adding the sherry; mix well. Add bouillon to form a gravy. Reduce heat to 350°. Cook until tender. Serve over a steaming bed of rice. Serves 6.

DUCK IN SWEET ONION SAUCE LaPLACE

Breasts of 6 small ducks, split
  and flattened
1 stick margarine
2 c. brown roux
1 c. onions, chopped
½ c. bread crumbs
1 lb. lean ground chicken

1 egg, beaten
½ c. milk
¼ tsp. sweet paprika
2 c. hot water
½ tsp. ground red pepper
½ tsp. white pepper
2 Tbsp. catsup

In a bowl, combine seasonings; set aside. In a large saucepan, melt margarine at 450°. Add ½ seasoning mix; stir in well. Add duck parts and saute for 3 minutes on both sides. Remove from pan and set aside. Add onions and remaining seasonings; saute until tender. Slowly blend in roux. Add hot water and simmer for 20 minutes. Remove from heat. In a separate bowl, combine ground chicken, bread crumbs, egg, milk, and catsup. Place duck breast, meaty part down, in a slightly oiled casserole dish. Spoon ground chicken mixture on top; pat into place firmly. Cover with roux mixture and bake at 350° for 30 minutes. Serves 6.

DUCK IN RED WINE GUEYDAN

2 ducks, dressed and cleaned
1 c. dry red wine
2 cans mushrooms
1 can white grapes
2 apples, cored and peeled
1 large onion, sliced

1 tsp. coarse black pepper
½ stick margarine
1 tsp. salt
½ tsp. white pepper
¼ tsp. ground red pepper

Place apples inside the cavity of each duck. In a bowl, combine seasonings. Melt ¼ stick margarine at room temperature and combine with seasonings. Thoroughly rub the seasoning on the ducks. Arrange the ducks in a broiling pan. Brown on both sides until golden. Remove pan from broiler. In a separate saucepan, melt remaining margarine at 350°. Add remaining ingredients and saute for 4 minutes. Pour over the ducks. Bake until tender at 325°, basting occasionally. Serve with wild rice. Serves 6.

QUAIL IN HOT LEMON BUTTER SAUCE COLFAX

1 doz. quail, split at the back
and flattened
Juice of 2 lemons

2 tsp. Worcestershire sauce
½ stick margarine

In a large saucepan, melt margarine at 450°. Saute quail on both sides until light brown. Remove the pan from heat and sprinkle quail with Worcestershire sauce and lemon juice; set aside.

Sauce:

¼ stick margarine
3 Tbsp. all-purpose flour
1 c. dry white wine

½ c. sour cream
1 tsp. ground red pepper

Melt margarine at 350°. Add flour; blend well until it gels. Add wine, blending well. Reduce heat to 250° and blend in sour cream. Add red pepper. Simmer until sauce thickens. Add quail and simmer for 30 minutes or until tender. Serve with steaming rice. Serves 6.

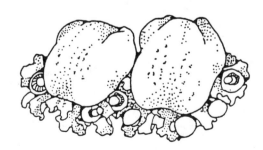

BAKED QUAIL KAPLAN

1 doz. quail
1 c. bread crumbs
3 chicken bouillon cubes
3 c. hot water
1/4 tsp. red pepper
1/4 tsp. white pepper

1/4 tsp. onion powder
1/4 tsp. garlic powder
1 large can mushrooms
4 Tbsp. truffle peelings
2 c. brown roux

Dissolve 3 chicken bouillon cubes in 3 cups hot water; set aside. In a small bowl, combine seasonings; thoroughly rub quail inside and out. In a separate bowl, combine mushrooms, bread crumbs and truffles. Stuff quail. In a large saucepan, bring the bouillon to a simmer. Slowly blend in roux, mixing well. Simmer for 10 minutes. In a lightly oiled casserole dish, arrange quail. Pour broth over quail. Bake at 325° until tender. Serves 6.

WILD DUCK IN RICE DRESSING GOLDEN MEADOW

2 large wild ducks
1 lb. duck giblets, chopped
1/4 stick margarine
1 c. onions, chopped
1/4 c. green peppers, chopped
1/4 c. celery, chopped
1/2 tsp. garlic powder

1/4 tsp. white pepper
1/4 tsp. red pepper
3 c. cooked rice
1 c. dark roux
2 chicken bouillon cubes
2 c. hot water

Dissolve chicken bouillon cubes in 2 cups hot water; set aside. In a saucepan, melt margarine at 450°. Add vegetables and saute until light brown. Add giblets and saute for 3 minutes. Stir frequently. Add bouillon; bring to a simmer. Add seasonings and slowly blend in roux. Simmer for 5 minutes. Add rice and simmer for 5 minutes. Arrange ducks in a slightly oiled baking pan. Pour sauce over ducks. Bake at 350° for 30 minutes or until done. Serves 6.

VENISON BACKSTRAP STEAKS OLLA

6 backstrap venison steaks, cut
   1 inch thick
1 stick margarine
1 c. all-purpose flour
Juice of 1 lemon
½ tsp. garlic powder

½ tsp. red pepper
½ tsp. black pepper
2 Tbsp. Worcestershire sauce
2 beef bouillon cubes
1 c. hot water

Marinade:

2 c. dry red wine
3 cloves, chopped

½ c. onion, chopped

Dissolve 2 beef bouillon cubes in 1 cup hot water; set aside. In a bowl, combine marinade ingredients. Add venison and allow to stand for 4 hours at room temperature. Remove venison from marinade. Discard marinade. Place the venison on a chopping board and pound with a tenderizing mallet until flat. In a bowl, combine seasonings and mix well with flour. Dredge venison thoroughly in the flour mixture; shake off excess.

In a large saucepan, melt margarine at 450° until a light smoke appears. Place steaks in margarine and brown on both sides. Slowly add the bouillon and remaining ingredients. Allow the venison to simmer for 10 minutes, forming a light gravy. Serve with mashed potatoes. Serves 6.

VENISON PATTIES JONESVILLE

1 lb. ground venison
¼ lb. ground seasoned smoke
   sausage
½ tsp. garlic salt
½ tsp. red pepper
½ tsp. coarse ground black
   pepper
¼ tsp. ground bay leaves

¼ tsp. thyme
1 c. bread crumbs
2 eggs, beaten
1 c. onions, finely chopped
2 Tbsp. parsley, finely chopped
¼ stick margarine
1 c. all-purpose flour

In a bowl, combine seasonings; set aside. In a large saucepan, melt margarine at 450°. Add sausage and saute until light brown. Remove from pan and allow the drippings to remain. In a large bowl, combine venison, sausage, ½ seasoning mix, onions, bread crumbs, and eggs. Form into ½ inch thick elongated patties. In a large soup plate, combine flour and remaining seasoning mix. Pat in venison burgers, shake off excess and fry at 350° until lightly browned on both sides. Reduce heat to 200°. Cover the pan and continue to cook for an additional 10 minutes. Serve on French bread. Serves 6.

CAJUN RABBIT IN BUTTERED RICE

1 rabbit, dressed and cut into
   quarters
¼ stick margarine
½ c. onions, chopped
2 c. rice (uncooked)
1 Tbsp. parsley, chopped
1 c. flour
½ tsp. garlic powder

½ tsp. onion powder
¼ tsp. red pepper
¼ tsp. black pepper
¼ tsp. sweet basil
¼ tsp. white pepper
3 beef bouillon cubes
3 c. hot water

Dissolve bouillon cubes in 3 cups hot water; set aside. In a bowl, combine seasonings; set aside. In a separate bowl, combine ½ seasoning mix with the flour. Rub rabbit parts thoroughly with the remaining seasoning mix, then dredge in the flour. Do not shake off excess. In a saucepan, melt margarine at 450°. Add rabbit parts and saute until brown on both sides. Remove the rabbit from the pan. Add vegetables and saute for 3 minutes. Slowly add bouillon liquid, whisking thoroughly. Add rice; blend in well. Return rabbit parts; cook until rice is tender. Remove from the heat, cover for 10 minutes and serve. Serves 4.

This is excellent with most game.

RABBIT STEW

2 rabbits, dressed and cut in
   parts
3 c. brown roux
1 c. onions, chopped large
½ c. green pepper, chopped
   large
4 celery stalks, chopped large
3 Irish potatoes, quartered
½ tsp. thyme

¼ tsp. bay leaf powder
½ tsp. white pepper
½ tsp. black pepper
¼ tsp. red pepper
¼ tsp. sweet basil
2 cloves garlic, chopped
1 can tomatoes
½ stick margarine
1 c. red wine

In a saucepan, melt margarine at 450°. Add rabbit and saute until light brown on both sides. Remove rabbit from the pan. Add vegetables and saute until tender. Slowly blend in roux. Add seasonings and tomatoes, including the juice. Reduce the heat to 350° and simmer for 10 minutes. Add remaining ingredients, except rabbit, and mix well. Return the rabbit parts to the mixture. If necessary, add hot water to control thickness. Simmer until tender. Serve with buttered rice. Serves 8.

CREOLE FRIED RABBIT IN MUSTARD SAUCE

2 rabbits, dressed and cut in
    parts
1 c. corn oil
1 c. flour
1 tsp. white pepper

¼ tsp. sweet basil
1 tsp. black pepper
3 eggs, beaten
¼ c. cream

In a bowl, combine seasonings; set aside. In a separate bowl, combine eggs, cream and ½ seasoning mix. In a separate bowl, combine remaining seasoning with the flour. Immerse rabbit parts in egg mixture, then dredge in the flour mixture. Shake off excess. In a saucepan, heat corn oil at 350°. Fry rabbit on both sides until golden brown. Remove rabbit from the pan and set on a paper towel. Discard oil from pan.

Sauce:

¼ c. Creole brown mustard
1 c. sour cream
2 tsp. Worcestershire sauce
1 tsp. prepared mustard

¼ tsp. red pepper
⅛ tsp. white pepper
⅛ tsp. black pepper
⅛ tsp. sweet basil

In a separate bowl, combine ingredients; mix well. Return rabbit to the pan and reduce the heat to 250°. Cover with mustard sauce. Allow to simmer for 20 minutes, turning rabbit frequently. Serve over steaming mounds of rice. Serves 6.

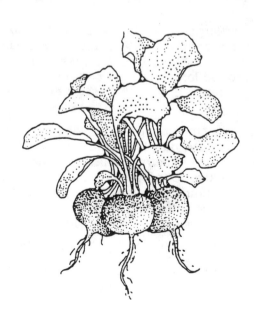

CAJUN HAWAIIAN DUCK

6 lb. boneless duck
½ stick margarine
2 eggs, beaten
¼ c. milk
1½ c. all-purpose flour

½ tsp. salt
⅛ tsp. white pepper
¼ tsp. black pepper
⅛ tsp. sweet basil

In a bowl, combine seasonings; set aside. In a separate bowl, add ½ seasoning mix, milk and eggs; whisk together well. On a plate, blend together the flour and remaining seasoning mix. Dip duck into the egg mixture, then dredge in the flour mixture; shake off excess. In a saucepan, melt margarine at 400°. Add duck and saute until light brown on both sides. Remove the duck from the pan and set aside.

Sauce:

1 c. hot water
1 c. dark brown roux
1 tsp. salt
¼ tsp. dark Oriental seasoning

1 Tbsp. blackstrap molasses
½ tsp. soy sauce
¼ stick margarine

In the same saucepan, add ¼ stick margarine. Blend in roux and remaining ingredients. Simmer until sauce becomes a consistency of a heavy cream. Remove from heat. In a lightly oiled casserole dish, pour in ½ of the sauce. Arrange the duck. Cover with remaining sauce and broil for 10 minutes. Serves 8.

DUCK IN PEPPERY WHITE WINE SAUCE BREAU BRIDGE

1 duck, cut in parts
¼ stick margarine
½ c. onions, chopped
1 c. dry white wine
1 c. tomato sauce
1 chicken bouillon cube

1 c. hot water
1 tsp. cinnamon
1 tsp. salt
½ tsp. red ground pepper
1 tsp. white pepper

Dissolve bouillon cube and cinnamon in 1 cup hot water. In a saucepan, melt margarine at 450°. Stir in seasonings for 1 minute. Add onions and saute until tender. Add duck parts and saute until brown on both sides. Add wine and simmer for 10 minutes. Add tomato sauce and bouillon liquid. Simmer until duck is tender. Serves 4.

RABBIT FRICASSEE

3 lb. young rabbit, dressed and
    cut into pieces
1 c. onions, chopped
½ c. celery, chopped
½ stick margarine
3 Tbsp. all-purpose flour
½ tsp. chicken bouillon, crushed

2 c. hot water
½ c. white wine
½ tsp. white pepper
¼ tsp. red pepper
¼ tsp. garlic powder
¼ tsp. oregano
¼ tsp. sweet basil

In a bowl, combine seasonings, including crushed bouillon; set aside. In a saucepan, melt margarine at 400°. Add rabbit and saute until light brown on both sides. Remove rabbit from the pan and set aside. Add onions and celery; saute for 2 minutes. Add the flour; blend until it becomes a rich brown. Add seasonings and 2 cups hot water; mix well. Add wine, blending well. Return the rabbit and simmer until tender at 250°. Serves 8.

QUAIL IN CREOLE PARSLEY SAUCE

1 doz. quail, cut in halves
½ stick margarine
2 Tbsp. flour
1 c. sour cream
2 chicken bouillon cubes
1 c. hot water
2 egg yolks, beaten

1 Tbsp. lemon juice
½ c. parsley, chopped fine
¼ tsp. red pepper
¼ tsp. black pepper
¼ tsp. white pepper
1 tsp. salt

Dissolve bouillon in 1 cup hot water; set aside. In a saucepan, melt margarine at 450°. Add quail and saute until light brown. Remove quail from the pan and set aside. Add flour, blending into the juices. Add sour cream and mix well. Add chicken bouillon liquid. Simmer until sauce thickens. Reduce the heat to 200°. Add parsley, lemon juice and seasonings; blend well. Add egg yolks slowly until thoroughly blended. Return quail parts. Simmer for 30 minutes. Serve over a steaming bed of rice. Serves 6.

ALLIGATOR IN SAUCE PIQUANT

6 pieces alligator tail, sliced
1 c. dark red roux
2 c. hot water
1 can tomatoes
1 c. red wine
½ stick margarine
1 tsp. dark brown sugar
3 Tbsp. Worcestershire sauce
¼ tsp. oregano
¼ tsp. sweet paprika
2 bay leaves

1 c. tomato sauce
2 onions, quartered
1 c. celery, chopped large
3 cloves garlic, chopped large
1 green pepper, chopped large
1 tsp. white pepper
1 tsp. ground red pepper
1 tsp. coarse ground black
   pepper

In a bowl, combine seasonings; set aside. Thoroughly rub ½ seasoning mix on the alligator pieces. In a saucepan, melt margarine at 450° until a light smoke appears. Braise the meat on both sides until brown. Remove from pan and set aside. Add vegetables and saute until soft. Add tomato sauce and canned tomatoes, blending well. Stir in the roux. Add hot water, Worcestershire sauce, sugar, and remaining seasoning mix. Stir well. Reduce the heat to 300°. Add wine. Return alligator meat to the mixture. Blend well. Add enough water to allow a brisk simmer. Cook until meat is tender. Serve over a mound of steaming rice. Serves 6.

FRIED ALLIGATOR IN POUPON MUSTARD SAUCE SLIDELL

3 lb. boneless alligator, cut in 2
   inch cubes
½ tsp. white pepper
½ tsp. dry mustard
½ tsp. red pepper
½ tsp. black pepper
½ tsp. thyme

1 c. Poupon mustard
1 c. heavy cream
1 c. seasoned fish fry
3 eggs, beaten
¼ c. milk
1 c. corn oil

In a bowl, combine seasonings; set aside. Place the alligator parts on a butcher's block and flatten with a tenderizing mallet. In a bowl, combine ½ seasoning mix with milk and eggs. In a soup plate, combine remaining seasoning mix and fish fry; blend well. Dip alligator parts in the egg mixture; stir in well. Drain off excess liquid and dredge in fish fry. Repeat this process until thoroughly coated; shake off excess.

In a saucepan, heat corn oil to 450°. Add alligator and saute on both sides until golden brown. Remove from pan and place on a serving platter. In a bowl, combine Poupon mustard and heavy cream. Use as dip for alligator. Serve. Serves 6.

ALLIGATOR CASSEROLE

3 lb. boneless alligator meat,
  sliced 1 inch thick
1 c. celery, chopped
½ c. green onions, chopped
½ tsp. bay leaf
½ c. green pepper, chopped
½ c. parsley, chopped
½ tsp. red pepper

½ tsp. black pepper
½ tsp. white pepper
½ stick margarine
2 Tbsp. basil
1 tsp. oregano
¾ c. onions, chopped
1 c. brown roux
1 c. hot water

In a saucepan, melt margarine at 450°. Add alligator meat and saute on both sides until brown. Add vegetables and saute until soft. Add seasonings, blending well. Add roux and 1 cup hot water; stir well. Reduce heat to 250°. Simmer for 10 minutes. Control moisture with hot water. In a lightly oiled casserole dish, pour in mixture. Bake for 25 minutes at 350°. Serve with rice. Serves 6.

ALLIGATOR, CREOLE STYLE

4 lb. boneless alligator, cut bite-
  size
1 c. dry white wine
1½ c. green pepper, chopped
Juice of 1 lemon
1½ c. onions, chopped
2 c. celery, chopped
3 large cans tomatoes
3 Tbsp. Worcestershire sauce

3 Tbsp. dark brown sugar
½ tsp. black pepper
¼ tsp. red pepper
½ tsp. white pepper
½ tsp. ground bay leaf
1 c. dark brown roux
1 stick margarine
1 Tbsp. cloves
½ tsp. garlic powder

In a large saucepan, melt margarine at 450°. Add alligator meat and saute on both sides until light brown. Add vegetables and saute until tender. Reduce heat to 250°. Slowly add the roux. Add tomatoes, stirring in well. Add the seasonings and bring to a boil at 300°. Add remaining ingredients; blend well. It may be necessary to add hot water to control thickness. Keep at a rapid simmer for 45 minutes or until meat is tender. Stir frequently. Serve over a steaming bed of rice. Serves 10.

FRIED FROG LEGS

1½ doz. frog legs
3 eggs, beaten
¼ tsp. red pepper
¼ tsp. white pepper
¼ tsp. black pepper

1 c. bread crumbs
½ c. lemon juice
¼ tsp. garlic powder
¼ tsp. onion powder
1 c. corn oil

In a saucepan, combine lemon juice with enough hot water to scald frog legs for 5 minutes. Remove frog legs from the pan; drain and discard the water. In a bowl, combine seasonings with onion powder, garlic powder and eggs. Dip frog legs in the egg mixture. Roll in the bread crumbs. In a saucepan, heat corn oil to 450°. Fry until golden brown. Serve with cream of wine or mustard sauce. Serves 6.

FROG IN SAUCE PIQUANT

1½ doz. frog legs
1 can large tomatoes
½ tsp. white pepper
1 tsp. black pepper
¼ c. parsley, chopped

¼ c. green onions, chopped
1 large onion, sliced
3 cloves garlic, chopped
1 c. flour
½ stick margarine

In a bowl, combine seasonings; set aside. Combine ½ seasoning mix to the flour and roll in frog legs generously. In a saucepan, melt margarine at 450°. Add frog legs and fry until light brown. Remove legs from heat and set aside. There should be a residue of flour on the bottom of the pan. Add 2 tablespoons flour and saute until light brown. Add vegetables and saute until flour is a rich brown. Add tomatoes, including juice; blend well. It may be necessary to add more water. Reduce the temperature to 250°. Return frog legs to mixture. Simmer for 20 minutes or until sauce thickens. Serve over a bed of rice. Serves 4.

CAJUN ROASTED WILD HOG

1 wild hog (hindquarter)
1 c. onions, chopped fine
1 c. green peppers, chopped
   fine
1 c. celery, chopped fine
1 Tbsp. garlic flakes
1 tsp. dry mustard

1 tsp. thyme
2 tsp. sweet paprika
2 tsp. black pepper
1 tsp. white pepper
1 tsp. red pepper
2 tsp. salt

In a bowl, combine seasonings; set aside. Rub the hog quarter thoroughly with ¼ seasoning mix. Place the hog in a large roasting pan with a rack. Braise under a very hot broiler until brown. Remove from heat and set aside; retain drippings. In a large saucepan, add the drippings. Combine the remaining ingredients and add to the drippings. Saute at 450° for 5 minutes. Remove from heat and set aside. Make numerous small slits in the hindquarter and place in a baking pan. Pour the sauce over the leg and bake at 350°, turning twice and basting frequently, until leg reaches your desired doneness. Serves 6.

DUCK SMOTHERED IN WILD RICE AND GIBLETS BOGALUSA

2 large ducks, cleaned and
   dressed
Duck giblets
½ c. onions, chopped
½ c. celery, chopped
¼ stick margarine
1½ c. ¾ cooked wild rice
1 tsp. salt

¼ c. green onions, chopped fine
¼ tsp. red pepper
¼ tsp. white pepper
½ tsp. black pepper
½ stick margarine
2 chicken bouillon cubes
2 c. hot water

Dissolve bouillon cubes in 2 cups hot water; set aside. Split the ducks at the back; spread and press flat. Rub with ¼ stick margarine. In a large skillet, melt margarine at 450°. Add seasonings, stirring for 1 minute, until a light smoke appears. Add giblets and saute for 2 minutes. Add vegetables and saute until brown. Add rice and bouillon liquid, stirring well for 2 minutes. Remove from the heat. In a roasting pan, place ducks meat side down. Cover the back with the rice mixture. Bake at 300° until ducks are tender. Serves 6.

OLD-TIME TURTLE STEW HAMMOND

4 lb. turtle meat
2 c. brown roux
¼ stick margarine
1 c. onions, chopped
2 cans tomatoes
1 can tomato paste
¼ c. celery, chopped
¼ c. green onion, chopped
1½ c. sherry wine
¼ tsp. white pepper
¼ tsp. black pepper
¼ tsp. red pepper
½ tsp. bay leaf
6 cloves
2 tsp. dark brown sugar
½ tsp. allspice
½ c. green pepper, chopped
6 hard-boiled eggs, chopped
2 c. hot water

In a saucepan, melt margarine at 450°. Add vegetables and saute until soft. Add tomatoes and tomato sauce; blend well. Reduce the heat to 300°. Slowly add the roux and bring to a simmer for 5 minutes. Add turtle meat and 2 cups hot water. Bring to a brisk boil. Add seasonings; blend well. Add wine and remaining ingredients. Simmer until turtle meat is tender. Serves 8.

TURTLE IN SAUCE PIQUANT

4 lb. turtle meat
1 c. onions, chopped
½ c. green pepper, chopped
½ c. celery, chopped
½ stick margarine
3 cloves garlic, chopped
1 can mushrooms
4 Tbsp. steak sauce
1 can tomatoes
¼ tsp. red pepper
¼ tsp. white pepper
½ tsp. black pepper
¼ c. green onions, chopped
¼ c. parsley, chopped
3 Tbsp. Worcestershire sauce
½ tsp. oregano
1 c. dark brown roux
4 c. hot water

In a saucepan, melt margarine at 450°. Add vegetables and saute until light brown. Add steak sauce, mushrooms and tomatoes. Add 4 cups hot water and bring to a brisk simmer. Blend in the roux. Add turtle meat and remaining ingredients; blend well. Cook until tender. Serves 8.

OLD-TIME CREOLE TURTLE SOUP

4 lb. turtle meat
2 onions, cut in eighths
1 c. celery, cut large
6 Tbsp. Worcestershire sauce
½ c. sherry wine
¼ c. green pepper, chopped
    large
5 cloves garlic, chopped

¼ c. parsley, chopped
1 tsp. black pepper
½ tsp. red pepper
3 Tbsp. allspice
¼ stick margarine
4 Tbsp. all-purpose flour
1 gal. hot water

In a small cooking sack with a thin mesh, add 3 tablespoons allspice and seasonings. Seal tightly. In a saucepan, melt margarine at 400°. Add vegetables and saute until soft. Add flour and saute until a rich brown. Add 1 gallon of hot water slowly; mix well. Add all remaining ingredients, including cooking sack. Cook until turtle is tender. Before soup is served, remove the seasoning sack. Add 1 cup of cooked rice and serve. Serves 8.

"We're not deviled eggs, Mr. Cajun.
We're good eggs!"

Eggs, Cheese and Extras

A CLOVICE COMMENTARY:

An egg is a serious cre'ature. It proves de aggressive eatin' habits of folks other den Cajuns. You see, when you eat an egg, one must realize dat you have just devoured de unborn child of a chicken.

Keep a sauce hot by putting it over hot water, never over a direct flame, no matter how low.

Salad dressings should accent, never overpower the flavor of salads.

If you want to peel a firm tomato, rub the skin gently all over with the side of a knife handle, then split the skin carefully and peel.

If you're learning about cheese, don't be put off by the way some kinds look. Many cheeses taste their best when they look their worst.

Rice wine vinegar is one of the softest and most pleasant of vinegars, especially in salad dressings. You can get it in most Oriental food stores and in the foreign food departments of most supermarkets.

Hollow out tomatoes with a grapefruit spoon; this will avoid punching holes in the sides while removing the pulp. Allow the skin to remain on the tomato if you intend to stuff them.

Shrimp should be barbecued on a hot grill covered with foil. In this way they will retain their juices.

EGGS, CHEESE AND EXTRAS

EGGS BENEDICT BASIN STREET

6 eggs
6 English muffins

6 slices ham

Lightly toast the English muffins. Cut ham slices the same size as the English muffin; place on top. Poach eggs; place on top of ham. Set aside.

Sauce:

4 sticks margarine
4 egg yolks
3 tsp. white wine

¼ tsp. white pepper
¼ tsp. ground red pepper
½ tsp. Worcestershire sauce

In a saucepan, melt margarine at 175°. Raise the heat to 400° and bring margarine to a boil. Set aside and skim the top. In the top of a double boiler, combine together all remaining ingredients and whisk well. Fill the bottom of the double boiler ½ full and bring to a simmer. Place the top boiler over the bottom and whisk the egg mixture well for 6 minutes or until mixture is fluffy. Remove the top of the boiler from the heat and whisk in margarine slowly. Pour over poached eggs and serve. Serves 6.

HOLLANDAISE SAUCE ST. CHARLES

1 lb. margarine
4 egg yolks, beaten
2½ tsp. white wine
½ tsp. Tabasco sauce

½ tsp. Worcestershire sauce
2 tsp. lemon juice
2 oz. brandy

In a saucepan, melt margarine at 400°. Bring to a rapid boil. Remove from heat and skim. In a double boiler, combine remaining ingredients except brandy; whisk thoroughly. Add water to the bottom of a double boiler and bring to a simmer. Do not work this too hot. Rapidly whisk egg mixture until air forms and liquid becomes light and creamy. Do not allow eggs to harden under any circumstance. Slowly blend margarine into mixture. Reduce temperature and whisk until totally blended. Remove from the heat and allow to cool. Whisk in brandy for 1 minute. Serves 8.

EGGS IN SMOKED SAUSAGE SAUCE RAMPART STREET

1 c. leftover cooked red beans
½ lb. ground Italian or Polish
   smoked sausage
3 eggs, beaten fluffy
1 tsp. sugar
1 tsp. baking powder
¼ tsp. white pepper
¼ tsp. ground cinnamon
⅛ tsp. ground nutmeg

½ c. all-purpose flour
1 tsp. salt
¼ c. milk
½ tsp. vanilla extract
2 c. cooked rice
1 c. corn oil
1 c. bearnaise sauce
½ c. hot water

In a large mixing bowl, add beaten eggs, sugar, baking powder, salt, pepper, cinnamon, and nutmeg. Whisk together well. Add flour and whisk until smooth. Add milk and vanilla; blend well. Add rice and form into rice patties. In a large saucepan, heat the corn oil to 350°. Fry patties until golden brown. Remove from pan and place on a paper towel. In a saucepan, reheat the leftover red beans with ½ cup hot water, stirring well. Add ground smoked sausage and bring to a simmer for 10 minutes. In a serving platter, form a bed with rice patties. Cover with red bean mixture. Top with bearnaise sauce and serve. Serves 8.

CAJUN SCRAMBLED EGGS

8 eggs
1 c. fresh mushrooms, sliced
¼ stick margarine
¼ c. green onions, finely
   chopped

⅛ tsp. marjoram
⅛ tsp. white pepper
⅛ tsp. black pepper
⅛ tsp. red pepper
¼ c. heavy cream

In a saucepan, melt margarine at 400°. Add mushrooms and onions; saute until light brown. Beat eggs and heavy cream until fluffy. Whisk in seasonings thoroughly. Pour over vegetables and stir until eggs are done. Immediately remove from the heat and serve. Serves 4.

CHEESE SOUFFLE

2 Tbsp. margarine
2 Tbsp. flour
1 c. hot milk
1½ c. grated cheese
1 c. cooked rice

4 egg yolks, beaten
4 egg whites, beaten stiff
¼ tsp. white pepper
¼ tsp. red pepper

In a saucepan, melt margarine at 250°. Blend in flour until it gels. Add hot milk slowly; do not boil. Stir constantly. Add cheese and continue to blend on medium heat. Add seasonings and rice. Remove from heat and allow to cool. Fold in egg yolks. Do not beat. Fold in egg whites. In a lightly oiled casserole dish, pour in mixture. Bake at 225° for 45 minutes. Before serving, sprinkle top with grated cheese. Serves 4.

BASIC OMELETTE

In preparing an omelette, I like to use a heavy Teflon skillet and a minimum amount of margarine. This keeps the omelette from sticking, but allows movement. I do not like to overbeat the eggs, it toughens the omelette. Unless I'm cooking a plain omelette, I add the filling to the center of the egg mixture. Cook at 350° until one side bubbles on the surface. Arrange the filling just off center. Use a wide spatula to fold the other half of the egg over filling. Allow to cook for 2 minutes and turn omelette over. Cook to your desired results. Serves 4.

SPICY SPANISH OMELETTE

8 eggs, beaten
½ c. green onions, chopped
1 small jalapeno pepper,
   chopped
2 Tbsp. margarine
1 pimento, chopped
6 olives, chopped

1 small can tomatoes
¼ tsp. ground red pepper
½ tsp. coarse ground black
   pepper
2 Tbsp. heavy cream
2 Tbsp. bell pepper, chopped
⅛ tsp. garlic powder

In a bowl, combine seasonings; set aside. In a saucepan, melt 1 tablespoon margarine at 400°. Add vegetables, except tomatoes, and saute until light brown. Add tomatoes; simmer until moisture evaporates. Add ¾ seasoning mix; blend in well. In a separate saucepan, melt remaining margarine at 400°. In a blender, combine eggs and cream and whip until fluffy. Pour in eggs and allow to cook until surface bubbles. Add filling in a neat line on one side of the eggs. Fold other half over filling. Cook for 1 minute. Turn omelette over and sprinkle with remaining seasoning. Cook until desired doneness. Serves 4.

OPEN-FACED CAJUN OMELETTE

6 eggs
3 c. onions, sliced thin
1 stick margarine
1 can tomatoes, drained and
   chopped

3 Tbsp. Parmesan cheese
1 tsp. coarse ground black
   pepper
⅓ c. fresh basil, chopped
½ tsp. salt

In a saucepan, melt ¾ stick margarine at 250°. Add onions and saute until light brown. Add tomatoes and salt; blend well. Raise the temperature to 350° and saute for 10 minutes, stirring frequently. Remove from the pan and strain to remove the oil; set aside. In a bowl, beat eggs thoroughly. Add the mixture, blending thoroughly. Add the pepper, basil and cheese; blend thoroughly with a whisk. In a small skillet, melt the remaining margarine at 350°. Add egg mixture and cook until the surface is bubbly. Remove from the heat and serve directly from the skillet. Serves 4.

CAJUN SAUSAGE GRAVY OMELETTE

8 eggs
½ lb. smoked sausage
3 Tbsp. all-purpose flour
½ stick margarine
⅛ tsp. basil
⅛ tsp. oregano
⅛ tsp. red pepper

½ tsp. coarse ground black
   pepper
¼ c. onions, chopped fine
2 Tbsp. green pepper, chopped
   fine
½ c. hot milk

In a bowl, combine seasonings; set aside. In a saucepan, melt ¼ stick margarine at 450°. Add vegetables and saute until light brown. Add flour and blend until a rich brown. Blend in hot milk and simmer until it reaches a heavy cream consistency. Remove from heat and set aside.

In a separate saucepan, melt ⅛ stick margarine at 450° until a light smoke appears. Add sausage and ¾ seasoning mix; fry until brown and crispy. Add vegetable mixture and cook until mixture thickens. Remove from the heat and set aside. In a deep skillet, melt remaining margarine at 300°. Pour in well beaten eggs and cook until surface bubbles, but still runny. Add sausage mixture and cover. Remove from the heat and allow to set for 10 minutes. Turn the mixture over carefully onto a heated platter. Sprinkle top of eggs with the remaining seasoning and serve. Serves 4.

CREOLE EGG AND CHEESE SANDWICH

8 eggs
1 loaf French or Italian bread
6 thick slices sharp Cheddar
   cheese
1½ c. milk

1 can cream of mushroom soup
¼ tsp. white pepper
½ stick margarine
2 oz. Creole mustard

Cut a loaf of French bread lengthwise, then in half, forming 4 sections. Place in a baking pan and under a hot broiler. Toast surface of the bread until a rich brown. Remove from broiler and spread with margarine. In a bowl, beat eggs, milk and seasoning thoroughly. Pour mixture over the bread and allow to stand for 10 minutes or until bread becomes soggy. Place the bread in a heated oven at 350° and bake for 10 minutes. Remove from the heat. Top with the cheese. Return to the oven until cheese begins to melt. Remove from the heat. In a bowl, blend mustard and cream of mushroom soup. Pour over bread. Return to the oven at 350° for 15 minutes. Serve. Serves 4.

EGGS IN MUSHROOM AND CHEESE SAUCE DAUPHINE

8 eggs
3 Tbsp. margarine
1 (6 oz.) can mushrooms, drained
2 c. Cheese Sauce (see recipe)

6 English muffins or bagels
1/4 tsp. red pepper
1/4 tsp. black pepper

Toast bread and arrange in a baking dish. In a saucepan, melt margarine at 400°. Add mushrooms and saute until brown. Pour mushrooms on top of bread. Poach eggs; arrange on top of mushrooms. Sprinkle with seasoning.

Cheese Sauce:

1 c. sharp cheese
1/8 tsp. white pepper
1/3 tsp. dry mustard
1/8 tsp. red pepper

4 Tbsp. margarine
4 Tbsp. flour
1 c. milk

In a saucepan, melt margarine at 400°. Add flour; blend well, but do not brown. Reduce the heat to 200°. Slowly add hot milk until mixture thickens. Stir constantly. Add cheese; blend until melted. Stir in seasonings; remove from heat. Pour over top of poached eggs. Place in a preheated oven at 300° for 10 minutes. Serve. Serves 4.

CHICKEN LIVER OMELETTE

6 eggs, beaten
1 c. dry white wine
4 Tbsp. margarine
3 Tbsp. heavy cream
1/4 tsp. red pepper
1/4 tsp. white pepper

1/8 tsp. oregano
1/2 lb. chicken livers, chopped
1/4 c. onions, chopped
1/2 tsp. sweet basil
1/2 tsp. salt

In a saucepan, melt 2 tablespoons margarine at 400°. Add onions and saute until soft. Add livers and seasonings; saute until livers are light brown, about 7 minutes. Reduce the heat to 250°. Add wine and allow to simmer slowly. In a separate saucepan, melt remaining margarine at 350°. In a blender, whip eggs thoroughly with cream. Pour into saucepan and cook until the surface bubbles. Arrange liver filling, which should be free of most of the moisture, on one side of the eggs. Fold over the other half of the eggs. Cover and cook until desired doneness. Serves 4.

SPICY POTATO OMELETTE PARADIS

8 eggs
1/4 c. American cheese, grated
4 Tbsp. heavy cream
1/4 stick margarine
2 potatoes
2 tsp. parsley, chopped
1/2 tsp. red pepper

1/2 tsp. white pepper
1/4 tsp. sweet basil
1/4 tsp. garlic powder
1/4 tsp. onion powder
1/2 tsp. paprika
1 tsp. salt

Peel potatoes and grate. In a saucepan, melt 1/8 stick margarine at 450°. Add potatoes and saute until light brown. Do not stir, but turn over and allow to form a patty. Sprinkle with seasonings except paprika. Do not stir. Add parsley. In a blender, whip eggs, cream and American cheese. In a saucepan, melt remaining margarine at 300°. Pour in egg mixture and cook until top bubbles, but is still runny. Carefully slide the potato patty over the eggs. Remove from the heat. Sprinkle with paprika. Cover for 10 minutes and serve. Serves 6.

CRABMEAT OMELETTE DESIRE STREET

8 eggs
1/4 stick margarine
1/4 tsp. red pepper
1/4 tsp. white pepper
1/4 tsp. black pepper
1/4 c. celery, finely chopped

1/4 c. onions, finely chopped
3 Tbsp. green pepper, finely
  chopped
1 lb. crabmeat, drained
1 tsp. salt
3 Tbsp. heavy cream

In a saucepan, melt 1/8 stick margarine at 400°. Add vegetables and saute until light brown. Add crabmeat and saute for 3 minutes. Add seasonings, blending well. If possible, do not break up crabmeat. Remove from heat and set aside. In a blender, whip eggs and cream. In a saucepan, melt remaining margarine at 350°. Pour in eggs. Cook until top is bubbly, but still runny. Pour in crabmeat filling on one side of eggs. Fold and cook until desired doneness. Serves 6.

SHRIMP OMELETTE CLAIBORNE

8 eggs
¾ lb. small shrimp, peeled and deveined
2 Tbsp. green pepper, chopped fine
¼ c. celery, chopped fine
¼ c. green onion, chopped fine

¼ tsp. red pepper
¼ tsp. white pepper
1 tsp. salt
¼ tsp. oregano
⅛ tsp. sweet basil
¼ stick margarine
¼ c. dark brown roux
½ c. cream

In a saucepan, melt ⅛ stick margarine at 400°. Add shrimp and saute until pink. Add vegetables and saute until soft. Add seasonings, blending well. At this point, the shrimp should become a deep red color and firm. Add roux and saute for 5 minutes or until it reaches a sticky consistency. In a blender, whip eggs and cream. In a saucepan, melt remaining margarine at 350°. Pour in eggs. Cook until bubbly, but still runny. Add ¾ shrimp mixture to center of the eggs. Fold in edges. Top with remaining sauce. Cook until desired doneness. Serves 6.

EGGS RANCHERO NAPOLEONVILLE

8 eggs, beaten
¼ lb. dried shrimp
1 c. Cheddar cheese, shredded
¼ tsp. black pepper
¼ tsp. white pepper
¼ c. green peppers, chopped
¼ c. onions, chopped

¼ stick margarine
¼ tsp. garlic powder
1 large can tomatoes, well drained and chopped
2 oz. chilies, drained and chopped
¼ tsp. chili powder

In a saucepan, melt ⅛ stick margarine at 400°. Add vegetables, including chilies, and saute until soft. Add dried shrimp and tomatoes and saute until moisture is removed. Add seasonings, except for 1 pinch of chili powder, blending well. Remove from heat. In a saucepan, melt remaining margarine at 350°. Pour in beaten eggs. Cook until bubbly, but still runny. Pour shrimp mixture into center. Fold in both sides. Cover with cheese. Remove from heat. Sprinkle with pinch of chili powder. Serve. Serves 6.

SWEET ONION OMELETTE IN CHEESE SAUCE BARONNE

8 eggs
1½ c. Vidalia onions, chopped
¼ lb. sharp Cheddar cheese,
    grated
1 c. hot milk
½ stick margarine

¼ tsp. dry mustard
¼ tsp. paprika
¼ tsp. red pepper
¼ tsp. white pepper
2 Tbsp. flour
1 tsp. salt

Place ¾ of cheese, hot milk, ⅛ stick margarine, mustard, salt, paprika, peppers, and flour in a blender on high for 15 seconds. Pour mixture in a saucepan and simmer at 200°, stirring constantly, until sauce reaches a sticky consistency. In a separate saucepan, melt ⅛ stick margarine at 400°. Add onions and saute until light brown. Add remaining cheese and cook until it melts. Remove from heat. In a separate saucepan, melt remaining margarine at 400°. Pour in well beaten eggs and cook until center bubbles. Add onions and fold in both sides. Cover with sauce and cook until desired doneness. Serves 6.

CRAB SPREAD ROYAL STREET

½ can cream of chicken soup
1 can cream of mushroom soup
1 small jar pimentos
1 jar Velveeta cheese
½ c. onions, chopped fine

1 can crabmeat
3 Tbsp. sherry
1 tsp. salt
½ tsp. red pepper
½ tsp. white pepper
1 Tbsp. margarine

In a saucepan, melt margarine at 400°. Add onions and saute until soft. Add crabmeat and saute for 5 minutes. Add chicken soup; blend well. Add mushroom soup; stir well. Reduce heat to 250°. Add cheese, stirring briskly. Remove from heat. Blend in sherry and seasonings. Allow to cool, then chill. Serve on saltine crackers.

OLIVE SPREAD CHARTRES STREET

5 egg yolks
1 egg
¼ c. white wine
2 tsp. margarine
2 Tbsp. Creole mustard
1 large bottle salad olives, finely
    chopped

3 Tbsp. parsley, chopped
¼ c. green onion tops, chopped
¼ tsp. white pepper
⅛ tsp. red pepper

Beat eggs thoroughly. Place wine in a saucepan; bring to a simmer. Remove from heat; blend in eggs. Beat constantly. Reduce the heat. Add mustard, olives, seasonings, and remaining ingredients. Blend thoroughly. *Makes an excellent spread.*

CREOLE MUSTARD SPREAD

2 tsp. prepared mustard
1/4 c. Creole brown mustard
1 Tbsp. Worcestershire sauce
1/2 tsp. salt
1/4 tsp. black pepper

1/4 tsp. white pepper
1/8 tsp. sweet basil
1/2 c. sour cream
1/2 c. heavy cream
6 oz. cream cheese

Soften cream cheese at room temperature. In a bowl, blend together cream cheese, sour cream and heavy cream, forming a thick creamy mixture. Add brown mustard, blending well. Add remaining ingredients, whisking until it becomes a smooth single color. Pour ingredients into a Teflon coated saucepan. Simmer for 15 minutes at 200°, stirring constantly. Remove from heat and cool at room temperature.

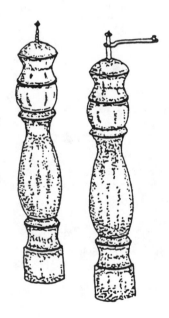

Notes

"It's not the dessert.
I've got big bones."

Desserts and Sundowners
or
How to Ruin Your Diet Without Even Trying

A WARNING FROM CLOVICE:

Dere is a very dear and helpful gentleman, who rightly say to offer de reader an approximate calorie count.

My wife has studied de calories to a doctor'ate proportion and has de ability to threaten each mouthful dat I take with those massive calculations. The calorie count per slice, for instance, of deep dish creole pecan pie:

1,000,000,000,000,000,000,000,000,000,000,000,000,000.

So dere you are. This formula per slice can be applied to any of de followin' desserts.

BASIC FOOD HINTS

Dried herbs will bring more flavor to your food if you crush or crumble them well between your palms as you add them to your cooking. This releases the bouquet.

Dried herbs keep best in containers which shield them from light. Use screw-top jars and keep them away from heat.

Snapper, grouper and any other fish of this nature can be substituted for this dish. Never stuff a fish over 6-8 lbs. It is better to cut a large fish into steaks than to stuff whole.

If you allow frozen fish to thaw slowly in the refrigerator there will be less leakage of the juices than if you thaw it at room temperature. Use frozen fish immediately after thawing.

After cooking, fish can be refrigerated in a covered container no longer than 3 days or frozen no longer than 3 months.

Bay scallops are small, cream-colored and tender. They're sweeter, have a more delicate flavor and are also more expensive than sea scallops, which are larger, often whiter and slightly tougher - but still good to eat.

Tuna comes in 3 forms: chunk, flake and solid pack. The solid pack is a continuous piece of fish, more expensive than the other two. I use solid pack for casseroles. Flake and chunk are good for salads.

DESSERTS AND SUNDOWNERS

DEEP DARK CREOLE PECAN PRALINES

2 c. dark brown sugar
1 c. light brown sugar
1 c. water

1 c. cream
3 c. pecans

Combine sugars, cream and water in a saucepan. Cook at 250° until it thickens to form balls. Stir frequently. Remove from heat. Beat until creamy. Fold in nuts. Drop spoon-sized amounts on a lightly oiled cookie sheet. Will set up immediately. Serve.

NEW ORLEANS BEIGNETS

¾ c. water
¾ c. flour
3 Tbsp. butter

8 eggs, beaten
2 tsp. vanilla
2 c. confectioners sugar

In a saucepan, combine water, butter and flour; mix well. Bring to a boil for 5 minutes. Remove from heat. Blend in eggs, 2 at a time. Beat thoroughly 3 to 4 minutes after each set of eggs. Add vanilla; blend well. For large beignets, drop tablespoon size of the mixture into a deep fat fry. Fry until golden brown on both sides. Dust thoroughly with confectioners sugar.

CAJUN PRALINES

3 c. pralines, chopped
2 Tbsp. butter
1 c. light brown sugar

1 c. canned cream
2 c. white sugar
2 tsp. vanilla

In a bowl, combine sugars and cream. Place in a saucepan, heated at 250°. Cook slowly until thickened. Test to see if it will form into balls by dropping a small amount into cold water. When the balls form, remove from heat. Add remaining ingredients; stir briskly until thickened. Drop large spoonfuls onto wax paper. Sets up immediately.

PECAN ISLAND PECAN PIE

1 unbaked pie shell
1 c. pecans
3 eggs, beaten
1 c. corn syrup
2 Tbsp. flour

1 c. dark brown sugar
1 Tbsp. butter
¼ tsp. salt
1 tsp. vanilla
¼ tsp. cinnamon

In a bowl, combine butter and sugar, using a whisk; blend well. Add flour, whisking steadily. Add syrup and eggs. At this point, whisking is important, so don't give up. Add remaining ingredients. Pour into pie shell. Bake for 45 minutes at 325°.

SOUTHERN PECAN PIE WITH A GLAZE PECAN FROSTING

1 c. dark corn syrup
1 c. pecan halves
1 c. brown sugar
3 Tbsp. butter

3 eggs, beaten
1½ tsp. flour
1 tsp. vanilla
1 unbaked pie crust

In a bowl, combine eggs and butter, blending with a whisk. Blend in remaining ingredients. Pour into a pie crust. Bake at 375° for 45 minutes. Remove from the heat and set aside.

Frosting:

½ c. dry roasted pecans,
    chopped fine
1 c. water

½ c. brown sugar
1 tsp. vanilla extract

In a saucepan, combine water and sugar and bring to a boil. Remove from the heat. Stir in vanilla; blend in pecans. Brush generously over top of the pie.

LEMON MERINGUE PIE LULING

1 unbaked pie shell
3 egg yolks, beaten
Juice and grated rind of 2
    lemons
¼ tsp. salt
2 Tbsp. cornstarch

¾ c. sugar
2 Tbsp. flour
1⅓ c. hot water
1 Tbsp. butter
1 baked pie shell

In a bowl, combine sugar, cornstarch, flour, and salt. Add lemon juice and rind. Blend well. Add hot water. Cook over a medium heat. Add beaten egg yolks. Cook until mixture begins to bubble. Remove from heat; add butter. When mixture cools, pour into pie shell.

Meringue:

3 egg whites
1¼ tsp. cream of tartar

6 Tbsp. sugar

Beat together egg whites until stiff. Blend in cream of tartar and 1 tablespoon of sugar at a time, beating well. Top pie with meringue. Bake at 350° for 15 minutes or until meringue is golden brown.

NEW ORLEANS RICE PUDDING

2 c. cooked rice
1½ c. milk
⅛ tsp. salt
3 eggs, beaten
1 tsp. vanilla
½ c. brown sugar

1 tsp. butter
1 tsp. grated lemon rind and
   juice
½ c. raisins
1 c. crushed cookies

Preheat oven to 325°. In a bowl, combine 2 cups cooked rice, milk, salt, and remaining ingredients except cookies. Blend continuously. This is more a folding action to avoid smashing the rice. Lightly oil bottom of a baking dish. Pour in mixture. Cover with crushed cookies. Bake for 45 minutes.

RICE PUDDING IN BRANDY CREAM

2½ c. milk
1½ c. uncooked rice
2 c. heavy cream
1 c. sugar
1 tsp. ground nutmeg

1 c. raisins
4 egg yolks
4 egg whites
2 Tbsp. vanilla extract

In the top of a double boiler, heated to 400°, combine milk, 1 cup cream, ¾ cup sugar, ½ cup rice, and ½ teaspoon nutmeg. Blend together well. Cover and cook for 20 minutes. Stir in raisins. Reduce heat to 300°. Cover and cook for an additional 30 minutes. Remove from heat and set aside. Set an electric mixer at medium speed. Add egg whites and beat until frothy. Add remaining sugar and beat until stiff and eggs peak. In a small bowl, beat egg yolks; gradually add 1 cup rice. Stir in remaining cream, vanilla and nutmeg. Pour into an ungreased baking pan. Bake at 250° until rice is tender.

Brandy Cream:

1 Tbsp. brandy
1 tsp. Grand Marnier
1 tsp. vanilla extract

⅔ c. heavy cream
¼ c. sugar
2 Tbsp. sour cream

Refrigerate a mixing bowl until cold. Combine brandy, Grand Marnier, vanilla, and cream. Beat together well with a hand mixer on medium speed. Add sour cream and sugar; blend until it peaks, about 3 to 5 minutes. Serve and cover with Brandy Cream.

BANANAS FOSTER BATON ROUGE

4 large bananas
1 qt. ice cream
½ c. dark brown sugar
½ stick butter
½ tsp. cinnamon

1 oz. banana liqueur
2 oz. rum
¼ c. dark roasted pecans,
   chopped

Combine butter and sugar in a saucepan. Cook over a medium heat until caramelized. Peel bananas; cut in quarters. Add to sauce; cook until tender. Take care not to crush. Add liqueur and cinnamon. Pour rum on top of mixture; do not stir in. As soon as brandy warms, light with a match. Slice ice cream in 1 inch thick pieces. Spoon over banana mixture. Sprinkle with pecans and serve.

BAYOU COUNTRY CHOCOLATE PECAN PRALINES

1½ c. semi-sweet chocolate
2 c. pecan halves
2 Tbsp. vanilla extract
1½ c. pecans, coarsely chopped

1 c. brown sugar
1 c. milk
½ c. heavy cream
1 c. sugar
1½ sticks butter

Before you begin this recipe, make sure you have all the ingredients and utensils at hand. Place chocolate chips in freezer and chill. In a large saucepan, melt butter at 350°. Add milk, sugars, cream, and chopped pecans. Cook for 5 minutes, whisking steadily. Reduce heat to 250° and continue to cook for 10 minutes. Don't forget the whisking. Add pecan halves and cook for 10 minutes. Drop a small amount in cold water to see if it forms a ball. At that time, blend in vanilla. Add ¼ cup chocolate chips to ¼ of the batter at a time. Stir in lightly and quickly drop heaping teaspoons of batter on a Teflon cookie sheet. Continue this process until all the material is used.

CREOLE CHEESECAKE

3 large pkg. soft cream cheese
4 eggs, beaten

1 tsp. vanilla
¾ c. sugar
1 graham cracker pie crust

In a bowl, cream sugar and cheese together thoroughly. Add eggs, one at a time; blend in well. Add vanilla; blend well. Pour into pie crust. Bake at 350° for 20 minutes.

Topping:

1 pt. sour cream

½ c. sugar

Whip together sour cream and sugar. Cover over cheesecake; bake for 10 minutes. Chill and serve.

CREOLE SWEET POTATO PECAN PIE

Filling:

1 can sweet potato yams
¼ c. brown sugar
1 egg, beaten heavily
2 tsp. sugar
1 Tbsp. butter
1 Tbsp. heavy cream

1 Tbsp. vanilla extract
⅛ tsp. nutmeg
⅛ tsp. allspice
¼ tsp. ground cinnamon
¼ tsp. salt

Combine all the ingredients in a mixing bowl. Beat thoroughly at a medium speed with a hand mixer until batter is smooth, about 3 minutes. Do not overbeat and set aside.

Syrup:

¾ c. sugar
¾ c. dark corn syrup
2 eggs
2 tsp. vanilla extract
¼ tsp. salt

¼ tsp. ground cinnamon
2 Tbsp. butter
1 c. pecan halves
1 (8 inch) pie shell

In a mixing bowl, combine all ingredients except pecans. Mix thoroughly with a hand mixer at medium speed until syrup darkens. Stir in pecans and set aside.

Pour filling into the pie plate. Pour syrup over top and bake at 325° until it will stand a fork test. Remove from the heat; set aside and allow to cool.

Glaze Topping:

½ c. dry roasted pecans,
    chopped fine
1 c. water

½ c. brown sugar
1 tsp. vanilla extract

In a saucepan, combine water and sugar and bring to a boil. Remove from the heat. Stir in vanilla; blend in pecans. Brush generously over top of the pie.

LOUISIANA APPLE STRAWBERRY CRISP

1½ lb. apple slices
1 qt. frozen strawberries
1 tsp. cinnamon
1 c. uncooked, quick rolled oats

½ c. flour
1¼ c. brown sugar
½ c. butter

In a square baking dish, arrange apple slices and sprinkle with cinnamon. Spoon in strawberries. In a bowl, add oats, flour and brown sugar; blend together well. Melt butter at room temperature. Add to mixture and blend in well. Spread over strawberries. Bake at 350° until apples are cooked.

LOUISIANA BREAD PUDDING WITH LEMON SAUCE

2 c. milk
3/4 c. raisins
1/2 c. dark roasted pecans,
    chopped
1/2 c. butter
1 1/2 tsp. ground cinnamon

1 tsp. nutmeg
1 1/2 tsp. vanilla extract
3 eggs
1 1/4 c. sugar
5 c. bread cubes

In a large bowl, using a hand mixer, beat the eggs at a high speed until frothy, about 4 minutes. Add vanilla, sugar, butter, cinnamon, and nutmeg; blend together well. Add milk. Note: Stir in raisins and pecans. In a lightly buttered casserole dish, arrange bread cubes and arrange egg mixture over top. Soak cubes thoroughly before continuing. Place mixture in a preheated oven at 350°. Lower to 300° and bake until pudding is brown.

Sauce:

1 lemon
1/2 c. water
1/4 c. sugar

1 tsp. vanilla extract
1/4 c. water
2 tsp. cornstarch

Squeeze 1/2 a lemon in a saucepan. Cut remaining in slices. Add lemon halves, sugar and 1/2 cup water; bring to a boil. In a small bowl, dissolve cornstarch, 1/4 cup water and vanilla. Blend in well into the mixture. Cook for 1 minute at 400°, stirring constantly. Remove from the heat and strain well. Pour over pudding.

CINNAMON PEACH PIE WITH BRANDY CREAM TOPPING

6 large peaches, peeled and cut
    in halves
1 c. sugar
1/2 tsp. cinnamon

2 Tbsp. butter, melted
2 eggs, beaten
1 unbaked pie shell

Place peaches into pie shell, round side down. Combine melted butter, sugar, eggs, and cinnamon, blending well. Pour over peaches. Bake at 400° for 35 minutes.

Topping:

2 oz. peach brandy
1 oz. Triple Sec

1/2 c. cream cheese, softened at
    room temperature

In a blender, add peach brandy, Triple Sec and cream cheese by the tablespoon. Blend together for 2 minutes. Pour 2 tablespoons over each pie slice when served.

BASIN STREET DEEP DISH APPLE PIE AND RAISINS

1 flat pastry crust	1 tsp. cinnamon
6 c. apples, pared and sliced	½ c. sugar
1 c. raisins	1 tsp. lemon juice
¼ c. flour	2 Tbsp. butter
½ c. water	¼ tsp. salt
½ c. dark brown sugar	½ tsp. nutmeg
⅓ c. cinnamon candies	1 pastry crust

In a double boiler on medium heat, add water, sugar and candies; melt until creamy. In a bowl, combine apples, raisins, flour, nutmeg, brown sugar, and salt. Add cinnamon, lemon juice and candied syrup. Blend well. Pour into a deep pie dish; dot with butter. Cover with pastry crust and seal edges well. Make 1 small cut on top to allow moisture to escape. Bake at 375° for 45 minutes.

FRENCH QUARTER STRAWBERRY CHEESECAKE

16 graham crackers	1 pt. sour cream
¼ c. butter	3 (8 oz.) pkg. cream cheese
1 c. sugar	4 eggs whites
1 tsp. vanilla	4 egg yolks

Preheat oven to 350°. Lightly oil the bottom of a 9x3 inch baking dish. Roll graham crackers. Place them in a bowl and combine with butter. Cover bottom of baking pan, creating a crust. In a separate bowl, beat egg whites until stiff; set aside. In a large mixing bowl, combine egg yolks, cream cheese, ¾ cup sugar, and vanilla. Beat until smooth. Fold in egg whites. Pour mixture carefully on top of cracker crumbs. Bake for 40 minutes until light brown. Remove from the oven. Combine sour cream with remaining sugar. Pour slowly over the top of the pie. Return to oven for 5 minutes. Remove and allow to cool.

Topping:

1 pack frozen strawberries, defrosted	1 c. sour cream
	¼ c. sugar

Combine together strawberries, sour cream and sugar. Chill and pour over top of pie. Chill before serving.

COCONUT CRUNCH CAMP STREET

1 c. coconut	¾ c. butter
1 c. pecans, chopped	1 Tbsp. baking powder
3 eggs, beaten	1 tsp. salt
1½ c. sugar	1½ tsp. vanilla
3 c. brown sugar	¼ tsp. nutmeg

Preheat oven to 350°. Lightly oil a 9x12 inch baking pan. Melt butter at room temperature and combine with sugars. One at a time, add remaining ingredients, blending well. Pour into baking dish. Bake for 45 minutes. Cut into healthy squares.

HAMMOND MACAROON SOUFFLE

1 doz. almond macaroons	⅛ tsp. salt
1 c. milk	½ c. hot water
3 egg whites	½ pt. whipping cream,
3 egg yolks	thoroughly whipped

Bring milk to a simmer. Blend in macaroons and remove from the heat. Pour into a bowl. In a separate bowl, thoroughly beat egg yolks with a pinch of salt. Place saucepan over low heat. Blend in hot water and remove from the heat. In a separate bowl, beat egg whites and fold into the mixture. Combine all ingredients and pour into a slightly oiled baking dish. Bake at 250° for 30 minutes and serve.

STRAWBERRY SHORTCAKE

2 c. all-purpose flour	4 Tbsp. baking powder
½ c. sugar	½ tsp. salt
½ c. shortening	1 pt. frozen strawberries
1 c. milk	Whipped cream

In a bowl, combine shortening with dry ingredients. Mix well. Add milk; beat mixture until well blended. Scrape mixture out onto a floured surface and knead until smooth. Form 1 large cake or cut into squares. Bake at 400° until light brown. Remove from the heat and split in half. Fill center with ½ frozen strawberries. Top with remainder and top with whipped cream.

STRAWBERRY COBBLER

1 pt. frozen strawberries	½ tsp. baking powder
⅓ c. butter	1 c. milk
1 c. flour	½ tsp. salt

In an ovenproof skillet, melt butter at a low temperature. In a bowl, combine dry ingredients with milk to form a batter. Pour into skillet. Place 2 cups strawberries over the batter. Bake at 350° until brown.

ALMOND PECAN TORTE

1 lb. pecans
1/2 lb. almonds, chopped
Grated rind of 3 lemons
Grated rind of 3 oranges
12 eggs, separated
1 box Zwieback crumbs
1 Tbsp. flour

1 tsp. cinnamon
4 c. light brown sugar
1/2 lb. butter
1/2 tsp. cloves
1 c. milk
2 oz. bourbon
2 oz. baking powder

In a small bowl, combine bourbon and baking powder. In a separate bowl, combine butter, egg yolks and sugar; blend until fluffy. Add dry ingredients, one at a time. Add milk, blending slowly. Add baking powder and brandy mix; blend thoroughly. Beat egg whites until stiff. Fold into mixture gently. Pour into a lightly buttered baking dish. Bake at 350° for 40 minutes.

PECAN ROLL

2 c. pecans, chopped fine
2 Tbsp. wild honey
2 Tbsp. brown sugar

1/2 lb. butter, melted
1/2 c. milk
2 1/2 c. flour

In a bowl, add melted butter and flour; blend together. Add milk. Combine well and knead into a soft dough. If more flour is necessary, feel free to use it. Dough should be soft and not sticky. Cut off spoon size amounts of dough and flatten into rolls. In a bowl, mix pecans, sugar and honey. Sprinkle over dough. Pat gently. Place in a cookie sheet and bake for 20 minutes at 350°.

Syrup:

2 c. dark brown sugar
1/4 c. blackstrap molasses

1 c. hot water

In a saucepan, add hot water and molasses; blend in sugar until it forms a syrup. Dip rolls into the syrup. Place on a wax paper sheet and allow to cool.

BROWNIES, CAJUN STYLE

1/4 c. butter
2 eggs
1/4 c. sugar
2 packs chocolate pudding
2 c. sifted flour

1/4 tsp. baking powder
1/4 tsp. salt
1/2 tsp. vanilla extract
3/4 c. chopped pecans
3/4 c. chopped walnuts

In a bowl, combine butter, sugar and eggs. In the order that the other ingredients appear, add to mixture. In a lightly buttered baking dish, spread mixture well. Bake at 350° for 25 minutes or until fork done. Cut into squares while brownies are still warm.

CREME DE MENTHE PARFAIT

24 large marshmallows
1 c. milk
2 oz. creme de menthe

1 oz. creme de cacao
1 c. heavy whipping cream
1 c. cream cheese

In a saucepan, combine marshmallows and milk. Simmer at a low heat until marshmallows melt and blend. Remove from heat and allow to cool. Add creme de menthe and creme de cacao. Gently fold in whipping cream. Pour into loaf pans and freeze. Remove from freezer and allow to partially thaw. Whip remaining cream cheese until it peaks. Cover creme de menthe mixture with whipping cream and serve.

TAPIOCA CREME PUDDING

2 c. milk
2 eggs, beaten
3/4 c. sugar
1/2 c. granulated tapioca

1/8 tsp. salt
1 tsp. vanilla extract
1 tsp. butter
Whipped cream

Combine milk and tapioca in the top of a double boiler. Cook at a medium heat, stirring frequently. Add eggs, sugar and salt; cook for an additional 5 minutes. Combine all ingredients. Pour into individual molds and chill. Top with whipping cream and serve.

BLACK CHERRY CUPCAKES

1 large can black cherries
1 c. cherry juice
1/2 c. light brown sugar

2 Tbsp. corn starch
1/4 c. cherry brandy
12 baked cupcakes

Drain cherries; save juice. Cover top of cupcakes with cherries. In a saucepan, bring juice to a boiling point. When reached, immediately add corn starch and sugar, stirring constantly. When mixture returns to a boil, stir vigorously for 1 minute and remove from the heat. Allow to cool; whisk in brandy. Chill and pour over cupcakes.

DEADLY BROWNIE PIE

1 c. fine chocolate wafers
1 c. pecans, chopped
1 c. sugar
4 egg whites
1 tsp. vanilla extract
1 c. cream, whipped and
  sweetened

1 sq. unsweetened chocolate,
  shaved
½ c. marshmallow
⅛ tsp. salt

In a bowl, beat together egg whites and salt until it peaks. Gradually add sugar and whisk until stiff. Fold in wafers, pecans and vanilla thoroughly. Spread evenly in a lightly buttered 10 inch baking dish. Bake at 325° for 25 minutes. Remove from the heat and cool thoroughly. Pour on a layer of marshmallow. Cover with whipping cream. Spread on a layer of shaved chocolate. Chill and serve.

CHOCOLATE FUDGE CAKE

4 oz. bitter chocolate
4 eggs
2 c. sugar
1 c. all-purpose flour

2 c. pecan halves
1 tsp. vanilla extract
1¾ sticks butter

Grease and line two 8 inch layer cake pans. Preheat oven to 350°. In the top of a double boiler, melt chocolate and blend with butter. Remove from heat and allow to cool. Add sugar, eggs and vanilla, whisking thoroughly. Dredge pecans in flour and combine with mixture. For a moist effect, place a pan of water in the oven while baking. Bake until fork done.

Icing:

2 boxes powdered sugar
2 Tbsp. cocoa
¼ stick butter

Evaporated milk
1 tsp. vanilla
1 c. pecans

In a bowl, blend cocoa and sugar thoroughly. Cream in butter. Add vanilla and milk, a little at a time, to form a thick icing consistency. Spread a layer between cakes. Cover with icing and top with pecans.

CHERRY COBBLER CAKE

½ c. cocoa
3½ c. cake flour
2 eggs
2 c. sugar
2 sticks butter

1 tsp. vanilla
⅛ tsp. salt
2 c. buttermilk
2 tsp. soda, dissolved in water

In a bowl, cream together sugar and butter. Add eggs. In a separate bowl, sift together cocoa and flour. Add alternately to egg mixture the flour, salt, milk, soda, and vanilla. Bake in a large pan at 350° for 45 minutes.

Topping:

1 can cherries
1 c. sugar

1 tsp. cornstarch

In top of a double boiler, heat cherries and juice to a simmer. Add sugar, blend in cornstarch and remove from the heat. Allow to chill. Pour over cake.

GERMAN CHOCOLATE CAKE

¼ lb. sweet chocolate
2 c. sugar
½ c. walnuts, chopped
½ c. pecans, chopped
1 c. shortening
4 egg yolks
½ c. boiling water

1 c. buttermilk
1 tsp. soda
2½ c. flour
1 tsp. vanilla
⅛ tsp. salt
4 egg whites, beaten stiffly

In a bowl, cream together sugar and shortening. Add egg yolks, one at a time, blending well. Melt chocolate in ½ cup boiling water. Blend into mixture. In a bowl, add buttermilk, flour, salt, and soda. Blend together thoroughly. Add vanilla. Fold in egg whites. Fold in nuts. Pour into three 9 inch cake pans. Bake at 350° until fork done.

Icing:

1 c. sugar
1 stick butter
1 c. evaporated milk
3 egg yolks, beaten

1 c. shredded coconut
1 c. pecans, chopped
1 tsp. vanilla

In a double boiler, while stirring constantly, add milk, sugar, butter, and egg yolks. Cook until mixture thickens. Blend in coconut, pecans and vanilla. Spread generously over cake.

COCONUT PINEAPPLE CAKE

2½ c. flour
4 egg yolks, beaten
4 egg whites, beaten stiffly
2 c. sugar
½ lb. butter

4 tsp. baking powder
1 c. milk
⅛ tsp. salt
1 tsp. vanilla extract

Lightly oil three 8 inch cake pans and set aside. Preheat oven to 350°. In a bowl, blend together sugar and butter. Add egg yolks; blend in well. Add baking powder, salt and flour; blend well. Add milk and vanilla; fold in beaten egg whites. Pour into pans and bake for 45 minutes or until fork done.

Icing:

1 egg yolk
1 c. milk
1 c. sugar
1 c. shredded coconut

1 c. pineapple preserves
1 tsp. vanilla extract
1 Tbsp. cornstarch

In a double boiler, mix together all ingredients except for coconut. When mixture thickens, allow to cool. Spread generously over cake and top with coconut.

OLD-FASHIONED CAJUN GINGERBREAD

½ c. molasses
1½ c. cake flour
2 eggs
½ c. butter
½ c. sugar

1 tsp. ginger
1 tsp. allspice
½ c. buttermilk
1 tsp. soda
1 tsp. cinnamon

In a bowl, cream together butter and sugar. Add eggs, beating well. Blend in molasses. In a separate bowl, combine flour, spices and soda. Fold flour into mixture. Add buttermilk. Bake at 350° until fork done.

Topping:

2 tsp. cinnamon
½ c. brown sugar
¼ c. flour

1 c. pecans, chopped
¼ c. butter

Blend together all ingredients until crumbly. Spread generously over cake. Return to oven for 5 minutes. Serve.

NEW ORLEANS COFFEE

1 c. dark chicory coffee

3 c. milk

Place milk in saucepan; bring to a boil. When starting to boil, add coffee. Remove from heat; stir well. Serve with beignets. Serve.

RIVER ROAD RED

6 oz. gin
2 c. tomato juice
2 c. frozen cranberries

12 oz. grapefruit soda
1 c. crushed ice cubes

In a blender, add frozen cranberries and 1 cup tomato juice and blend for 1 minute. Add remaining tomato juice, ice cubes and gin. Blend together well. Pour ingredients slowly over the soda. It may be necessary to pour it down the side of the glass to keep it from fizzing over. Garnish with a pineapple wedge and cherry. Serve.

SOUTHERN MINT JULEP

2 oz. bourbon whiskey
1 tsp. sugar

3 sprigs mint leaves

Crush mint leaves and sugar together in a bowl. Fill glass with crushed ice. Add whiskey. Shake well. Decorate with a sprig of mint and serve.

RUM PUNCH

1 qt. rum
½ qt. bourbon
½ pt. maraschino cherries
3 oranges, sliced

3 lemons, sliced
½ qt. unsweetened pineapple
   juice
2 pt. ginger ale

Combine ingredients; mix well. Dilute in crushed ice. Serve.

HOT SPICY PUNCH

1 stick cinnamon
1 tsp. allspice
½ c. sugar
¼ tsp. nutmeg

1 pt. grape juice
1 lemon, sliced thin
1½ pt. water
1 tsp. cloves

Combine ingredients in a saucepan. Bring to a boil. Serve.

DANISH COFFEE, VIEUX CARRE STYLE

¼ c. extra strong New Orleans
   coffee
¼ tsp. salt
1 qt. milk

1½ chocolate squares
½ c. sugar
⅓ c. chilled whipping cream

In a saucepan, add chocolate, sugar, coffee, and salt. Set over a low heat and stir until chocolate comes to a boil. Reduce heat to a simmer for 3 minutes, stirring frequently. Remove from the heat and blend in milk. Return to the heat and bring to a simmer. Remove from the heat. Set aside. Add whipping cream to a chilled bowl and whip until it peaks. Serve coffee piping hot and top with whipping cream.

HOT BUTTERED RUM ROYAL STREET

1 c. brown sugar
1 stick butter
1 c. powdered sugar
1 pt. vanilla ice cream

½ tsp. cinnamon
1 c. rum
½ tsp. nutmeg
Boiling water

In a bowl, melt butter at room temperature. Add sugars, blending well to a cream. Add ice cream and spices. Place in a freezer.

To serve: Place 1 ounce of mix into a mug. Add 2 ounces rum and 6 ounces boiling water. Stir vigorously. Sprinkle with a pinch of cinnamon and nutmeg.

CAJUN EGG FLIP

1 Tbsp. rum
2 egg whites
2 egg yolks
2 Tbsp. brandy

¼ c. sugar
Hot milk
Pinch of nutmeg

In a bowl, combine egg yolks and sugar; beat until stiff. Add egg whites; continue to beat until it peaks. Stir in brandy and rum. Pour 2 ounces in bottom of a glass. Add hot milk and sprinkle top with nutmeg.

CAJUN BANANA SMOOTHIE

1 large, fully ripe banana, sliced
   thin
½ c. fresh strawberries, sliced
   thin
¼ c. skim milk

¼ tsp. grated orange peel
1 tsp. brown sugar
½ c. banana yogurt
1 oz. dark rum
1 oz. banana brandy

Garnish:

3 whole strawberries
3 slices banana

3 sprigs mint

Place bananas and strawberries in a bowl and freeze. Remove after frozen and place in a blender. Add yogurt, skim milk, orange peel, and sugar. Blend at a medium speed until thick. Add rum and brandy. Pour into a chilled champagne saucer. Arrange strawberry, banana and mint on long toothpicks. Rotate into drink and serve.

Notes

Notes

Notes

INDEX OF RECIPES

VEGETABLES AND SALADS

SHRIMP IN ITS MANY MOODS AND TASTES

CHICKEN ON THE RUN

EGGS, CHEESE AND EXTRAS

DESSERTS AND SUNDOWNERS

BASIC FOOD HINTS

Baked potatoes can be re-baked if you dip them in water then, place them in an oven at 325 degrees for 25 minutes.

To remove the intestinal vein on shrimp, try using the blunt end of a toothpick under cold running water.

To crisp corn flakes, pour into a cake pan and heat in a moderate oven.

Curry powders differ too much that the safest rule to follow is to use half the amount of curry powder called for in a recipe. You can always add more to taste before serving.

Retain the bone in canned salmon; they are edible and especially rich in calcium and flavor.

To tell if a salmon steak is cooked, lift the center bone with the point of a fork. If you can raise it with none of the flesh clinging, then it is done.

Flounder is sometime called sole; it is the same in taste and texture. Always try to use a whole flounder, it retains its taste better than fillets. It is much easier to remove the backbone after a flounder is cooked.

BASIC FOOD HINTS

Trout is delicate and will break apart easily. Any handling of the trout other than turning over in a pan should be done before cooking. Turn trout over only once when frying.

Use a metal mold for aspic - it makes unmolding much easier.

When you boil pasta of any kind, add 1 teaspoon of salt to the water.

Amount of fish to buy per serving: whole fish - 1 pound
Drawn fish - 3/4 pound
Dressed or pan ready - 1/2 pound
Fish steaks -cross-sliced 3/4" thick about 1/3 lb. each
Fish fillets - 1/4 lb. per serving
Butterfly fish fillets - 1/4 lb. per serving
Fish sticks - 4-6 per serving

Certain times of the year clams may contain a lot of sand. They will usually discharge the sand if you cover them with a mixture of salt and water. Let them stand undisturbed for about an hour. You can store clams in the refrigerator by covering them with a wet towel.

Frying with a corn flake batter should be done on a low heat to keep the flakes from burning.

Oysters toughen quickly - they should rarely be cooked more than 2 minutes by themselves.

BASIC FOOD HINTS

Buy oysters freshly opened for frying; they hold together better. Freshly opened oysters also hold crumbs or corn meal coating longer.

A safe timetable for frying shellfish:

Deep-fried

1 lb. shrimp   - 2-3 minutes
10 oz. scallops - 3-4 minutes
1 pint oysters - 2-3 minutes
1 lb. clams   - 2-3 minutes

Batter-fried

1 lb. shrimp   - 4-5 minutes
12 oz. scallops - 3-4 minutes

Meat: How much should you buy?

Boneless meat - 1/3 lb. per serving
Boneless roast (veal, pork, beef, lamb) 1/3 lb. per serving
Small cuts, bone-in - 1/2 lb. per serving (pork loin, rib roast, ham)
Large bone-in - 3/4 lb. per serving (spareribs, back ribs, short ribs, shanks)
Medium bone-in - 1/2 lb. per serving (pot roast)

Buy pork chops from 3/4" to 1" thick; any thinner and they dry out during prolonged cooking that pork requires. To test doneness, prick it with a sharp fork. If the juices are pink continue to cook.

REMOVING THE MYSTERY FROM ROUX AND SAUCES

A roux is a mixture of flour and oil cooked together slowly until the flour has lost its raw taste and has expanded so that it can combine with liquid. This is used as a thickener for sauces for fish, meat, vegetables and chicken.

The basic colors of roux are white, cream, light brown, dark brown and rich dark brown. Each has its own taste and is controlled by the time and temperature of cooking.

To make a basic white roux, melt the butter until heated well. Reduce the heat and blend in equal parts of flour cooking slowly for several minutes. Remember, never stop stirring. When the flour gels with the oil, add the hot liquid of your choice. Using a roux, like a panada eliminates the raw flour taste of uncooked flour. White roux is used for bechamel, cream soups and souffles.

To make a basic brown roux, heat the flour in a dry pan over a medium heat, stirring constantly until it becomes the color of cinnamon. Add a little heated oil, stir well and then add the hot liquid of your choice. Cook on a low heat, then add this to the sauce or gravy. Use this as a thickener for brown sauces and meat and game gravies.

Roux may be prepared ahead of time. It is easily stored and keeps well in airtight containers. Keep roux in its thickest form; liquid and a whisk will create the thickness you desire.

ORDER FORM

Cooking Country With Shotgun Red $15.95

Is This Country Cooking? This Is $15.95
    Country Cooking!

How They Owned A Boat And Didn't Spend Any $ 9.95
    Money

The Cajun Gourmet Afloat And On The Road $15.95

All I Ever Wanted To Know About Cooking $14.95
    I Learned From Momma

The Upper Crud Cookbook $15.95

The Wing'ed Whale From Woefully $14.95

P lease select your choice of books and add $2.75 per book for shipping and packaging. *Send to:*

HAWK PUBLISHING AND DISTRIBUTING
P.O. Box 8422
Longboat Key, FL 34228

Mail Books To:

NAME _____

ADDRESS _____

CITY _____ STATE _____ ZIP _____